Book Club
for Middle School

Taffy E. Raphael
Marcella Kehus
Karen Damphousse

SMALL PLANET COMMUNICATIONS, INC.
Lawrence, Massachusetts

Acknowledgments

Editorial: Liz Grube
                    Kim L. Beaudet
                    Danielle Martin
                    Kristi L. McGee

Design and Production: Natalie MacKnight

We gratefully acknowledge the following teachers who reviewed portions of this guide and provided valuable feedback.

Kate Brueckman, Jane Addams Middle School, Royal Oak, Michigan
Alice Fournier, Morgan Park High School, Chicago, Illinois
Sally Harpool, Mata Intermediate School, Houston, Texas
Jean A. Samples, Herod Elementary School, Houston, Texas

Visit www.PlanetBookClub.com.

Small Planet Communications, Inc.
15 Union Street
Lawrence, MA 01840
www.smplanet.com

ISBN: 0-9656211-2-X   2 3 4 5   06 05 04 03 02 01

Contents

Preface

Book Club started over twelve years ago with the goal of creating an alternative context for reading instruction—one that would get students excited about reading and discussing books. We began developing the program in upper elementary classrooms. Since those early days, Book Club's combination of excellent literature, relevant writing activities, and student-led discussion groups has proven effective in classroom after classroom.

Our success with elementary students prompted us to bring Book Club to other age groups. Middle school students are ideal Book Club candidates for a variety of reasons—they enjoy talking with their peers, they're ready and eager to grapple with abstract ideas and real-world issues, and there's a wealth of excellent adolescent fiction written just for them. We developed *Book Club for Middle School* to help both beginning and experienced teachers implement Book Club in their middle-level classrooms. Chapters 1–5 of this guide explain the program and offer teaching strategies. Chapters 6–8 provide detailed lesson plans for several theme-based units.

In addition to this teacher's guide, you can use the Book Club web site to involve your class in book discussions with students at other schools, interact with other Book Club teachers, obtain additional novel guides, and access a variety of professional development resources. You'll find our web site at:

www.PlanetBookClub.com

We wish you the best as you implement Book Club in your middle school classroom. We think you'll discover that the program does more than teach literature and language arts skills—it sets students on a path to becoming confident, lifelong readers.

Book Club Theory and Curriculum

Rethinking Literacy

Picture a typical classroom of children studying literature. The students sit in rows with thick textbooks open on their desks. The teacher stands at the front of the room drawing a plot diagram on the chalkboard or reviewing a numbered list of questions at the end of a selection. Now consider the following questions.

- Are the students engaged in lively, thoughtful discussion?

- Are they taking responsibility for their own study of the literature?

- Are they growing to be confident and eager readers?

Unfortunately, traditional methods of teaching literature often fail to foster a genuine enthusiasm for reading. In a classroom entrenched in such methods, the answer to the above questions is likely to be no. In a Book Club classroom, however, time and again the answer to these questions is a resounding yes.

The Book Club program started taking shape in 1989, when a team of university researchers and classroom teachers set out to explore new ideas about literacy learning. Small, student-led discussion groups, or book clubs, form the core of the reading curriculum that we've since developed. The children in these groups learn to direct the course of their own conversations about literature, focusing on what they feel is important. Student responsibility and autonomy are crucial goals, but the book club conversations also take place within a context of balanced, literature-based instruction that effectively integrates reading, writing, speaking, and listening skills.

Book Club is an effective teaching tool because it's grounded in an understanding of literacy as a process. Good readers find meaning in a text by bringing their own ideas to it, discussing it, and connecting it to the world and to their own lives. This process allows readers to become truly engaged in their reading. Unfortunately, many classroom methods steer students down unnatural and unsatisfying paths for exploring literature. For example, think about the last time you read an interesting book. When you discussed the book with a friend, did you begin the conversation by quizzing each other about the book's setting? Did you ask your friend to name the book's main characters or identify three events that led to the story's climax? People don't usually discuss the books they love in this manner, yet in too many literature classrooms students are forced to respond to books in this way.

Many children learn to view reading as a hunt for facts and "right" answers. In school, they respond to short-answer questions without being given the chance to raise and explore topics that interest them. Teachers direct and dominate any discussions about a text, so students are unable to follow through with their own lines of thinking. By contrast, Book Club creates opportunities for students of *all* ability levels to engage in real conversations about books—not just conversations designed to ensure that comprehension has occurred. We want students to love talking about books, so we help them develop the literacy skills they need to be successful in book discussions. Book Club stresses students' personal responses to and engagement with books—factors that are crucial to their literacy development as well as to their lifelong enjoyment of reading and discussing literature.

Encouraging Students as Members of a Literate Community

A defining characteristic of Book Club is its transformation of the traditional classroom into a literate community. Through book clubs and whole-class discussions, students grow to see themselves and their peers as active contributors to the learning environment—contributors who can support one another and direct the course of discussion with their unique responses. The classroom community helps make students feel safe and important, gives them a sense of belonging, and allows them to assume ownership of their learning. All of these factors are crucial to the self-esteem and development of adolescent students.

The importance of students' individual identities within the Book Club classroom is supported by the work of educational researcher James Paul Gee.[1] Gee maintains that membership in any group leads an individual to develop an "identity kit" for being part of the group. In a school setting, this kit depends heavily on expectations about teachers' and students' roles. For students, a typical identity kit includes following directions, looking for answers that the teacher has in mind, and conceding ownership to the teacher.

Students just starting Book Club will need to go through a process of adjustment, since the program requires them to assume greater control over their own responses to and interpretations of texts. Book Club invites students to take responsibility for facilitating discussion, a role traditionally reserved for the teacher. Students must learn to view themselves as individuals who have ideas to share, who can assist their fellow students in their learning, and who can take responsibility for their own learning.

Book clubs and whole-class discussions give students practice in constructing their own meanings from texts and give them a sense of identity as members of a literate community. They learn to focus on how others use language and create meaning, and they learn to evaluate themselves as communicators. With these components of the program, we empower students as readers, thinkers, and guides. We've found that even students who usually struggle with reading and communication skills can open up and flourish in book clubs and in larger class discussions.

Recognizing How Readers Construct Meaning

While developing the Book Club curriculum, we gained valuable insights from various studies of reader response. We paid special attention to work that focused on the role of the reader. This research helped us understand reader-text relationships, the types of responses that readers can use, and the process by which readers respond to literature.

The work of Louise M. Rosenblatt[2] supports our belief that each student's unique response to a text must be valued and cultivated. Rosenblatt argues that meaning results from the interaction between reader and text—not solely from the reader *or* solely from the text. She explains that the literary experience is a synthesis of what the text brings to the reader and what the reader brings to the text. In other words, the reader brings meaning to the symbols (or words) on the page, while the structure of the text guides the reader toward meaning. Rosenblatt adds that the reader's first response is only a starting point of instruction. Personal response must be elaborated through a social exchange of ideas.

Another literacy scholar, Wolfgang Iser,[3] describes how a reader fills in gaps in the structure of a literary work by making metaphors or inferences, thus creating his or her own interpretation. Because every reader has unique experiences and a unique knowledge base, interpretations often differ. He stresses that there is no single "correct" interpretation of a work, although a complete interpretation takes into account all the information supplied by the author. An effective work of literature leaves room for the reader's imagination, but it also presents some surprises. The experience of reading is similar to real life in that the reader can impose order on the text to some extent—until something unexpected happens. This active process makes readers eager to share their experiences with a text with other readers.

Book Club both draws upon and helps support each of these theories. The program gives students many opportunities to interact with text, both privately and socially. Students are encouraged to honor and develop their own responses to a text and also to respect and learn from others' interpretations of the same text. The program also contains a strong writing component that allows for a variety of written responses throughout the reading of a book. See Chapter 2, page 16, for more information about the writing component of Book Club.

Taking a Sociocultural Approach to Learning and Development

From the very beginning, we've had specific goals in mind for Book Club. First, we want to introduce students to a love of literature and thus combat aliteracy—children's decision not to read even though they know how. This means that the program must provide something more engaging for young readers than the usual vocabulary, basic comprehension, and factual recall. Second, we want students to love talking and raising questions about books. To achieve this goal, the program must build discussion skills and provide ample opportunity for students to hold real conversations about literature. And third, we want our program to allow for direct instruction that helps students develop their reading skills. These goals resonate with research into "dialogic teaching"—a family of theories that focuses on the social bases for a student's development. Dialogic teaching emphasizes that an individual's learning is mediated by others who are more knowledgeable. These mediators help to interpret and encourage the learner's experiences.

While the ideas of many scholars in this area contributed to the creation of Book Club, the work of Russian psychologist Lev S. Vygotsky[4] proved especially valuable. Vygotsky argues that language and social interaction promote intellectual development. His theory focuses on what students can accomplish with the support of "knowledgeable others" in a group, and he stresses the importance of language for the development of thought.

The Role of More-Knowledgeable Others Students do not learn new skills automatically as they grow older. They need support from knowledgeable others who can guide them along the path. Vygotsky defines the "zone of proximal development" as the set of tasks that are just beyond the grasp of a student working independently. With the support and guidance of an instructor, the student can learn how to achieve these tasks. In Book Club, teachers provide instructional support that ranges from a helpful nudge in a "teachable moment" to direct instruction in a formal lesson. For more information on the role of the instructor in Book Club, see page 8.

The Role of Language in the Development of Thought Vygotsky explains that higher mental functions—such as reading, interpreting, and composing—are social in origin; they are learned first through interaction with others. Further, he argues that these higher mental functions are mediated by the use of sign systems, such as language. Building on these ideas, we believe that learners develop the ability for logical memory, selective attention, decision making, and language comprehension as they use signs and symbols within a social context. The more opportunities they have to use signs and symbols as tools to construct and communicate meaning, the greater the development of higher-order thinking.[5] Book Club allows students to learn about literature and acquire critical-thinking skills through their interactions with teachers and with fellow students in various contexts.

Vygotsky's sociocultural perspective is reflected in the basic structure of Book Club. Students first are encouraged to engage with text and develop their personal responses to it. Then, in both small-group and whole-class discussions, they share their responses and learn how others have responded to the same text. In these social contexts, students have many opportunities to hear and use the language of literacy and critical thinking. They learn from their peers as well as from their teacher. The knowledge that they gain through social interaction becomes part of the repertoire of skills that they can apply independently and for their own purposes.

Achieving a Balanced Literacy Curriculum

Book Club supports a balanced literacy curriculum that both honors the literature and gives teachers ample opportunities to teach conventional knowledge about reading and language. We define four Book Club curriculum areas: comprehension, language conventions, literary aspects, and composition.

- **Comprehension** Providing instruction in this area takes some of the mystery out of the reading process for students. It gives them the tools to gather information, connect ideas, identify important issues, and monitor their success as readers. Areas of instruction include vocabulary, text-processing strategies such as making inferences and sequencing, and monitoring strategies. If you teach and model the strategies that experienced readers use and encourage your students to practice these strategies, you'll see a marked improvement in your students' reading comprehension.

- **Language Conventions** This area includes all aspects of how written and oral language works. It addresses sound/symbol relationships, grammatical structures, mechanics such as spelling and punctuation, and interactions within small and large groups to discuss text. In considering the current debates that surround language instruction (e.g., phonics versus a more integrated curriculum), Book Club operates on the premise that it is unwise to focus exclusively on any single type of language instruction. Students should be given as many tools as possible as they build their language skills.

A Balanced Literacy Curriculum

Comprehension

Background Knowledge
- Make predictions
- Draw on prior knowledge
- Build knowledge as needed
- Use context clues
- Make intertextual connections

Processing Text
- Make inferences
- Summarize
- Sequence
- Build vocabulary
- Organize and use knowledge of text structure
- Analyze characters, setting, plot sequence

Monitoring Own Reading
- Ask questions
- Clarify confusions

Language Conventions

Sound/Symbol
- Spell conventionally
- Read with fluency

Grammar
- Use appropriate language choices (verbs, syntax, punctuation) in oral reading, discussion, and writing

Interaction
- Work with peers to set goals
- Interact with peers in literacy contexts

Literary Aspects

Literary Elements

Theme
- Author's purposes
- Connections to life

Point of View
- Characters' POV
- Author's POV

Genre/Structures
- Story structure
- Expository structures
- Types of genres

Author's Craft
- Style
- Text features

Response to Literature

Personal
- Share experiences
- Share personal feelings
- Place self in situation
- Compare self to characters

Creative
- Ask "What if?" (change event in plot and explore impact)
- Dramatize events and characters' attitudes or actions
- Illustrate events and characters

Critical
- Explain changes in beliefs or feelings
- Use evidence from text to support ideas
- Critique texts using specific examples
- Discuss author's purposes
- Identify author's craft
- Use text as mirror of own life and as window into lives of others

Composition

Process
- Plan
- Draft
- Revise

Writing as a Tool for Thinking
- Reading logs
- Think sheets

Writing from Sources
- Paraphrase
- Avoid plagiarism
- Cite sources
- Synthesize information

On-Demand Writing
- Essay test
- Assigned topic

- **Literary Aspects** This component teaches students to honor and appreciate a work of literature and the author's craft. Students strive to understand the structure and elements of a literary text, such as genre, plot, characterization, and figurative language. They also respond to literary texts in a variety of ways. These responses might include personal essays, journal entries, creative writing, dramatization, and critical essays.

- **Composition** This component of the curriculum is based on research that shows important relationships between reading and writing. Book Club features two different kinds of writing activities designed to support students' understanding of the texts they read. The first is writing as a tool to promote critical and higher-order thinking about texts. This kind of writing generally takes place through reflections, journals, notebooks, and dialogue. The second is process writing about issues and topics that relate to texts students read during Book Club. Students are also encouraged to gather information from multiple sources, synthesize information, and present it to peers in written form.

Fostering Ownership of Literacy

Students have ownership of literacy when they place personal value on their abilities and experiences as readers. Students who have ownership of literacy

- enjoy reading.

- have confidence and pride in their reading.

- share their reading with others.

- choose to read for their own purposes, both in and out of school.

- make personal connections to literature.

- set goals and evaluate their own progress as readers.

▶ **Ownership of Literacy** [6]
Students who gain ownership of their literacy become lifelong readers. Ownership encompasses and is supported by all four Book Club curriculum areas.

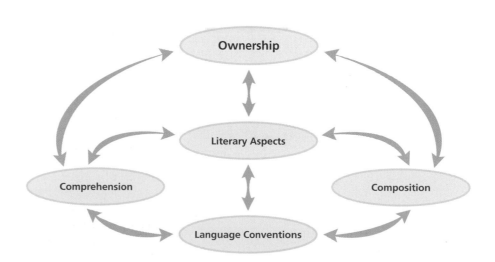

Developing students' sense of ownership over their learning is especially crucial in the middle grades. Adolescents stand at the crossroads between craving independence and desiring adult guidance. When teachers can give students the practical tools to pursue their own academic interests, both yearnings are satisfied. Book Club provides a framework within which teachers can instruct students in the skills they need to gain both knowledge and enjoyment from their interactions with literature. Instruction in each of the four curriculum areas provides students with tools to support their ownership of literacy. As students become competent in these knowledge areas, they can use literacy to achieve their own goals and meet their own needs.

Understanding the Role of Instruction

Students' active role in their own learning does not take away the need for guidance and instruction from the teacher. The teacher's role in Book Club is complex and varied. Depending on students' needs and the teacher's instructional goals, the teacher participates in literacy instruction in each of the following ways:

- The teacher provides explicit instruction during mini-lessons, when he or she takes on a more traditional teacher role. For example, a teacher might give background information on a topic or historical era that will enhance the students' reading.

- The teacher models cognitive processes. For example, during a read-aloud, a teacher might pause to "think out loud" about the text, sharing his or

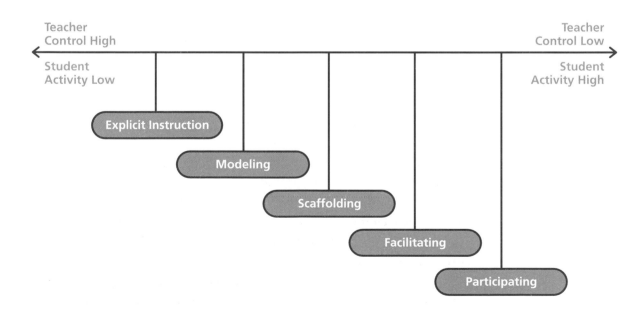

Teacher's Roles in Instruction[7]

Teacher Control High

Teacher Control Low

Student Activity Low

Student Activity High

Explicit Instruction

Modeling

Scaffolding

Facilitating

Participating

her thoughts or asking rhetorical questions. At other times, the teacher might share his or her own written response to a text or read sections of text aloud to highlight clues to characterization or theme.

- The teacher provides "scaffolding talk" to support students in their discussion. Scaffolding can consist of a teacher's asking questions to promote deeper levels of discussion. For example, if a student provides a partial answer to a text-based question, the teacher can pose further questions and then ask the student to provide a piece of textual support. In this way, the teacher guides the student to answer a question fully and to support that answer with textual evidence—skills she or he hopes the student will soon use independently.

- The teacher can be a facilitator in large-group discussions. In this capacity, the teacher simply directs the flow of conversation and helps students interact but does not dominate the conversation. For example, the teacher might merely direct the turn-taking or help students build on each other's ideas.

- The teacher can participate in group discussions as an equal member of the group. In this situation, the teacher's contributions are no more or less important than the contributions of the students. Because this is a distinctly different role than the others, especially in terms of power and authority, the teacher may need to reinforce this role by qualifying his or her input with phrasing such as "In my opinion . . ." or "As I was reading, I thought . . . What do you think?"

Within this flexible framework, the teacher has opportunities to have a great deal of control over instruction as well as opportunities to sit back and allow students to direct their own learning. The key is to achieve a balance that allows the teacher to provide background information and help students develop important strategies while not taking voice and responsibility away from students.

Final Thoughts

First and foremost, Book Club is about helping students of all reading abilities find a love of literature. Being lifelong readers and thinkers enhances their lives in ways that cannot be measured. As Lee Galda[8] has suggested, "literature mirrors our own lives and provides a window into distant peoples, times, and places." In the process of learning about literature, Book Club students are taught to value their own ideas and opinions, develop their understanding of our language, and exercise interpersonal, writing, and critical-thinking skills.

In short, Book Club opens doors to students' understanding of literature through guidance by an instructor, interaction with peers, and opportunities to talk and write about what they read. One of the best ways to examine the effectiveness of the program is to hear from the students themselves. Justin Ross, a student who experienced Book Club in his fifth-grade class, told a group of teachers:

> One of my favorite things about Book Club is that we get a chance to talk with our peers. When we talk with our peers we find out about other people's ideas, have a chance to say something really important, get to tell what the author should do better or different, ask questions about the book, and express our feelings and ideas. Also, sometimes books were hard for me to understand. In Book Club, other students, or the teacher, helped one another to understand the story. [9]

Our hope is that Book Club will help many students see themselves as capable readers and critical thinkers. Armed with strong reading, communication, and thinking skills, as well as a positive attitude toward reading, students are bound to succeed in whatever they do.

References

1   James Paul Gee, *Social Linguistics and Literacies: Ideology in Discourses* (London: Falmer, 1990).

2   Louise M. Rosenblatt, *Literature as Exploration* (New York: Noble & Noble, 1976).

3   Wolfgang Iser, *The Act of Reading: A Theory of Aesthetic Response* (Baltimore: Johns Hopkins University Press, 1978).

4   Lev S. Vygotsky, *Mind in Society: The Development of Higher Mental Psychological Processes* (Cambridge, MA: Harvard University Press, 1978).

5   Susan I. McMahon and Taffy E. Raphael (eds.), *The Book Club Connection: Literacy Learning and Classroom Talk* (New York: Teachers College Press, 1997).

6   Chart adapted from Kathryn H. Au and Taffy E. Raphael (eds.), *Literature-Based Instruction: Reshaping the Curriculum* (Norwood, MA: Christopher-Gordon Publishers, 1998).

7   Ibid.

8   Lee Galda, "Literature as Mirror and Window," in Kathryn H. Au and Taffy E. Raphael (eds.), op. cit.

9   Susan I. McMahon and Taffy E. Raphael (eds.), op. cit., page 24.

Chapter Two

Components of the Program

Understanding the Book Club Classroom

How exactly does the Book Club program operate? What are its components and how do they fit together? To begin to answer these questions, we present two typical classroom scenarios.

In the first classroom, students are several chapters into a novel that deals with racial conflict in the United States in the early 1960s. The teacher begins the day's lesson by reading aloud from articles about Rosa Parks and the bus boycott in Montgomery, Alabama. The read-aloud is followed by a discussion of the readings and a brief introduction to America's civil rights movement. These opening activities provide historical context that will help students appreciate the next few chapters of their novel. Students are then given time to read silently from the novel and write responses to their reading in reading logs, or journals. As students work, the teacher walks through the classroom, offering individual instruction and answers to questions.

The next day, the teacher breaks the class into small groups. For fifteen minutes or so, several groups of four to five students engage in lively conversation about their reading. As the students talk with one another, the teacher moves from group to group, listening and recording information that will shape instruction, assessment, and whole-class discussion. Finally, the teacher reconvenes the class and facilitates a whole-class discussion to share ideas and written responses and to clarify themes.

In another Book Club classroom, students are reading a novel about characters who are dealing with personal tragedy. Understanding similarities and differences between characters is an important part of appreciating the novel. So, after the students take time to read silently from the novel, the teacher gives a short lesson on using comparison and contrast to understand characters. The class works together to create a Venn diagram charting the similarities and differences between two characters in the novel. Then students are asked to respond individually in their reading logs by summarizing ideas they recorded in the class chart. When their responses are finished, students gather in their book clubs. The teacher, walking through the classroom, can hear that the lesson on comparison and contrast has helped the students focus their discussions and look more deeply into the characters. The teacher then brings the students together for a whole-class discussion, in which students share final thoughts about the day's lesson.

These two scenarios are examples of what you might encounter if you were to visit a Book Club classroom. However, Book Club lessons can and do unfold in a variety of ways—as long as they include the following components: high-quality literature; small, student-led discussion groups; opportunities for students to read and to write about what they read; and whole-class discussions and activities. Although these features vary from day to day and from classroom to classroom, they always form the foundation of the program. Book Club teachers have found that this foundation allows them to meet the essential goals set forth by the National Middle School Association for a developmentally responsive middle school education, including providing a curriculum that is challenging, integrative, and exploratory; providing varied teaching and learning approaches; and providing flexible organizational structures. Meeting these goals, in turn, fosters literacy and a positive attitude toward reading and learning.

When discussing Book Club, we find it useful to divide the program into four major components: reading, writing, community share, and book clubs. Keep in mind, however, that these components frequently overlap when they are actually put into practice in a classroom. As an introduction to the program, we will examine and discuss each component separately.

Reading

Reading is the most fundamental part of the Book Club program. While it seems logical that reading would be central to any literature/reading program, our review of research and our own observations have presented a different and rather disheartening picture. We've found that in many classrooms, the kinds of texts students read and the amount of time they spend reading are quite restricted. All too often, little consideration is given to students' interests and prior knowledge or to incorporating texts that are strong models of language and meaning. Students spend more time answering simple questions and completing workbook activities than engaging with literature that both inspires them and teaches them about language.

In designing the crucial reading portion of our program, we remained committed to the following goals: using quality literature, using texts that

► **Components of Book Club**

All elements of the program support students' book club discussions. In order for students to succeed in Book Club, the teacher must provide direct instruction in how to use reading skills and strategies, how to use writing as a tool for thinking, and how to participate in both whole-class and small-group discussions.

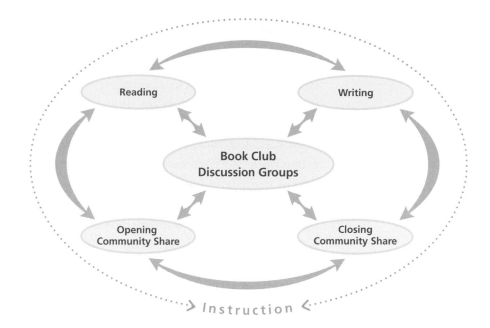

relate to students' interests and that help build students' knowledge, and providing extended periods of time each day for students to interact with texts—through reading aloud or silently, with a partner or independently, or through listening to a teacher or classmate read aloud to the class. A program that meets these goals provides students with multiple opportunities to interact with and find meaning in a variety of texts.

The reading component of Book Club has three important aspects: (1) reading "contexts"—various situations within which reading activities can occur; (2) texts—the books, essays, articles, and poems that students read; and (3) instructional focus areas drawn from national, state, and district guidelines.

Offering a Variety of Reading Contexts

Book Club involves three key reading contexts that move from greatest to least amount of teacher control. These are the teacher read-aloud; book club reading; and independent, sustained silent reading.

Teacher Read-Aloud The teacher read-aloud allows you to share with students a novel, story, article, or poem that relates in some way to the book students are reading and discussing in their book clubs. The piece might involve a similar topic, theme, or genre, or it might be by the same author. A good read-aloud selection may expose students to text at a higher level than that which they can read independently, thus expanding their vocabulary and oral comprehension. A single read-aloud selection may span an entire unit, providing continuity for the classroom community, informing discussions of theme and issues, and encouraging ties to other readings. If the entire class is reading the same book for book club discussions, the read-aloud can be used to support students' reading of that book. For example, you might alternate reading a chapter from the book aloud with having students read a chapter silently. This strategy can help students read the book more quickly, clarify confusing passages, and help struggling readers access the book more easily. Reading aloud can occur at any time during the lesson, and it has proven to serve a number of important functions.

First, reading aloud can encourage and teach students to make intertextual connections. We want students to realize that a book can remind us of or help us understand another book. Using a read-aloud book that has connections to the book students are reading for their discussions allows you to model how to make such intertextual links. We've found that students quickly learn to make these kinds of connections on their own. Their discussions and written responses become richer when they can draw from material in several related texts.

Second, you can use the read-aloud to model how good readers connect literature to their own lives. By pausing to talk about what you think and feel as you read, you can demonstrate for students how they might use a book to make sense of their own world. This technique also shows them how a reader can use personal experiences and prior knowledge to bring meaning to a text.

Third, listening to you read aloud helps students develop their own fluency and improves their use of language in writing and speaking. As they hear you read with good intonation, inflection, and emotion, students begin to develop an appreciation for language. They might hear beauty or rhythm that they would have missed in their silent reading. We've noticed that students' language use in both discussions and written work expands to include words and concepts from our read-aloud books.

Finally, the read-aloud helps build a literate community within your classroom. You and your students share a common experience within which you can work together to search for meaning, build knowledge, form opinions, express beliefs, and grow as a community of readers.

Book Club Reading In the book club reading context, students meet with their book clubs to read the book they are currently discussing or related texts. The teacher's role is minimal most of the time; occasionally you might work directly to support struggling readers, but rarely would you teach a formal lesson or model during this time. In the same way the teacher read-aloud supports students' understanding of their reading, students' reading in pairs or with a group of peers can help them reach a greater understanding of texts. Students might alternate reading silently with reading chapters aloud to one another. Some might even enjoy a chance to "perform" portions of a book for their peers. Another option is to allow readers to listen together to a professional reading of a text. This context asks students as a group to take more responsibility for their own reading comprehension and for the comprehension of their peers. (Chapters 3 and 5 discuss inclusion strategies and provide tips on helping all students to access literature.)

Independent Reading Sustained silent reading gives the greatest amount of choice for students and requires the least teacher involvement. When a class embarks on a Book Club unit, the classroom should be filled with high-quality books that relate to the theme or themes in the unit. This special classroom library should include books from a variety of genres that are below, at, and above the average reading level for the classroom. Students should then be given regular intervals of time in which they can read to build their own intertextual connections and background knowledge. Independent reading gives students a chance to both challenge and reinforce their learning from the other reading contexts. Furthermore, research has demonstrated that daily reading significantly increases students' vocabulary and improves their performances on standardized tests.

Choosing Literature: A Focus on Quality and Content

Although what constitutes "quality" literature is a subjective judgment, we have developed criteria for choosing books to be used in Book Club units and classroom libraries. First, of course, we rely on our own judgment as readers and educators. We also turn to reviews in professional journals such as the *Journal of Adolescent and Adult Literacy* and *Language Arts*. Additionally, we examine books that have received the Newbery Medal, the Caldecott Medal, the Coretta Scott King Award, and other notable honors. We try to choose books that will be enjoyable to students, that demonstrate an effective use of language, and that students may not choose to read on their own.

Besides looking for high-quality literature, we seek books with content that will interest young readers. These books might include characters that are of the same age or just a bit older. This seems to help students connect to a variety of characters across settings and cultures. We also like to choose books with cross-curricular connections that allow students to relate litera-ture to other subject areas, such as science or social studies. Book Club books should also feature content that promotes dialogue and discussion, since this is a key part of the curriculum. As students read the books, they should be eager to discuss them with their peers. (For detailed information on selecting and acquiring Book Club titles, see Chapter 5, pages 51 and 53.)

Providing Explicit Literacy Instruction

The Book Club program never overlooks opportunities to provide students with explicit instruction in literacy skills, strategies, and knowledge bases. This instruction happens most often in opening community share (see page 20). It can also happen when you meet with individual students in conferences, when you work with struggling readers to support their understanding of a book, and when you help students record their ideas in reading logs (see page 17). The Book Club curriculum can be adapted to meet national, state, and district

⬧ BUILDING A LIBRARY

What types of books might you include in your classroom library? The civil rights unit in Chapter 8 of this guide provides an excellent example. To support their reading in book clubs, students have opportunities to read poetry by Langston Hughes, essays and a letter by Martin Luther King, Jr., speeches by Malcolm X, relevant picture books, autobio-graphical accounts from the time period, and origi-nal source materials such as newspaper and maga-zine articles about events of that time. The class-room library for this unit provides a wide variety of materials that accommo-date many reading levels.

standards. Book Club is unique in that it builds knowledge and literacy that students need to pass tests and succeed in school while also fostering a love of reading and a sense of self-confidence as readers that will last a lifetime.

Writing

Traditional reading workbooks are structured around literal comprehension questions. As we've said before, this approach to reading as a hunt for right answers does not turn students into readers. The Book Club program asks students to respond to their reading in more open-ended ways. As a result, our students sharpen their writing skills and their critical-thinking skills. They take ownership of writing as they learn to use it as a tool to facilitate their own thinking. They also come to see ideas in books as complex, interesting, and relevant to their own lives, rather than just material for tedious worksheets.

Emphasizing Three Categories of Response

Our program emphasizes three categories of response to literature: personal, creative, and critical. Personal response deals with a student's emotional response to a text and encourages the student to relate the text to his or her own life through writing. For example, a student might write a journal entry or a personal essay that explains why he or she has something in common with a particular character or situation. Creative response allows a student to use his or her imagination to explore ideas in a text. For example, a student might write a poem based on a book's theme, write a dialogue based on the text, describe a situation from a character's point of view, or imagine what

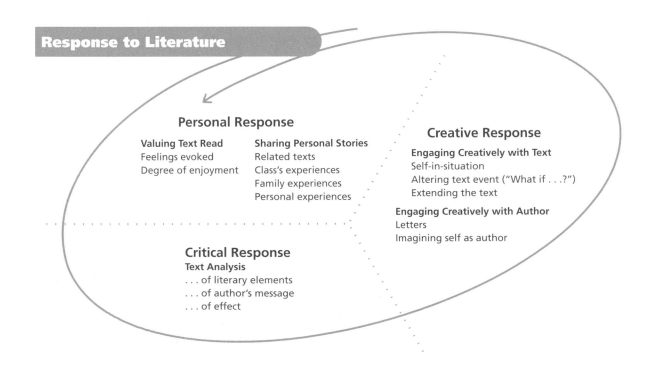

Response to Literature

Personal Response

Valuing Text Read
Feelings evoked
Degree of enjoyment

Sharing Personal Stories
Related texts
Class's experiences
Family experiences
Personal experiences

Creative Response

Engaging Creatively with Text
Self-in-situation
Altering text event ("What if . . .?")
Extending the text

Engaging Creatively with Author
Letters
Imagining self as author

Critical Response
Text Analysis
. . . of literary elements
. . . of author's message
. . . of effect

might happen next in a book. A student engages in critical response when he or she analyzes aspects of a literary work in an essay or a paragraph. Critical response might involve critiquing the author's use of literary techniques, explaining in writing why the techniques are effective or ineffective. The chart on page 16 provides more details about the response types on which Book Club's writing component is based.

Focusing and Recording Student Responses

Students who are used to answering factual-recall questions on worksheets will not automatically start writing personal, creative, and critical responses once they begin Book Club—nor will they have a conscious understanding of the difference between these response types. Students need instruction and support to develop their skills in using writing as a tool for thinking and as a means for personal expression.

Reading Logs Book Club students are encouraged to record their ideas, feelings, and questions in reading logs as they read. These logs can consist of both blank and lined pages that allow students to diagram, draw, or write their responses. At the beginning of the year, it's important to provide instruction and to model for students the various response possibilities that are open to them. Students should also be encouraged to invent new ways of responding and to share their inventions with the class.

The main purpose of reading logs is to help students focus on issues that they can discuss in their discussion groups. Reading logs are also places where they can record puzzling vocabulary words and questions that they would like their peers or teacher to help them answer. Writing in reading logs solidifies students' thinking, pushes them to explore new ideas, challenges them to approach their reading from multiple angles, and prepares them for subsequent reading assignments and discussions.

Think Sheets Think sheets work effectively with reading logs to help students examine what they read. They are open-ended worksheets that introduce students to new ways of thinking about and responding to texts. They can also help students organize their thoughts. For example, the think sheet on page 18 gives students topics to help them respond in their reading logs. Notice that the sheet also invites students to work with their peers to create and define their own topics.

Think sheets can be specific to the content or theme of a book that students are reading. Beginning on page 153 of this guide, you'll find a full range of think sheets—some that can be used with any Book Club unit, some that relate directly to Lois Lowry's novel *The Giver* (see Chapters 6 and 7), and some that relate to a multi-book unit on civil rights (see Chapter 8). For example, Think Sheets 4 and 12 provide students with specific reading log/discussion ideas for *The Giver*. Think Sheet 16 guides students to recognize and understand the author's use of foreshadowing throughout this novel.

Think sheets also play an important role in guiding students to assess their own work and monitor their own progress in Book Club. For example, Think Sheet 10 provides students with a revision checklist that will help them finalize essays related to their reading. Evaluation Sheets 7 and 8 (see the section following page 187) encourage students to set goals for their reading logs and their book club groups at the start of a unit. Evaluation Sheets 9 and 10 help students assess their work on completing a unit.

You might use think sheets to guide students toward using reading strategies and skills that are required by your school's curriculum. For example, a think sheet might ask students to create a sequence chart, summarize events, make predictions, generate questions, identify themes, locate examples of figurative language, or answer questions about characterization or

▶ **Tripod Think Sheet**
We developed this think sheet to remind and encourage students to approach literature from more than one angle. The "angles of literary response" in this tripod format are Text, Critical Response, and Personal and Creative Response. Whenever possible, students are expected to select response types from more than one angle. The think sheet promotes balance in the way students respond to their reading, allows teachers to address specific literary skills, and gives students a goal list to help them monitor their own reading awareness.

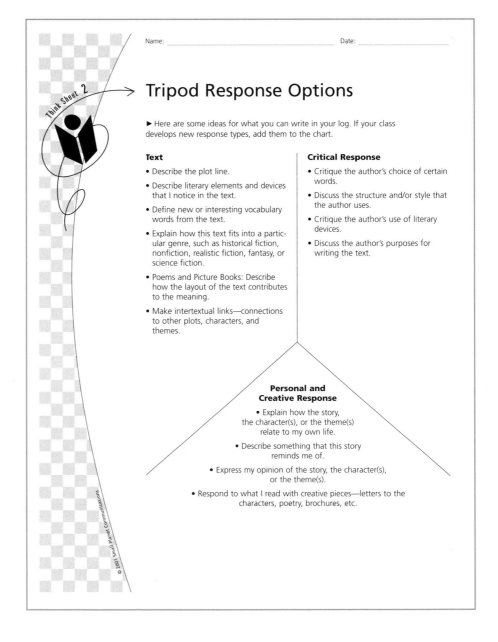

Name: _____   Date: _____

Think Sheet 2

Tripod Response Options

▶ Here are some ideas for what you can write in your log. If your class develops new response types, add them to the chart.

Text
- Describe the plot line.
- Describe literary elements and devices that I notice in the text.
- Define new or interesting vocabulary words from the text.
- Explain how this text fits into a particular genre, such as historical fiction, nonfiction, realistic fiction, fantasy, or science fiction.
- Poems and Picture Books: Describe how the layout of the text contributes to the meaning.
- Make intertextual links—connections to other plots, characters, and themes.

Critical Response
- Critique the author's choice of certain words.
- Discuss the structure and/or style that the author uses.
- Critique the author's use of literary devices.
- Discuss the author's purposes for writing the text.

Personal and Creative Response
- Explain how the story, the character(s), or the theme(s) relate to my own life.
- Describe something that this story reminds me of.
- Express my opinion of the story, the character(s), or the theme(s).
- Respond to what I read with creative pieces—letters to the characters, poetry, brochures, etc.

© 2001 Small Planet Communications

point of view. Think sheets model for students responses that will help them respond to literature independently in their reading logs. In Book Club, log responses that students create themselves on blank or lined paper (instead of on preformatted think sheets) are called *share sheets.* As students master more sophisticated methods of analyzing literature, you might ask them to brainstorm a share-sheet idea list to be displayed in the classroom. Allowing students opportunities to use and share their own ideas gives them a sense of confidence and a voice in their own literacy learning.

Incorporating Process Writing

In addition to asking our middle school students to respond directly to their reading in various ways, we've expanded the writing component of our program to include process writing and extended writing assignments. Our students complete research papers and presentations; creative pieces such as poetry, short stories, or skits; and extended essays on various themes or topics. For example, in our civil rights unit (Chapter 8), students are asked to "write into the unit" by planning and completing a research report on a civil rights topic. They "write through the unit" by responding to their reading assignments in their logs, by writing a poem, and by writing a final essay. Students then "write out of the unit" by completing a speech, children's book, or other creative piece on a social issue of their choice. We have found that extended assignments complement reading log responses to strengthen students' writing skills and build their knowledge of a topic, theme, or genre. Through extended assignments, students learn to budget time, work cooperatively, and complete a full revision process. Extended assignments can also be used as a means for assessment or as a way to connect a novel or theme to other curriculum areas.

Community Share

Community share is our name for all whole-class discussions within Book Club. This component, which is divided into opening community share and closing community share, is where students and teachers can bring ideas from their reading, writing, and small-group discussions to the wider classroom community. Because community share is firmly grounded in our understanding that learning is a social process and that higher-order thought processes are encouraged by social interactions, it is especially integral to the Book Club curriculum. Community share allows the teacher, as both a leader of and a participant in the conversation, to introduce skills and new ideas, to assist students who are struggling or misinterpreting information in their reading, and to facilitate the sharing of personal ideas and feelings between students. During this time, the teacher should encourage and support students in making intertextual connections and in responding to the text in a variety of ways.

Opening Community Share

Opening community share often involves a lesson in which you can discuss and teach response options, discussion skills, comprehension strategies, author's craft, or background information. It's important to keep in mind that opening community share can "float" in the daily schedule of activities, depending on the purpose you want it to serve. (See the chart on page 21.) For example, if you want to provide historical information to help students appreciate the next chapter they will read, it makes sense to provide this information before they begin reading. If you want to review or suggest a type of written response, it makes sense to instruct students after they read and just before they respond in their logs. If you want to suggest a particular discussion technique, it makes sense to hold community share just before students meet in their book clubs. Some teachers even divide the opening community share instruction by beginning the day with a lesson and then holding another meeting after the reading. In short, place opening community share wherever you feel it will be most beneficial to your students on a particular day.

Closing Community Share

Closing community share occurs after book clubs. We consider it a "debriefing" session during which students can make final connections, tie events in their reading to themes in the book as a whole, revisit past lessons, discuss their feelings about the most recent lesson, and examine interesting and confusing words from the reading. You might ask students what they found most difficult or interesting about the lesson taught in opening community share or about their group's discussion. You might also invite students to bring up any problems or sources of confusion so that the whole class can discuss these issues. It's crucial that students have this time so that they can start the next day's reading feeling confident and ready for new information.

Book Clubs

Student book clubs are the crux of the Book Club program, and all the other program components work to support these discussions. Through book clubs, students learn about the relationship between spoken and written language and practice valuable communication skills. It is the program's goal to have students engage in real conversations in which they take an interest in their peers' ideas and opinions while also taking responsibility for their own learning. When students read, write in their reading logs, and take part in community share, they are preparing themselves to do just that.

To help our student book clubs be successful, we first give careful thought to the grouping of students. We have learned over the years that groups of four or five students tend to be most effective. This number provides stability and allows for a variety of ideas while still giving every student a chance to

Placement of Community Share

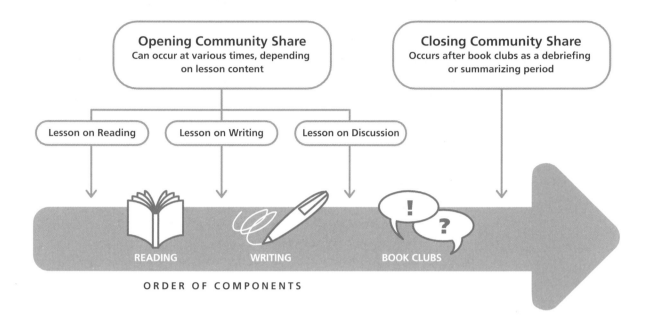

talk. We also take into consideration the personalities, communication styles, and ability levels of our students. At the beginning of a unit, it's important to listen in on conversations and check in with students to find out which groupings are working and which are struggling. For more information on forming groups, see Chapter 5, page 56.

Another way we ensure the success of book clubs is by offering discussion tips and strategies throughout a unit. The goal is to have students lead their own conversations, but we know that instruction and guidance are keys to helping them reach this goal. The way you lead discussion during community share provides a solid model for students to follow in their book clubs. In community share, you demonstrate the kinds of ideas, questions, and topics that can be explored in a real book discussion. Lessons on specific, conventional skills also give students structure from which to work. These lessons help students focus on necessary reading skills, develop conversational skills that they can bring to their groups, and gain practice in discussing literature. We also give our students concrete tools that they can take with them to their book groups. In community share, the class might generate a list of the features of a good book discussion. Students can add to this list and refer to it throughout a unit. Think Sheet 7, Questions for My Book Club, is another tool that can help students begin conversations in their groups. We also encourage students to use their reading logs as starting points for their discussions. As students gain more experience in community share and book club settings, their discussions become both more sophisticated and more natural. Chapter 5 expands on these ideas and offers additional tips for guiding and supporting book club groups.

Ownership

All components of Book Club ultimately emphasize the concept of ownership. This is the idea that students can feel a sense of empowerment and control when it comes to their own literacy activities. Only when they have this confidence in themselves as readers can they truly begin to delight in reading and in sharing ideas about books. Ownership allows students to be true participants in their reading and learning and in the learning of others. Book Club teacher Kathy Highfield[1] tells the following story to illustrate the idea of ownership:

> At the conclusion of reading and discussing *Charley Skedaddle,* [a student named] Natalie's written response shows ownership. She clearly values reading, has a positive attitude, enjoys reading, and shows a strong desire to share her love of reading with her family. . . . Natalie writes:

> "This book was just wonderful! I love this book, as a matter of fact, I think I'll take it home and read it to my mom or just have my sister read it, but I can't have my brother read it cause it takes forever for him to read a 12 page book! This is because he doesn't take pleasure in reading. (What I said about the 12 page book isn't true, but it sure feels like it!) I love all the books you read to us. I want to take them all home and read them to my brother or just have him read them. I want him to be in this class so he can read all of these books cause there just so wonderful! (By the way have you noticed a strong liking between me and the books.)"

> True to her beliefs, the following year, when Natalie discovered that her brother was not placed in my room, she came to me and asked what I could do to have him moved to my room, so that he could learn to love reading. While it was beyond my control, her follow-through and genuine interest in another's literacy learning further emphasizes Natalie's ownership and sense of agency around literacy learning.

Through their interactions within Book Club's components, students learn to share in their own learning process, set goals, identify ways to meet these goals, and develop positive, lifelong habits of literacy.

Reference

1   Kathy Highfield, "Evidence of Literacy Learning in a Literature-Based Reading Program," in Kathryn H. Au and Taffy E. Raphael (eds.), *Literature-Based Instruction: Reshaping the Curriculum* (Norwood, MA: Christopher-Gordon Publishers, 1998).

Chapter Three

Adolescents and Book Club

Understanding Young Adolescents

How do we best characterize that distinct stage of life called adolescence? We all know the image of the sullen, uncommunicative youth. Or the hormone-driven preteen drawn to loud clothing and loud music. Or the painfully self-conscious young person caught between childhood and adulthood. What is myth and what is truth in our beliefs about young adolescents? And how do we view this challenging period in a positive light and tap into the enormous learning potential that our young adolescents possess? As Book Club teachers, we have the opportunity to explore these questions through reading and talking about books—activities that work well with the special strengths and interests of young adolescents.

The developmental changes to the body and mind that mark early adolescence affect the work we do in our middle school classrooms—particularly in classrooms that regularly call on interpersonal skills, personal expression, and cooperative learning. The distinguishing traits of adolescents shown in this chart highlight the complex social needs of adolescents as they seek to define themselves. Understanding these needs is the first step toward creating a learning environment that will allow our students to succeed.

Distinctive Traits of Adolescents[1]

Adolescents continually strive for . . .

- competence.
- autonomy and personal identity.
- positive interaction with peers and adults.
- physical activity.
- meaningful participation in school and community.
- structure and clear limits.

It's helpful to examine the various kinds of change experienced by adolescents—physical, intellectual, social, and emotional—and to observe how these kinds of change affect one another and influence the feelings and actions of our students.

Physical Development

Physical development—the most visible of changes that occur in adolescence—often affects how students view themselves and interact with one another. It's a somewhat unkind reality that just as early teens are becoming more self-aware, they must deal with growth spurts, hormonal increases, and other physical changes that increase their feelings of self-consciousness and insecurity. The fact that same-age students mature physically at vastly different rates only complicates these circumstances. We know that late or early physical development can affect students' behavior and can even affect our expectations of students. For example, a student might appear more or less mature than he or she actually is. We also know that, on average, girls' growth spurts peak about two years earlier than boys' do. Being among the first or among the last students in the class to deal with these kinds of physical changes can be hard on self-esteem.

Girls tend to struggle the most with appearance issues during this volatile time. As a result, self-consciousness can lead many of them to try to hide in the background and avoid drawing attention to themselves in class. Extra support and encouragement in the classroom can help both girls and boys who are painfully self-conscious. However, we must recognize that we are constantly fighting peer opinions as well as media images that promote gender stereotypes. These have a powerful effect on the minds of growing and changing adolescents and influence how our students treat themselves and others.

In addition to changes in physical appearance, young adolescents often experience changes in their energy and activity levels. Fluctuating hormones, controlled by the pituitary gland, cause intense restlessness and a need for physical activity as well as periods of lethargy and fatigue. Activities that allow students to move around the classroom and/or engage in hands-on projects accommodate students' need for movement. Giving students a different kind of activity every 15 to 20 minutes also helps prevent boredom and restlessness.

Intellectual Development

As early adolescents experience physical changes, they also experience changes in their intellectual functioning—changes brought on by brain development as well as by new experiences. Students at this age have an increased capacity for abstract thought and a strengthening ability to analyze and solve hypothetical problems. Jean Piaget [2] describes this stage of human development—when a person is no longer limited to dealing with concrete objects—as "formal operational." Aspects of formal thought include the ability to examine abstract ideas and make connections to solve problems; the ability to think about and plan for the future; the ability to be self-reflective; a sense of idealism; and a need to explore new possibilities.

As teachers, we see that these newly developing abilities can result in students who are endlessly questioning and curious, as well as thoroughly fascinated by and absorbed in their own thoughts, beliefs, and questions about the world. An effective middle school curriculum taps into this natural curiosity and capacity for critical thought. Ideally, these students—hungering for new ideas, answers to big questions, and outlets for self-expression—should be active participants in their own learning. Creative writing or creative projects allow them to explore their identities and personal beliefs; critical essays allow them to explore and challenge ideas; discussions allow them to exchange ideas with others, get feedback on their ideas, and expand their thinking; and reading offers them an opportunity to explore new worlds and search for answers. These are just some of the ways we can encourage and honor the intellectual growth of young adolescents.

Social and Emotional Development

Young adolescents' social interactions and emotional growth are directly affected by the physical and intellectual changes they experience. As anyone who works with these students knows, socialization plays the most important role in the life of any young adolescent. Study after study reveals that middle school students consider making friends and fitting in with their peers to be the most challenging and most important aspects of going to school. And, just when students are searching for a sense of security amid dramatic physical and intellectual changes, they find themselves leaving the safe world of elementary school behind to face new social and academic challenges. We've found that we can best serve these students' needs if our middle school curriculums meet students' social needs as well as their academic needs.

In organizing and facilitating classroom activities, it's especially important to keep in mind the crucial role of peers in the lives of young adolescents. Students look to peers for models of behavior and for approval. Some "perform" for their peers to get attention. Others refrain from doing or saying anything that might invite ridicule or stand out as "different" in any way. These feelings and behaviors obviously affect classroom activities that call for collaboration and an open exchange of ideas. Book Club's use of small discussion groups provides a safer, more intimate environment in which students who are shy in whole-class discussions can participate and blossom. When grouping students in book clubs, teachers must consider the personalities of individual students and how their presence may affect the behavior of other individuals in a small-group setting.

Additionally, we must take into account students' emerging interest in the opposite sex. Most middle school students still prefer the companionship of their own gender. However, influenced by the media and by older students, boys and girls do begin to engage in casual flirting and sometimes develop increased levels of self-consciousness around one another. When grouping students for discussions or collaborative projects, we pay close attention to the nuances of peer relationships; these relationships are at the heart of social and emotional development in middle school. (For more on grouping, see Chapter 5, page 56.)

We know that people define themselves in relation to others. During the teen years, these "others" are most often peers, fictional characters, public personalities, and adults whom young people can admire. In their quest for identity, adolescents continually compare and contrast their appearance, values, and ideas with those of others in order to formulate an identity that fits. In the area of language arts, much of this identity work can be done through reading good adolescent fiction, which typically deals with relevant "coming of age" issues. The other role our classrooms can play in enabling adolescents to explore their own identities is to provide a safe and meaningful context in which they can discuss their ideas with their peers.

As middle school teachers, presenting activities and learning experiences that support adolescents' developing sense of autonomy, self, and values should rank high on our list of goals. In fact, this quest for identity is often seen as the most important task of adolescence, crucial in building self-esteem. If we base our school environments and instructional methods on what we know about adolescent development and support our students in their search for self, we are more likely to guide them toward success.

Meeting the Developmental Needs of Adolescents in the Classroom

Building a Safe Learning Environment

Responding to the call for more supportive learning environments for young adolescents, many teachers have worked to strike a balance between students' interests and opportunities to teach. These teachers focus on students' developmental needs, recognizing that meeting these needs can reduce stress and contribute to greater academic and personal success. In all subject areas, it's important to help students build interpersonal skills, practice decision making, and feel safe expressing their ideas and taking academic risks.

Some middle schools achieve these goals through advisory programs. In an advisory program, an advisor (usually a teacher) meets regularly with a small group of students for the purpose of helping them develop safe, trusting relationships. These groups help students in the areas of understanding the self and others, problem solving, developing community awareness, sharpening communication skills, planning for the future, and working through academic stresses. Through a variety of cooperative activities, students learn to communicate with their peers constructively and to give and receive support. Advisory projects often involve community outreach as well.

We've found that a literature/language arts program can benefit from adapting some of the principles of advisory programs to its own purposes in literacy instruction. In Book Club, we constantly look for opportunities to reflect on feelings in the context of literature discussion. For example, we often ask students to analyze the feelings/behaviors of characters and relate those feelings/behaviors to their own. In forming book clubs, we use grouping to encourage interaction among students who might not normally interact with one another. We try to separate close friends and create groups that reflect the racial, ethnic, and gender diversity of the community. If your school has an advisory program, consult with your students' advisors to find out how each student functions in his or her advisory group. This information can help you form effective book clubs in your classroom.

We also spend time explicitly naming and discussing problematic behaviors (as well as positive ones) through opening community share, mini lessons, and fishbowl (see page 59). Problems that students learn to avoid include quitting, interrupting, disagreeing, arguing, shouting, name calling, etc. Students learn techniques for negotiation and conflict resolution. We've found that establishing supportive peer groups and allowing students to have some control in their study of literature builds confidence and enthusiasm in the classroom. This type of curriculum fosters students' intellectual, social, and emotional development—all while building literacy.

Establishing a Differentiated Classroom

A classroom environment that meets the developmental needs of its students must part ways with certain traditional but limiting educational practices. In our own classrooms, we have seen firsthand the benefits of moving toward a differentiated classroom—that is, a classroom that honors the diversity and special needs of its students. In a differentiated classroom, we follow some of these basic principles:

- Planning is built around student differences, not on the idea that all students learn in the same manner.

- Assessment is ongoing and informs instruction, rather than occurring only at the end of a unit to catch those students who failed to learn.

- Teachers use a variety of activities that focus on multiple intelligences and learning styles.

- Students are graded and evaluated on individual growth.

- Students are given more responsibility for their own learning (e.g., through self-assessment) and are encouraged to communicate their own interests and concerns.

Placing these ideas at the crux of a curriculum allows for students who represent a variety of interests and ability levels to succeed.

Designing an Effective Literacy Program

In continually planning and updating our Book Club program, we've had success drawing from the principles of advisory programs and differentiated classrooms. We also look to numerous studies that outline the components of an effective literacy program for young adolescents. Citing case studies of proven adolescent literacy programs, Judith Davidson and David Koppenhaver [3] have noted five essential components:

1. vision and definition
2. developmental responsiveness
3. academic effectiveness
4. access to the world of the written word
5. organization to ensure success for all

Book Club contains all of these components. The program's vision is clear: we aim to develop students' ownership of literacy by providing them with both excellent literature and the tools they need to read, write about, and discuss this literature. Book Club for the middle grades is grounded in our understanding of adolescent needs and interests. The program is responsive to the unique physical, intellectual, social, and emotional characteristics of young adolescents and takes advantage of their natural inclinations toward wrestling with serious issues and sharing ideas with their peers. Book Club has proven academic effectiveness: Our research indicates that not only do Book Club students perform well on standardized tests, they also tend to outperform their peers in more authentic assessments, such as writing essays, creating responses to literature, and informal evaluations such as Quality Reading Inventory (QRI). Our commitment to keeping students in heterogeneous groups and to providing even our most struggling readers with age-appropriate texts ensures access to the written word and success for all of our students.

Engaging Adolescent Readers in Literature

In addition to highlighting adolescents' needs in the curriculum, there are several other crucial areas that we need to address to make a literature program successful for middle school students. First, we must invite students into the literature by selecting excellent books worthy of discussion. We must also invite them into each theme, perhaps even before they encounter the books, by choosing themes that young adults can relate to and discuss. Then, remembering our commitment to heterogeneous classrooms and groups, we must provide the assistance or scaffolding necessary to help struggling readers gain access to texts containing age-appropriate content. Last, if we want

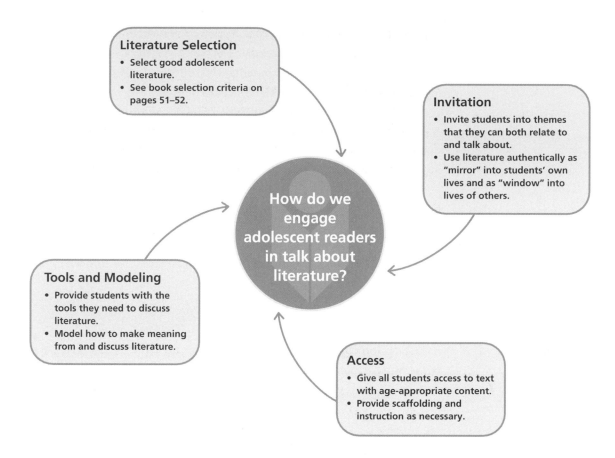

Literature Selection
- Select good adolescent literature.
- See book selection criteria on pages 51–52.

Invitation
- Invite students into themes that they can both relate to and talk about.
- Use literature authentically as "mirror" into students' own lives and as "window" into lives of others.

How do we engage adolescent readers in talk about literature?

Tools and Modeling
- Provide students with the tools they need to discuss literature.
- Model how to make meaning from and discuss literature.

Access
- Give all students access to text with age-appropriate content.
- Provide scaffolding and instruction as necessary.

students to be truly successful, we must provide them with the tools necessary for reading, writing about, and discussing good literature. This requires a combination of explicit instruction and continual modeling of the necessary skills for complex meaning making. For example, borrowing a term from the emergent literacy community, we must "lend them the language" for substantive talk about text, so that they may eventually appropriate this in their own contexts, even those beyond our classrooms.

Practices of Good Readers[4]

Good readers . . .

1. make connections.
2. monitor their own comprehension.
3. repair faulty comprehension.
4. distinguish important from less important information.
5. synthesize information within and across texts and experiences.
6. visualize.
7. make inferences.
8. ask questions of themselves, authors, and texts.

Working with Proficient Adolescent Readers

One of the dilemmas of the middle school language arts teacher is "Exactly what should I be teaching?" Though national, state, and district guidelines may provide some guidance, and good teachers are always moving their students forward, this question comes loaded with assumptions, some valid and some not. Certainly the most popular assumption of our middle school students is that they already know how to read. Although this may be true for the majority of them, this is an assumption worth checking out. The ability to read is more complex than most of our current assessments would have us believe. Even our very best readers can benefit from instruction in practices we know to be true of good readers. The list on page 29 summarizes some of these practices.

To strengthen the skills of students who are already reading on level, we suggest continually reviewing the practices of good readers. One way to outline these practices for students is to present them in three parts: before-reading practices, during-reading practices, and after-reading practices.

Before Reading
- Preview text.
- Determine text type and analyze structure of text.
- Build background information. (What do I know about this topic? Have I read other pieces like this?)
- Set a purpose for reading. (What am I reading to find out?)

During Reading
- Adjust reading for different purposes.
- Visualize what is described in text.
- Continually monitor understanding and fix comprehension. Use strategies such as questioning, determining the most important ideas, making inferences, and rereading.
- Integrate what I read with what I already know.

After Reading
- Decide if my goals for reading have been met.
- Evaluate my understanding of what I've read.
- Summarize my ideas about what I've read.
- Apply what I've learned to new situations.

Working with Struggling Adolescent Readers

Besides working on the comprehension strategies mentioned above, our most struggling readers need extra support and instruction. What exactly should be the teacher's role in literacy education for these students? We often describe the dilemma inherent in this question as the "dual obligations of reading instruction." On one hand, we're obligated to provide students with reading materials at their *age level,* or text containing content relevant and intriguing to students of that particular age. This is especially important if we want our students to enjoy reading, make connections, see legitimate reasons for reading, and become lifelong readers. On the other hand, we're also obligated to teach students at their *reading level,* defined roughly as the level at which they achieve 70 to 90 percent accuracy/comprehension/fluency. In this way we can build on students' current skills and, through scaffolding, improve their reading overall.

Yet, for the struggling reader, these two obligations often appear at odds—and at the expense of the student. If students experience text only at their reading level, presumably a level significantly lower than that of their same-age peers, the texts themselves are likely to be uninteresting and/or obviously "baby stuff" written for younger readers. It's no wonder that struggling readers tend not to enjoy reading such materials, and we know this to be a vicious circle in which their lack of enjoyment causes them to read less, which in turn puts them further behind.

With this understanding, Book Club has been designed to meet both of the "dual obligations" of reading instruction. We are committed to providing all our students with age-appropriate texts. This means that struggling readers will need a good deal of support to access this text. And so we promote using books on tape, allowing buddy reading, and enlisting the help of parents and support personnel to make sure all readers have access to the book at hand. We've found that inclusion in book clubs gives struggling readers an added incentive to work on their comprehension of text. They are inspired to read because they want to be able to join the conversation around each book. Moreover, book clubs allow these children, many of whom have oral language abilities that outstrip their reading and writing skills, to capitalize on their strengths.

It's important to keep in mind that some students simply need a few more tools and strategies in order to read as well as some of their peers. Scaffolding from the teacher—in the form of background information, read-aloud sessions, guided reading questions, and reviews of the practices of good readers—can give struggling readers the boost they need to enjoy and understand their reading. Reminding students of the KWL strategy (what you **know**, what you **want** to know, and what you want to **learn**) is one helpful strategy that encourages active reading.

The QAR (Question-Answer Relationships) strategy gives readers useful tools for analyzing questions about text as well as for creating effective questions for literature discussions. Reading is a process of combining information from a text with the reader's own knowledge. The four types of questions defined by QAR give students a framework for understanding the sources of specific information. "Right There" questions are answered in a single sentence within a text. "Think and Search" questions require information from more than one sentence or paragraph. "On Your Own" questions can be answered from the reader's background knowledge alone. "Author and You" questions pull information from both the text and the reader's own knowledge. In Book Club, QAR can help students answer questions provided by the teacher (e.g.,

Teaching Strategies for Struggling Readers

✔ Scaffolding to give certain students the head start they need to be successful (background information, guided reading, reading aloud)
✔ Information-processing practices such as KWL
✔ Questioning practices such as QAR and SQ3R
✔ Reciprocal teaching
✔ Summarizing
✔ Encouraging recreational reading

writing prompts for their daily reading logs), and it can facilitate better discussions because teachers and students have a vocabulary for talking about good questions. For example, if a teacher notices that the students in one book club are asking each other lots of "Right There" questions, he or she can suggest that the students formulate more "Author and You" and "On Your Own" questions.

SQ3R (Survey, Question, Read, Recite, Review) is a reading strategy familiar to many teachers. It is most often used for nonfiction texts but may be applied to fiction as well. Before students read, they survey the text. This might include examining the book cover, reading any text on the back of the book, and reviewing chapter titles. Students formulate questions as they survey, perhaps turning chapter titles into questions or asking themselves what they already know about the setting or subject of the book. When students begin reading, they look for answers to their survey questions, monitor their comprehension, and employ fix-up strategies as needed. After reading, students may "recite" by asking themselves questions about the text, taking notes, and recording page numbers of important passages. Finally, students review what they've read, perhaps taking additional notes or looking for information related to unanswered questions.

Another strategy to use with struggling readers is reciprocal teaching. In this technique, the teacher and students take turns leading a dialogue on sections of a text. Students involved in this technique are continually checking their own understanding of what they read, generating questions, and summarizing. This approach allows for plenty of teacher support while giving students the chance to take control of their own reading and questioning. When they aren't acting as facilitators, students are observing their teacher model the habits of a good reader.

As a final note, keep in mind that students often read more regularly than we realize. In their spare time, they read email messages, comic books, magazines, song lyrics, cereal boxes, instruction manuals, and games. These aren't the kinds of texts we study in school, but they can still provide opportunities for students to build their reading and critical-thinking skills. Encourage students to pursue the kinds of reading they enjoy, reminding them that all reading is good practice. Whenever possible, make explicit connections between the reading skills students are learning in the classroom and the kinds of reading they do on their own. Chapter 5, page 62, provides more tips for helping all students in a heterogeneous classroom access literature written for their age level.

Read-Aloud and Picture Books in Middle School?

Though they may be reluctant at first, middle school students of all reading levels can learn a great deal from picture books and from listening to you read books aloud. Besides providing a common experience for the class, reading aloud offers a number of instructional opportunities, including modeling thoughtful reading, stimulating whole-group discussion, making connections (both personal and textual), and developing fluency. When choosing a read-aloud book, consider the book selection criteria on pages 51–52. You should also choose a book above the reading level of your students, as their verbal comprehension abilities are higher than their reading levels. You might choose a novel that you will read throughout an entire unit to help tie the unit together, or you might choose shorter works that you can read in one session and use to extend the unit or theme.

Picture books can create a shared reading experience in which students are able to follow both pictures and text more closely. Many picture books offer abstract topics, engaging themes, and vivid images that strengthen literature units. The visual dimension adds depth to the reading experience and offers another layer to be considered in students' reading, writing, and discussion. Picture books can provide an easy, non-threatening way to enter a unit, approach a difficult topic, or fishbowl to improve discussions. Keep in mind that picture books are for everyone, not just struggling readers; they offer an enjoyable extension to any unit for students of all ages and abilities, and they build students' confidence as they explore a unit theme and practice their reading and discussion skills. When gathering literature for a teaching unit, select picture books that present opportunities for thematic, intertextual, and interpersonal connections.

Building on Our Students' Strengths

Book Club perfectly matches the needs of adolescent students. By definition, the program gives students a strong voice in the classroom and presents literature as a way for them to grapple with issues relevant to their own lives. As a middle school teacher, you may sometimes feel frustrated by the constant need to quiet students down and bring them back to task. In Book Club, one of students' daily tasks is to converse with each other. Book Club provides a learning environment that builds on one of the adolescent learner's greatest strengths—talk.

Speaking and listening are commonly recognized as important components of the "language arts." Still, in most programs, there is far less instruction focused on oral language skills than on their textual counterparts. Instructional materials and goals that do promote oral language seem to overemphasize formal speaking, such as giving a persuasive speech to a group, at the expense of less formal types of speaking, such as small-group discussions. And even when we recognize that these less formal listening and speaking skills are more relevant to real life, there is a dearth of materials and curriculum that show what instruction in these skills might look like. Granted, our students come to us able to speak, particularly with their peers in casual settings, but they generally lack the social skills required to carry on extended conversation about literature or other substantive topics. Conversational groups such as book clubs provide the perfect context within which to teach and practice these social skills.

In addition to satisfying adolescent students' desire to talk about significant issues, Book Club provides an authentic means to make reading more interesting and meaningful to them. Too often we find ourselves teaching with the same tired collection of literary works simply because they are "classics" and because their reading levels match the grade levels of our students. Time and again, students find it difficult to relate to the insane older characters in Poe's horror stories or to the language and context of *Johnny Tremain*. Yet, on the same day, the same students might beg to read aloud from *Holes*. Book Club emphasizes choosing excellent literature to which students can relate. With Book Club, you can provide your students with high-quality literature while taking into account their interests and the books' relevance to their lives.

As a nation, we are more literate than ever before. But the problem of aliteracy—capable readers choosing not to read—is cause for great concern. As teachers, we aim to make our students more proficient readers, and, further, we expect them to like reading and writing. Positive experiences with books in a middle school classroom can shape students' attitudes toward reading for years to come. We feel we can increase the odds of our students' becoming outside-of-class readers and lifelong readers if we incorporate relevant, engaging literature into reading instruction and allow students' ideas and concerns to help shape the curriculum. By raising our expectations and giving students the tools to meet these expectations, we've seen remarkable results with our adolescent Book Club students.

References

1   Adapted from Joan Lipsitz, *Successful Schools for Young Adolescents* (New Brunswick, NJ: Transaction Books, 1984).

2   Jean Piaget, *The Development of Thought: Elaboration of Cognitive Structures* (New York: Viking, 1977).

3   Judith Davidson and David Koppenhaver, *Adolescent Literacy: What Works and Why,* Garland Reference Library of Social Science, vol. 828 (New York: Garland Publishing Company, 1993).

4   P. David Pearson and Laura Roehler, "Developing Expertise in Reading Comprehension," in S. Jay Samuels and Alan E. Farstrup (eds.), *What Research Has to Say About Reading Instruction* (Newark, DE: International Reading Association, 1992).

Assessment

Changing the Way We Think About Assessment

Imagine that you and your students have reached the end of a Book Club unit. Students have spent weeks completing a novel, reading at various times independently, with you, and with their peers. They have also read poetry that relates to the novel and learned to make intertextual connections. They have written critical, creative, and personal responses to their reading and expressed their ideas about literature in student-led discussion groups. They have collaborated with their peers to answer questions about the literature and to explore related topics. How do you now evaluate the learning that has occurred in your classroom and communicate this information to students, parents, school administrators, and the larger community? Do you distribute a multiple-choice or short-answer test? Could this type of test, by itself, measure all that students have learned during the Book Club unit?

If you've adjusted your teaching style to accommodate new ideas about literacy, it just doesn't make sense to fall back on a one-dimensional method of measuring students' progress. Many traditional methods of testing are rooted in the belief that reading is a collection of isolated skills, and they measure reading achievement by focusing exclusively on students' command of those skills. In the context of our new understanding of reading, we know that concentrating only on isolated, low-level skills is not a sound way to measure literacy. Worse, this approach gives students the impression that we value the ability to demonstrate these skills on a test more than we value achievement in the authentic literacy events that take place in the classroom every day.

Fortunately, many educators have realized the need to close the gap between current instructional goals and outmoded assessment methods. Research has led to the development of new approaches to assessment—approaches that make use of practical tasks instead of contrived test items. The National Middle School Association (NMSA) calls such methods *authentic assessment.* Authentic assessment does not replace all other forms of assessment, but it can be an important component of a system that includes a variety of assessments and evaluations. This variety has been missing for too long in many of our standardized test–centered schools, yet incorporating it is the best way to get a complete and accurate picture of a student's performance level. We've found that an assessment system involving authentic assessment matches perfectly the overall goals of the Book Club curriculum.

Understanding the Role of Authentic Assessment

The word *assessment* comes from the Latin root *assidere,* meaning "to sit beside as an assistant judge." Authentic assessment is conducted with this meaning in mind. As described in one NMSA research summary,[1] "teachers and students work together to determine what is being learned, how well it's being learned, and what both the student and the teacher might do to facilitate learning." Authentic assessment depends on the concept of accountability. Both teacher and students accept responsibility for planning, implementing, and demonstrating learning. Both have a voice in designing assessments that will not only demonstrate learning but also *enrich* learning. Authentic assessment is non-judgmental; its purpose is not to place students in a spectrum from best to worst. Instead, this kind of assessment is part of the learning process. Students participate in the process by setting goals for themselves, evaluating their work, conferencing with their teacher, and using information from the assessment to define future learning goals. Teachers use their knowledge of each student to make rich, nuanced assessments that will inform future instruction.

The most popular types of authentic assessment include performance-based assessment, in which a teacher observes students in their normal classroom setting during a specific block of time; portfolios, which provide samples of student work over a period of time; student self-assessments, which encourage students to take an active role in conceptualizing and meeting their own learning goals; and other concrete evidence of students' thinking and learning, such as peer assessments, journals, logs, and projects. A standard test gives students only one chance to share what they know about a limited number of topics. Authentic assessment activities allow both teacher and students to observe a range of skills, abilities, and ideas over a longer period of time. Authentic assessments create a more accurate picture of students' abilities. They also emphasize to students the value of pursuing original ideas, monitoring one's own progress, and accepting trial and error as an important part of the learning process. Because activities like these assess every student as an individual, they are useful for students at all reading levels. The chart on page 37 summarizes some of the essential characteristics of authentic assessment.

A BALANCED APPROACH TO ASSESSMENT

"All students who make reasonable effort should see their efforts rewarded. Emphasis should be on what the student has accomplished, not the failure to reach some arbitrary uniform standard. It also is important to help students and their families see how a student's performance corresponds with national or state norms. Such information is useful for planning careers and further education, yet it should not be the dominant concern during the middle level years."

—The National Middle School Association [2]

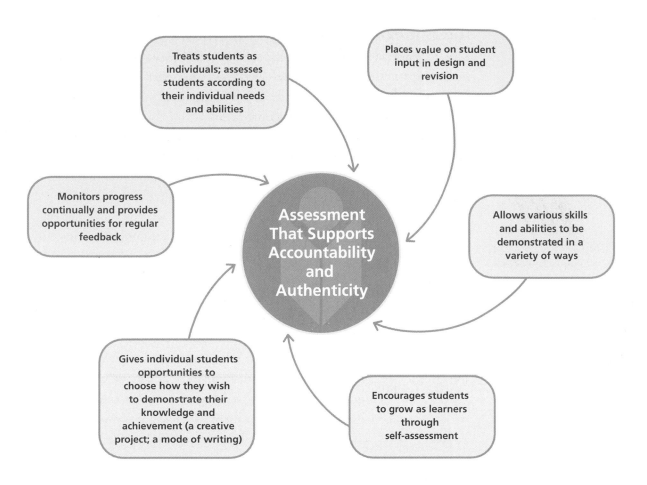

Treats students as individuals; assesses students according to their individual needs and abilities

Places value on student input in design and revision

Monitors progress continually and provides opportunities for regular feedback

Assessment That Supports Accountability and Authenticity

Allows various skills and abilities to be demonstrated in a variety of ways

Gives individual students opportunities to choose how they wish to demonstrate their knowledge and achievement (a creative project; a mode of writing)

Encourages students to grow as learners through self-assessment

By far the most important element of an authentic assessment plan is teaching students to think for themselves and to assess and evaluate their own work. Assessment should help students grow in self-knowledge, preparing them for the day when they will not have teachers and parents around to guide their efforts. Educator Fred M. Newmann,[3] who has researched and written about authentic instruction and assessment, stresses that assessment activities should require students to organize information and consider alternatives. He identifies three qualities that mark authentic pedagogy: the construction of knowledge, disciplined inquiry, and value beyond school. This third quality, in particular, shows a distinct departure from traditional testing. Completing a multiple-choice test has no relevance to anything students might do in the real world. Authentic assessments, by contrast, require students to complete meaningful projects in which they acquire knowledge that can be applied to their lives outside school.

Book Club's assessment strand is a solid reflection of these ideas. Like the other components of the program, assessment is organized in terms of accountability for both teachers and students, and it is grounded in the authentic activities that constitute literate practices.

Integrating Assessment into the Book Club Program

We know that Book Club's components—reading, writing, small discussion groups, and community share—work together effectively to support literacy learning. The challenge, then, is to determine how best to gather concrete evidence of students' literacy learning. In creating the assessment strand of Book Club, our goal was to rely on practical assessment methods that fit naturally into the Book Club curriculum.

We did not want our assessment methods to intimidate students but to extend learning and give us a truthful, detailed picture of each student's progress and abilities. At the same time, we needed a system that would help us know how well we were addressing curricular target areas and meeting district, state, and/or national standards. The assessment system we've built through trial and error reflects our belief in principles of authentic assessment as well as the need to teach specific skills and meet various educational standards and guidelines. The chart at left gives a brief overview of assessment within the various components and activities of Book Club.

Assessment in Book Club

✔ **Book Club Discussions**

❑ Quality of contributions
❑ Amount of contribution
❑ Support for peers' contributions

✔ **Writing**

❑ Log entries (variety and depth)
❑ Sustained writing
❑ Process writing

✔ **Contributions to Whole-Group Discussions**

✔ **Oral and Written Fluency**

✔ **Text Comprehension**

✔ **Self-Assessment**

❑ Reading logs
❑ Checklists
❑ Recorded discussions

Curricular Target Areas

In Chapter 1, we outlined Book Club's curricular target areas: comprehension, language conventions, literary aspects, and composition. Comprehension refers to how students make sense of text. Targeted skills include developing background knowledge, processing text, and monitoring one's own comprehension during reading. Language conventions refer to the workings of written and oral language. These include grammar, sound/symbol relationships, spelling, and fluent reading. In Book Club, language conventions also include the social skills used in discussing literature. Literary aspects include both literary elements and students' response to literature. Examples of literary elements we want students to understand and appreciate are story structure, genre, author's purpose, and point of view. Response to literature encompasses personal, critical, and creative responses. Composition refers to the various ways students can respond to texts in writing. They are taught to use writing as a tool for thinking, and they learn practical techniques (planning, drafting, revising) for more long-term process writing.

A variety of activities and learning opportunities within Book Club support the curricular target areas and can play a role in assessment. Student-led discussion groups, reading logs, think sheets, structured written responses, and projects are the most significant sources of learning evidence. Through student discussions you can assess students' understanding of what they are reading and find out what they know about characters, plot, setting, point of view, and theme. You can also observe over time how well students can organize and express their thoughts and support their ideas and the ideas of their peers. If you combine these observations with a review of students' reading logs, think sheets, written responses, and completed projects, you will have accurate and valuable information about each student's developing literacy.

Think Sheets and Evaluation Sheets as Assessment Tools

This teacher's guide provides blackline masters that can serve as tools for assessment in your classroom. We've divided the blackline masters into two sections, Think Sheets and Evaluation Sheets. (See pages 153 and 187.) Think sheets are designed primarily to support students' thinking as they interact with text. However, both you and your students can also use think sheets to inform assessment. They provide "traces" of students' thought processes as well as evidence of reading comprehension. By evaluating the evidence of literacy learning that think sheets provide, you can determine where additional instruction may be necessary. Students can review their think sheets at the end of a unit to assess the depth of their thinking about a particular book or theme and to set goals for future learning.

Evaluation sheets are more directly aimed at assessment. Some evaluation sheets are for students to complete, such as goal-setting and self-assessment sheets. These sheets provide structures that students can use to plan for and evaluate their own learning. Evaluation sheets for the teacher include some that help you observe and record students' progress. For example, Evaluation Sheet 2, Book Club Observation Sheet, provides a format for you to jot down quick notes about students' behavior during book club discussions. Later, you can return to the sheet to summarize or elaborate on these observations. Evaluation Sheet 1, Reading Log Evaluation, offers standards for assessing students' reading log entries. Other evaluation sheets help you report students' progress to students and parents. For example, Evaluation Sheet 6, Language Skills Checklist, complements a standard report card, allowing you to give details about what each student is learning through his or her participation in Book Club.

Keep in mind that our blackline masters are merely a sampling of the kinds of assessment tools you'll need in your classroom. Some you'll want to copy and use as they are; others will provide ideas for the tools you'll craft to suit your own purposes. Each curriculum and each classroom is unique, and assessment tools must reflect the specific learning goals of teachers and students.

Student Self-Assessment

In many classrooms over the years, teachers' opinions of student work were the only opinions that counted and went on record. In Book Club, however, we believe strongly that students' opinions about their own work are crucial to assessment and growth. Student self-assessment is valuable to our program for the following reasons:

1. It encourages students to be clear about your classroom's criteria for high-quality participation. If they must actively judge their own work or the work of their peers, they will gain a stronger understanding of classroom standards.

2. Students assume responsibility for their own learning and for Book Club participation. Students set their own goals and then work to meet these goals. This can be an empowering experience for young readers. Classroom activities and experiences become more than just ways to please the teacher—they are also personal challenges.

3. The fact that learning is a process becomes much clearer to students. They are asked to review their reading logs and observe the ways in which their classroom discussions have improved. This helps them see how they've grown and how activities and experiences have built on one another.

The Evaluation Sheets section of this guide (see page 187) contains tools for student goal setting and self-assessment. We hope that our sheets will give you ideas for creating your own assessment tools based on the particular learning goals of your classroom.

Rubrics for Book Club Behaviors

When you implement Book Club in your classroom, your students will spend a lot of time writing and talking about literature. How will you measure their accomplishments in these areas? How can you assign a score or a grade to a book discussion or to a reading log entry? As we developed Book Club, we confronted these questions in our own classrooms. To help us define our expectations for students' behavior, we created detailed scoring rubrics. Our rubrics for book clubs and reading logs appear on pages 41–42. Each score on the five-point scale represents several criteria, allowing you to judge each body of work holistically.

You'll probably want to design rubrics based on your own teaching goals and curriculum requirements, as well as the goals of your students. Rubrics are especially effective when students participate in their creation, but at the very least students should have access to rubrics before they begin Book Club. In this way, rubrics become part of instruction and learning because students know what is expected of them and can set goals for themselves.

Rubric for Book Club Discussions

Score	Criteria
5	• Focuses on major themes, issues, questions, or characters • Effectively uses evidence from text, content area, and/or personal experience to support ideas • Appropriately introduces new ideas • Builds/expands on others' ideas • Respects others' ideas • Talks for a clear purpose • Appropriately supports less active members of the group
4	• Focuses on some major themes, issues, questions, or characters • Effectively uses some evidence from text, content area, and/or personal experience to support ideas • Occasionally introduces new ideas appropriately • Occasionally builds/expands on others' ideas • Respects others' ideas • Purpose for speaking is usually clear • Sometimes supports less active members of the group
3	• Focuses on secondary themes, issues, questions, or characters OR lacks detailed discussion of major themes • Uses little evidence from text and/or personal experience to support ideas OR use of evidence is less than effective • Demonstrates some sense of purpose for speaking • Builds some on others' ideas but may resort to round-robin turn taking • Demonstrates some respect for others' ideas • Less than effective at introducing new ideas
2	• Makes few references to important themes, issues, questions, or characters OR lacks detailed discussion of any themes • Uses little evidence from text and/or personal experience to support ideas OR use of evidence is ineffective • Purpose for speaking is unclear or lacking • Seldom builds on others' ideas and may resort to round-robin turn taking • Demonstrates little respect for or attention to others' ideas • Seldom introduces new ideas • Speaks infrequently
1	• Superficial response with minimal reference to the text or personal experiences • Talks about trivial textual details or irrelevant personal experiences • Perseverates on ideas—does not build on them • Does not introduce new ideas • Demonstrates no clear purpose for speaking • Speaks very infrequently • Raises hand before speaking and/or resorts to round-robin turn taking

Rubric for Reading Log Entries

Score	Criteria
5	• Focuses on major themes, issues, questions, or characters • Effectively uses evidence from text, content area, and/or personal experience to support ideas • Produces multiple, related, and well-developed responses • Writes for a clear purpose • Generates a well-focused, connected, and coherent response • Dates entry
4	• Focuses on some major themes, issues, questions, or characters • Effectively uses some evidence from text, content area, and/or personal experience to support ideas • Produces several related responses • Purpose for writing is fairly clear • Generates a focused, connected, and generally coherent response • Dates entry
3	• Focuses on secondary themes, issues, questions, or characters OR lacks detailed discussion of major themes • Uses little evidence from text and/or personal experience to support ideas OR use of evidence is less than effective • Demonstrates some sense of purpose for writing • Generates a somewhat focused, connected, and coherent response
2	• Makes few references to important themes, issues, questions, or characters OR lacks detailed discussion of any themes • Uses little evidence from text and/or personal experience to support ideas OR use of evidence is ineffective • Purpose for writing is unclear or lacking • Response has inadequate focus, connection between ideas, and overall coherence
1	• Superficial response with minimal reference to the text or personal experiences • Writing is a string of trivial textual details • Demonstrates no clear purpose for writing • Generates an unfocused, unconnected, and incoherent response • Does not date entry

Planning for Assessment

You can incorporate authentic assessment into your Book Club classroom in two basic ways. One is through planned assessment "events," during which you collect information based on specific tasks that your students complete. These assessments require some planning beforehand and analysis afterward, so you probably won't have time for more than a few of them each year. The second way is through ongoing assessments—more frequent, informal assessments that can take place at any time. Both approaches contribute to the overall success of assessment during a unit or grading period.

Assessment Events/Summative Assessment Some Book Club teachers plan week-long performance-based assessment events. One of these events might take place in the middle or at the end of a unit, as a form of summative assessment. Each event centers around a particular text that relates to a theme students are studying. During the event, students participate in all the activities that would normally be part of a Book Club unit: they read a selection, create reading log entries, meet for discussion in book clubs, and engage in whole-class discussions. Individual students also assess their own group participation and log entries. Each of these tasks, with the exception of independent reading, provides concrete evidence of student performance that you can later evaluate. These pieces of evidence include students' log entries, audio- and/or videotapes of both book club and community share discussions, and students' written self-assessments. The chart below shows two sample schedules for performance-based assessment events.

Sample Schedules for Week-Long Assessment Events

45-minute periods

Monday	Tuesday	Wednesday	Thursday	Friday
• Read Chapters 12–13 of *The Giver* • Respond in logs	• Discuss in book clubs (Tape groups 1 and 2) • Meet for closing community share	• Read Chapters 14–15 of *The Giver* • Respond in logs	• Discuss in book clubs (Tape groups 3 and 4) • Meet for closing community share	• Review tape of book club discussion and write self-assessment • Select one log entry and write self-assessment (May complete as homework)

90-minute periods

Monday	Tuesday	Wednesday	Thursday	Friday
• Read Chapters 12–13 of *The Giver* • Respond in logs • Discuss in book clubs (Tape groups 1 and 2) • Meet for closing community share	• Regular Book Club activities for Chapters 14–15 of *The Giver* (no formal assessment)	• Read Chapters 16–17 of *The Giver* • Respond in logs • Discuss in book clubs (Tape groups 3 and 4) • Meet for closing community share	• Review tape of book club discussion and write self-assessment • Select one log entry and write self-assessment	• Return to regular Book Club activities

● TECHNOLOGY AND SELF-ASSESSMENT

In some Book Club classrooms, students assess their performances in book club discussions by reviewing audio- or videotapes of their conversations. Since some classrooms have limited equipment, each individual group might be taped only once toward the end of a unit. Students can later assess their taped discussions in small groups with you or with the whole class during a special community share. After reviewing the tapes, each student should be encouraged to create a written self-assessment noting what was good and what needs improvement in his or her interactions.

It's important to keep several factors in mind when choosing texts for performance-based assessment events:

1. Texts should represent the range of literature that you want your students to be able to read and respond to. We suggest one work of fiction and one work of nonfiction.

2. Texts should relate to a theme or topic your students are studying at the time the assessment takes place. Some teachers use the event as a time to make cross-curricular connections, choosing texts that relate to science or social studies topics their students are studying.

3. If you're using a longer book as an assessment text, avoid using the first few chapters of the book. Instead, wait until students reach the "heart" of the novel and are comfortable discussing it. It isn't fair to assess them when they are still trying to figure out characters and settings and perhaps also adjusting to new discussion groups.

4. Remember that you can opt to use a short story, rather than a section of a novel, for your performance-based assessment. We've found that both novels and short stories work well in the assessment process and provide strong examples of students' achievement in Book Club.

Ongoing Assessment Students' progress can be checked at any time and in a variety of ways. Reading logs provide information about their understanding of what they're reading and their performance in Book Club. Teachers can collect logs at any time for review. Teachers can also move through the room during small-group discussions, monitoring and recording the participation of individual students in their book clubs. During community share, teachers can again observe which students seem to be grasping key concepts and participating and which students might be falling behind. As in the structured assessment events, audio- and videotapes can be helpful in ongoing assessment. If the technology is readily available, students and teachers can review taped discussions throughout the unit.

Student self-assessment is also used throughout a unit. The forms we've developed for self-assessment can serve a variety of purposes: some are meant to be used at the beginning or the end of a unit, while others can be used at any time. A teacher can review a student's self-assessment form and then write back to the student with questions. In this way, student and teacher maintain a dialogue throughout the unit.

The chart on page 45 shows one teacher's notes on how she divided assessment for the novel *The Giver.*

Accommodating Standards-Based Assessment

So far in this chapter, you've heard many arguments in favor of authentic assessment. We believe strongly that this kind of assessment is best for our

► **Sample Outline for
Assessing a Book
Club Unit**

Assessment

Ongoing Assessment
- Teacher's anecdotal notes
- Student reading logs
- Tapes of discussions
- Student self-assessment

Summative Assessment
- Discussion record, recording, and self-assessment
- Complete reading log
- Student poem on conformity
- Test: Looking at the conformity issue in a different text
- Debate: Discussing a conformity-related issue
- Expository essay
- Hands-on project

students, but we also recognize the practical needs of teachers working in standards-based schools. You may need to demonstrate your students' mastery of specific learning objectives and/or prepare your students to take standardized tests. Fortunately, you can accomplish these goals within the structure of Book Club. With some advance planning, you can cover all of your required skills while your students engage in authentic interactions with literature.

Book Club teacher Jean Samples teaches in Houston, Texas. She must ensure that her students achieve competency in a wide range of skills outlined in the Texas Essential Knowledge and Skills (TEKS). At the same time, she is committed to providing her students with meaningful literacy instruction through Book Club. Here's how she describes her approach:

I have my TEKS in a list form. I look over what will be covered in a particular book—usually I can find opportunities for almost all of the TEKS at least once in each book—and simply teach each objective in the form of a mini-lesson before we begin to read a specific chapter. I also use books of reproducible reading activities related specifically to the novel. Some of the activity pages we do quickly on the overhead as a class; some we do in pairs; some we do individually. How I do it and how much time I spend on each activity depends on the group and what their needs are. The combination of mini-lessons, reading, writing, book clubs, whole-class discussions, and reading activities is extensive enough to cover all of my requirements for TEKS by the time we take the TAAS (statewide) test.

The Book Club units in this guide provide correlations to national standards that can serve as a model for your own correlations. See pages 69–70, 104, and 125 for charts correlating individual lesson plans to language arts standards established by the National Council of Teachers of English and the International Reading Association (NCTE/IRA). Our lesson plans and extended unit activities are also correlated to national standards for social studies; see pages 71, 105, and 126.

Building an Effective Assessment System

We see effective assessment as a system that must serve a variety of purposes. The major areas in a complete assessment system are student self-evaluation, rubrics, a teacher's anecdotal notes, standardized testing, and report cards. Ways to track students in these five areas typically include work samples in a portfolio, standardized tests, teacher records and observations, pre- and post-evaluations of student book discussions, and final projects. Using these methods, you can build an assessment system that satisfies the goals of all stakeholders in a student's education: you, the student, parents, the administration, the district, the state, and the nation. The scenarios on page 47 demonstrate how this can be done.

Components of an Effective Assessment System[4]

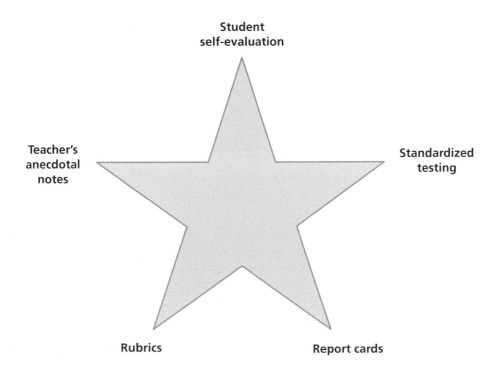

Student self-evaluation

Standardized testing

Report cards

Rubrics

Teacher's anecdotal notes

Scenario 1: A Book Club teacher must show evidence of meeting specific NCTE/IRA standards. One standard states: "Students participate as knowledgeable, reflective, creative, and critical members of a variety of literacy communities." The teacher wants to reword this formal language, using language he or she would naturally use with students. So, working with students, the teacher begins to write clear statements based on this standard. These statements will then be turned into a rubric that both teachers and students can use for assessment. For example:

- voices opinions

- backs up opinions with facts

- stays on topic

- asks good questions

- introduces original ideas

- is open to the opinions of others

- maintains eye contact

- displays active listening skills

The teacher can create a similar rubric for every standard on the list. This includes standards that address reading, writing, and content learning. This process can be used to adapt specific state guidelines as well.

Scenario 2: A teacher asks students to write a final essay to assess their achievement at the end of a unit. The assessment process begins with a student's self-evaluation of the essay, which helps the teacher and the student understand if the student has met his or her own learning goals. During this meeting and this initial review, the teacher takes anecdotal notes that will inform his or her teaching in the future. The essay is then evaluated more formally, using a rubric based on district guidelines for essay writing. The results of the evaluation with the rubric are translated into a number or letter grade that is placed on a report card. Doing this helps the teacher communicate student progress to parents and the school. The work can then be evaluated holistically according to other state or national standards. Thus, the teacher has assessed at a variety of levels for a variety of audiences.

In developing our program, we've come to realize how complex and multifaceted literacy training can be. We believe our way of assessing students—using a system of evaluation that depends on variety—satisfies all the necessary requirements of a language arts program and still protects the integrity of Book Club.

▼ MODIFIED REPORT CARDS

Traditional report cards often do not reflect all the skills that students learn in Book Club. So, how do you share with parents the wealth of assessment information that you've gathered? To solve this problem for ourselves, we developed checklists to be attached to our schools' report cards. These checklists covered various aspects of students' achievement in literacy and were much more comprehensive than simple letter grades. See Evaluation Sheet 6, in the section following page 187, for a sample checklist.

Developing Your Own Assessment Methods for Book Club

As with any component of Book Club, these ideas about assessment are not meant to be prescriptive or unchangeable. Any teacher will want to adapt our assessment system to meet the needs of specific students or a specific school system. Your own creativity and experiences will help you adapt our ideas and materials so that they benefit your own students and help you meet your own goals. Our strongest hope is that educators will gain a new perspective on the process of assessment and try to design systems that extend learning while they evaluate performance and achievement.

References

1 National Middle School Association Research Summary #16: "What Are Appropriate Assessment Practices for Middle School Students?" (See www.nmsa.org/resources/).

2 National Middle School Association, *This We Believe: Developmentally Responsive Middle Level Schools* (Columbus, OH: National Middle School Association, 1995), page 28.

3 Fred M. Newmann and Associates, *Authentic Achievement: Restructuring Schools for Intellectual Quality* (San Francisco: Jossey-Bass Publishers, 1996), pages 28–32.

4 Adapted from Taffy E. Raphael, Susan Florio-Ruane, Marcella Kehus, MariAnne George, Nina Hasty, and Kathy Highfield, "Thinking for Ourselves: Literacy Learning in a Diverse Teacher Inquiry Network," *The Reading Teacher* 54, no. 6 (2001): 596–607.

Chapter Five

Classroom Management

Pulling It All Together

As with any innovation, starting a new instructional program with your class may seem like an intriguing but formidable goal. True, there are many decisions to make and questions to answer for yourself and for your students. It's not as difficult as you might think, though. In this chapter, you'll find practical tips for incorporating Book Club in your classroom.

As always, we draw from our experiences teaching with Book Club, and we know that you will draw from your own experiences and expertise. Your instincts as a teacher are your most valuable resource—you know your students, your schedule, and the expectations of your school system. We aim simply to provide you with information and suggestions that will help you feel comfortable teaching in a Book Club setting.

We've divided this chapter into five major sections. **Preparing for Book Club** shows you how to choose themes and literature, get books for your classroom, and plan your curriculum. **Getting Started** deals with grouping students, scheduling your Book Club activities, teaching students how to behave in discussion groups, and building a community in your classroom. **Supporting Students Throughout a Book Club Unit** explores ways to facilitate students' reading and discussions. **Using Inclusion Strategies** discusses ways of helping diverse learners access age-appropriate literature and feel comfortable in student discussion groups. **Troubleshooting** provides tips for handling issues and problems you may encounter along the way. Topics in this final section include helping students who struggle with sustained silent reading, accommodating fast readers, dealing with disruptive students, and improving students' social and conversational skills.

Preparing for Book Club

Particularly at the middle school level, Book Club works best in the context of integrated, theme-based teaching units. The reading, writing, and discussing that students do in their book clubs are enriched when they can draw upon previous work involving related topics, genres, and themes. In the same way, Book Club can enrich theme-related activities that your team implements across disciplines. Here are some suggestions for planning a theme-based teaching unit.

Choose a Relevant, Engaging Theme

Before selecting the literature for a Book Club unit, think about the kinds of themes you want circulating in your classroom. For example, you might want to invite discussion about a particular literary genre, a social issue, a historical era or event, interpersonal relationships, or various stages of life. Good classroom themes are not arbitrary or superficial; they invite real discussion. Above all, you want your themes to show students how literature can help them better understand their lives, one another, and the world around them.

It's helpful to frame your themes as open-ended questions. These "big theme questions" signal to students that the class is conducting an inquiry and that everyone is responsible for finding his or her own answers. We suggest that you post the "big theme questions" in your classroom for the duration of the unit. Students should return to the questions continually, revising

Theme/Topic Ideas

- abuse
- adolescent characters
- animals
- author study
- coming of age
- conformity
- death/dying/grief
- differences
- disabilities/ challenges
- divorce
- drugs
- family
- fears

- fitting in/ being left out
- friendship
- gender
- heritage
- history
- human rights
- humor
- illness
- immigration
- inspirations
- male/female point of view
- mental illness

- peer issues
- prejudice/ discrimination
- relationships
- risk
- self image
- sibling rivalry
- sports
- suicide
- survival
- time travel
- women's rights

Qualities of a Strong Theme

A Strong Theme . . .

- invites discussion.
- helps students connect to the literature.
- motivates students in their reading.
- explores human values.
- provides for in-depth learning.
- is open-ended and has no single right answer.
- is relevant to people of all ages.
- investigates the "gray areas" of life.
- explores our humanity in archetypal stories.
- takes time to sort through.
- allows for explicit teaching.

and refining their answers as they read and discuss the literature. See pages 72 and 127 for examples of big theme questions.

Whenever possible, consult with your teaching team partners to select themes that you can apply across the curriculum. With the help of social studies, science, and math teachers, you can encourage students to approach a theme from a variety of interesting angles. For example, a unit on immigration in the United States could combine reading and discussing relevant literary texts in the Book Club classroom with analyzing historical information in the social studies classroom. Students could complete a final research/writing project that satisfies requirements for both classes. To extend the theme to include math, teachers might have students manipulate statistical data to present in new and meaningful ways the numbers of immigrants entering the United States or living in one part of the country at various times. A science teacher might focus on environmental changes that result from a rapidly increasing population and an increase in industry.

Select Appropriate, High-Quality Literature

The success of any Book Club unit depends on the selection of appropriate literature. We suggest that you first choose the book that students will read and discuss in their book clubs. Then build your collection of support materials: books for reading aloud, shorter works (poetry, short stories, articles) for sharing, and books for your classroom library. All of your materials should support and enrich your theme. You'll probably need to do some research to locate relevant materials, but don't forget to draw upon the knowledge of your colleagues, too. Other teachers and librarians are likely to have lots of helpful suggestions. As you collect your materials, you'll obviously want to choose well-written, high-quality literature. In addition, bear in mind the following criteria.

Potential for Discussion Look for books that students will want to talk about. Books that raise interesting, real-life issues give readers something to discuss, sort out, and form opinions about. At the same time, consider your students' personal situations and maturity levels. If a particular issue makes you or your students uncomfortable, you might want to avoid it.

Content Choose books with subject matter that your students can connect with. This means they should know something about the book's content from the start. You can give your class an appropriate knowledge base by teaching a brief inquiry unit related the story's context before students begin reading the book. This might include research and writing activities that help students become familiar with the setting. Related short readings, such as picture books and news articles, can also help students build background knowledge.

Consider whether your students will find the content of a book interesting and relevant. Look for stories that students can relate to their own lives. Books with adolescent main characters are a good choice. Think about the "gender gap" in your classroom, and try to pick books that will appeal to both girls and boys. Over the course of the year, strive for a balance between male and female main characters.

Readability It's important to select books that most students in the class can read. If reading and comprehending a book present problems for a significant number of students, their discussions will fall flat. In a mixed-ability classroom, you can employ strategies to support lower-ability readers such as reading aloud, partner reading, and books on tape. It's important that all students receive an opportunity to explore issues raised by age-appropriate literature. Students reading above grade level can supplement their reading with other books by the same author or within the same theme and then share their insights with their groups. For more on inclusion strategies, see page 62.

Your Own "Thumbs Up" Remember that your own experience with a book will affect your success in using it with Book Club. If you couldn't honestly recommend a book to a friend, don't expect your students to feel excited about it, either. On the other hand, when you present students with a book that you've enjoyed reading or teaching in the past, your passion for the book will filter down to them. They'll approach their reading with a positive attitude and look for what's good in the book.

Tips for Selecting Books

- Consult reviews and book lists in journals and magazines.
- Choose a theme to focus your selection of books.
- Ask other teachers about books they've enjoyed using.
- Ask a librarian which books children are borrowing.
- Invite student input. What books have they heard about? What topics interest them?
- Pick something you like. Your enthusiasm will rub off on your students.

Plan Your Curriculum Goals

Once you've selected solid literature linked by a common theme, it's time to consider how you will use these materials to meet your curriculum goals. While students are reading and discussing a book, you'll have many opportunities to focus on literary elements such as plot, theme, characterization, setting, mood, and so on. Book Club also provides a natural context in which to teach speaking and listening skills. Students will need these skills to interact in their book clubs as well as with the whole class during community share. Such informal speaking and listening activities are often overlooked in the language arts curriculum, but they are authentic and relevant to students' lives. If your curriculum goals require more formal speaking and listening activities, you can easily add theme-related presentations, speeches, or debates to your unit.

GOOD LITERATURE FIRST

Don't try to teach every last skill within the structure of a single Book Club unit. You'll lose focus on what is truly important—getting students engaged in the literature. You can abuse good literature by trying to force it to accomplish too many narrow goals. Let it be good literature first, a teaching tool second.

Required Curriculum Standards Many teachers are required by their state or school district to meet specific curriculum standards. You might wonder if teaching with Book Club will help you cover your own set of mandatory standards. The answer is yes. As you plan your daily lessons for Book Club, look for opportunities to teach your required skills. Many language arts skills will flow naturally from your teaching of the literature (e.g., genre, author's craft, plot, making inferences, predicting, comparing and contrasting). The literature will also provide a context from which you can extract grammar and comprehension activities. As students interact in various contexts, you'll find opportunities for direct instruction in speaking and listening skills. The writing that students do before, during, and after Book Club allows you to teach the writing process and specific composition skills. For a model of how to correlate a Book Club unit to a set of language arts standards, see the theme-based unit for Lois Lowry's *The Giver,* page 67.

Cross-Curricular Connections Book Club integrates well with other content areas. If you select appropriate literature and structure your unit accordingly, you'll find many opportunities to make cross-curricular connections. For example, you can work with your colleagues to select a Book Club book to fit with social studies or science content, such as historical fiction or a novel that deals with how people treat the natural environment. Then you can gather nonfiction materials that deal with the same topics and have students build background in the weeks leading up to Book Club. You can also have students do their own research projects and present them to the class. When they eventually read the Book Club book, they'll have a solid foundation on which to build understanding of the book.

Acquire Books

When choosing your books, of course, you'll have to consider the availability of the titles. We encourage you to make sure all students have their own copies of the book they'll be reading in their book clubs. Students' sense of ownership increases when they can hold books in their hands and actually touch the words with their eyes and their fingers. Also, students often like to have their books readily available during discussions. They can refer to the text to support their opinions, remind themselves of important passages, and reinforce points they are making. Finally, if students have the books in their possession, they have more opportunities to reread sections that they had trouble understanding or that they especially enjoyed.

In trying to acquire multiple copies of books for our own classrooms, we've looked for existing class sets in our schools or districts, traded sets of books with fellow teachers, and borrowed from libraries. Other options include the following:

- Buy a set of books jointly with other same-grade teachers in your school or district.

Contexts for Reading

Context	Description	Number of Copies Needed
Book Clubs	In their book clubs, students read and discuss an age-appropriate text central to the unit's theme.	Class set
Read Aloud	Read-aloud selections (short stories, poems, essays) can bring discussions to a higher level and help tie the unit together. These materials can reinforce themes or aid students' understanding of a genre or an author.	1 copy
Shared Reading	Shared reading accomplishes some of the same goals as the read aloud. In this case, however, a piece is read as a whole group while students follow along in the text.	8–10 copies, 2–3 students per copy
Classroom Library	Books in the classroom library might be tied to the Book Club book by theme, author, or genre. They're great for encouraging independent silent reading.	1 or more copies of a variety of books

▲ This chart shows one model for the distribution of books in a Book Club unit.

- Ask the PTA/PTO to provide funds to purchase classroom sets of books.

- Call book distributors to ask about special prices on classroom sets.

- Use bonus points from commercial book clubs to purchase extra copies.

- Ask your school administrators if there are funds available.

- Contact district or county resources.

- Secure special education and Title I funds, if your classroom features inclusion.

Annotate Your Copy of the Book

It's a good idea to make "crib notes" in your book as you are reading. These notes will be valuable during community share and when you're trying to formulate questions or writing activities for your students. Mark passages you want to highlight for students in community share—passages that show a literary technique, exemplify a skill, reveal something about a character, or simply illustrate why you enjoy the book. You can also mark challenging spots in the book for which you might need to provide background information or other forms of support. Use your notes to help you model for students how you engage with a text and also how you can work through difficult sections. Furthermore, students can benefit from your sharing of the crib-note strategy itself. Show them how to mark important, favorite, or puzzling passages with sticky notes or strips of paper used as bookmarks, and encourage them to refer back to these passages in book clubs and class discussions.

Expand Your Unit with Creative Activities and Writing

During the Book Club portion of your unit, students will write informally in their reading logs as a tool for thinking. Throughout the unit, they should also be working on a variety of other writing assignments. One approach is to have students write their way into, through, and out of the unit. For example, students can "write into" the unit by answering one of the big theme questions in a brief essay. Then they can see how their views change or evolve during the course of the unit. If your unit begins with a research phase, students can write reports on their findings. "Writing through" the unit can include various book-related assignments such as log entries, character sketches, compare-and-contrast essays, poems, personal essays, persuasive writing, and so on. Students can "write out of" the unit with assignments that allow them to share, publish, synthesize, extend, and apply what they've learned. This writing can span genres and allow students to choose the best formats to express their ideas.

In addition to the many writing opportunities, don't forget to engage students' individual learning styles with other forms of creative expression. Think about artistic and musical links you and your students can make to the literature. Middle school students benefit from hands-on activities that allow them to respond creatively to their reading and discussions. As you build your unit, try to include activities in which students can use computers, draw, paint, build, and perform. Ideas for these activities should spring from the specific literature and themes in your unit.

You should have little trouble integrating formal speaking and listening activities into your unit. Students can present findings from their research in oral reports while their classmates listen and take notes. They can write and deliver persuasive speeches on issues that come up during the unit. They can debate questions that arise from unit themes or topics. They can present oral readings of poetry or other literature, including pieces they've written themselves. As with other activities, formal speaking and listening opportunities should arise naturally from well-chosen themes and literature. Your curriculum goals will also guide you in developing appropriate activities.

Start with a Great Book and Build Your Unit Around It

In the preceding pages, we've described a process that begins with selecting a theme for your unit and then gathering literature. But perhaps you have a particular book that you want to start with. The chart on page 56 describes a step-by-step process for building a complete unit around a chosen book.

Building a Theme-Based Unit

1. After your first reading of the central book for your unit, select a theme in the book that can be approached from several angles.

2. Create "big theme questions" to display in the classroom and discuss throughout the unit. They should apply to all the literature in your unit and should address several aspects of your theme. See pages 72 and 127 for examples of big theme questions.

3. Read the book a second time to determine the most dominant literary techniques. (Consider the literary skills you're required to teach at your grade level.) Choose the techniques you wish to emphasize. Think about how students may be able to practice these techniques in their own writing.

4. Find multi-genre selections to develop the theme. Consider poetry, picture books, nonfiction, short stories, and music.

5. Read the book a third time and, for each chapter, create writing prompts (questions) for students' logs. Try to emphasize equally the three major angles: text, critical response, and personal and creative response. (For more on the tripod log format, see page 18.) Also, note vocabulary words and select lesson topics for each chapter.

6. Develop at least two types of writing assignments that will naturally connect to the book and to your literary techniques focus. Connect some related prewriting activities to students' reading logs or to class charts developed in community share.

7. Decide what other issues or topics besides the big theme questions deserve to be tracked regularly on class charts as students read the book.

8. Identify and integrate the grammar skills and other language conventions that you want to emphasize.

9. Connect at least one hands-on project to the unit.

10. Try to link at least one meaningful Internet or technology activity to the unit.

11. Decide how you will fit all the pieces together. Arrange your activities in a logical order. You may have activities that precede the Book Club portion of the unit, activities that happen during Book Club, and activities that follow Book Club.

12. Decide how and what to assess, taking into account your required curriculum standards.

Getting Started

When you've finished your planning and preparation, you're ready to involve your students in Book Club.

Think Carefully About How to Group Your Students

Book Club's student-led discussion groups make the program unique and effective. Because group dynamics can have a large impact on how a book club functions, you need to give some thought to how you'll group your students.

Typically, a book club contains four to five students. This allows for differing opinions but not so many that chaos takes over. Also, if one student is absent on a given day, the group can still function. We like to keep group membership constant throughout a book or unit and then change groups for each new unit. These are some factors to consider when forming groups.

Diversity We try to make groups as diverse as possible, mixing gender, ethnicity, interests, reading abilities, verbal abilities, and personalities. If a group is diverse, its discussions are likely to be varied and interesting. Each unique point of view adds to the quality of the discussion. Students also benefit from the opportunity to interact with a diverse group of classmates. While interacting with their friends may come naturally, working closely with students outside their immediate circles stretches their social skills. Forming diverse groups can present a challenge at the beginning of the school year, before you know your students well. Obtain whatever information you can from student records, previous teachers, and advisors, and then just do your best. Form groups for subsequent units based on what you learn from earlier groupings.

Attitudes, Personalities, and Cliques It's also important to consider the personalities and attitudes toward school that are represented in each group. For example, two strong, outgoing personalities might dominate a group and intimidate the other members. On the other hand, four strong personalities might create a lively discussion. We've also found that couples and close friends as well as students who strongly dislike each other do not work well together in a group. Private conversations, flirtation, and intense animosity tend to distract the group from the task at hand—discussing the book.

Considering students' attitudes and personalities will inevitably lead you to the issue of cliques—a fact of life in most middle schools. Because cliques provide adolescents with an identity and a feeling of safety, when students are within these exclusive groups they are less likely to take risks and speak honestly about their own ideas. As best we can, we try to break up social and racial units so that students are forced to function as individuals. Splitting up cliques is also a step toward promoting tolerance and building unity in the classroom. Again, there are some combinations that probably will never work—their personal issues are just too distracting to a book club's discussions. However, we have found that mixing up groups of students generally makes for interesting and successful discussions.

Students' choice It's often valuable to allow students some choice in the grouping process. We want students to take ownership of their learning, and giving them a voice in forming their book clubs is one way to achieve this. At the end of a unit, you might ask students to list their group members and describe how they think their discussions progressed. Ask students to name two or three students they would like to have in their next book club and explain why. As the teacher, you should always have the final say. However,

WHEN TO REGROUP

We like to keep book clubs stable throughout an entire book or unit. However, if you discover midway through a unit that your groups are not working out, don't feel that you're stuck with them. You can regroup students at any time to create better-functioning book clubs.

TWO PAIRS DON'T ALWAYS MAKE A QUARTET

It's great to allow students some input regarding which other students will comprise their next book club. However, if each student works with one person of his or her choosing, you might end up with a foursome that functions as two pairs. Avoid grouping two students who are likely to talk exclusively to each other.

you can probably allow most students to be with at least one person of their choosing. Students will benefit from having choices and from being invited to think about how they can do their best work.

Consider Your Scheduling Options

Today's school systems use a variety of flexible scheduling options, from block scheduling to rotating schedules to alternate-day schedules. You can adapt Book Club to fit any of these formats. If you have large blocks of time, you can go through all the program components in one day—reading, writing, book clubs, and community share. If you have shorter periods, you can divide the components across two or more days. The chart below shows two possible weekly schedules, one for 45-minute periods and the other for 90-minute periods.

Arrange the Classroom to Accommodate Discussion

Meeting in book clubs requires each group to have its own little space in which to concentrate on discussion. A variety of approaches can work effectively. Some teachers arrange student desks in clusters of four or five. Others use tables or even allow students to sit in circles on the floor during their discussions. Alternative meeting places—such as the floor, library, or hallway (with supervision)—usually work best when students have learned the routine of book club discussions. Arrange your classroom in the way that will work best with your students. What's important is that students are able to face and hear one another without distracting or being distracted by other groups.

Sample Book Club Schedules

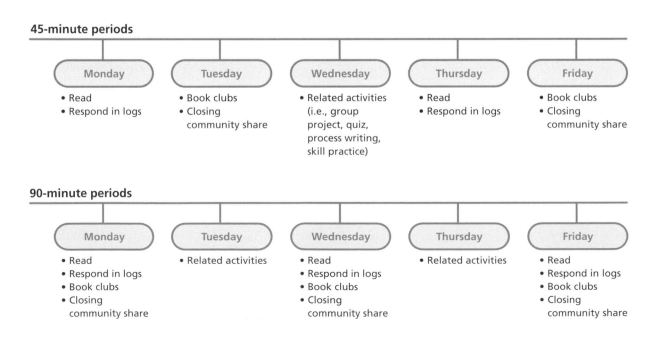

45-minute periods

Monday	Tuesday	Wednesday	Thursday	Friday
• Read • Respond in logs	• Book clubs • Closing community share	• Related activities (i.e., group project, quiz, process writing, skill practice)	• Read • Respond in logs	• Book clubs • Closing community share

90-minute periods

Monday	Tuesday	Wednesday	Thursday	Friday
• Read • Respond in logs • Book clubs • Closing community share	• Related activities	• Read • Respond in logs • Book clubs • Closing community share	• Related activities	• Read • Respond in logs • Book clubs • Closing community share

Build a Community in Your Classroom

For Book Club to succeed, students must feel comfortable sharing their ideas in small-group discussions. Therefore, you need to build a classroom community in which students feel safe, included, and valued as individuals. Before you begin your first unit, introduce students to the components of the program and talk about how discussions should be conducted. Remind the class that every individual has unique ideas, and that everyone in the class is entitled to speak. Make it clear that you won't tolerate disrespectful or dismissive behavior toward others—in any situation. In your interactions with students, model how to take everyone's comments seriously and how to ask questions to better understand others' ideas. If your school has an advisory program, look for opportunities to extend its community-building, interpersonal-relations, and conflict-resolution activities into Book Club.

Begin with Easy Texts and Short Amounts of Time

For students who are completely new to Book Club, it's a good idea to introduce them to the program with short, easy texts. They'll have a lot to absorb just getting used to the new format, so you shouldn't expect them to hold great discussions immediately. Be prepared to allow extra time for them to practice Book Club before they tackle the first chapters of a novel. Select theme-related poems, short stories, picture books, or articles that students can read and discuss as they learn how to function in book clubs. Allot shorter periods of time for their first discussions—perhaps just five or ten minutes. As the time allocated to students' book club discussions increases, inexperienced students may feel discouraged if they run out of things to say. However, you should require them to remain in their groups for the entire time. We've found that students become accustomed to the longer time frame, and even after a conversation appears to have run its course, it will pick up again. Also be aware that it will take some students a while to feel comfortable speaking in their groups and sharing their ideas.

The best way to get students started on the right foot is to be realistic in these important early stages. Spend plenty of time helping students identify and build on what is working well in their discussions. Use closing community share to discuss students' experiences in their book clubs. Ask them to describe conversations that flowed well and to analyze the specific behaviors that contributed to this success. The next section describes a strategy you can use to model good discussion techniques.

Use "Fishbowl" to Model Book Club Discussions

Some students have more trouble than others adjusting to book clubs. Most students are not accustomed to having so much responsibility, so they need guidance when participating in a book club for the first time. One effective way of showing students what's expected of them is to provide a concrete model. We've developed a modeling method that we call *fishbowl.*

A fishbowl is a book club discussion that takes place in the center of the classroom with the rest of the class observing. The model group might be comprised of you and other adults, or it could consist of randomly chosen students. Here's how you can use fishbowl in your class:

- Arrange the desks or tables in your classroom so that one book club is in the center and all other students have a clear view.

- Select a short, simple text that students can easily read and discuss. Have the entire class read the text to prepare for fishbowl.

- In the first part of the fishbowl exercise, members of the selected group should conduct their discussion as they normally would. Although it might be tempting, the teacher should avoid giving support to a student group. A certain amount of floundering through silent moments is part of the learning process. Students observing the fishbowl should have their reading logs available to write down ideas they'd like to contribute to the discussion and to note when fishbowl participants have made good contributions.

- Allow the discussion to continue as long as it is productive. Then hold community share to debrief students on the fishbowl. We generally involve only the fishbowl observers, not the participants, in this community share. Focus first on the substance of the discussion and then on behaviors that contributed to making the discussion work. Ask students: (1) What went well? and (2) What needs improvement? Have them

The Fishbowl Model

People within the fishbowl:
- Construct meaning from a text
- Work together to make connections
- Solve problems
- Practice literate talk
- Develop personal response skills
- Articulate and develop ideas
- Critique the text and the ideas of others
- Actively listen to others

People outside the fishbowl:
- Observe what goes well and what needs improvement
- Take notes
- Formulate questions as the discussion unfolds

identify specific behaviors, and discuss how these behaviors contribute to or detract from a good discussion.

Fishbowls allow students to see how a book club discussion occurs. Students learn to recognize and, later, self-assess what kinds of behaviors are acceptable and how group members can contribute to a good discussion. We've used fishbowls at the beginning of the Book Club program, during the year when book clubs needed a "boost," and at other times just for a break in the routine.

Model Thoughtful Reading and Discussion

As a reader yourself, you should be prepared to show students how a literate person approaches a book and shares his or her ideas with other readers. You might display your own reading responses using an overhead projector or a chart. During discussions, bring up your own ideas and discuss some of the notes you made while reading. While doing this, model good discussion etiquette by not dominating the conversation. You might also role play or show a videotape of an effective book discussion.

Supporting Students Throughout a Book Club Unit

Once your Book Club unit begins, you can support your students in a variety of ways. We find the following techniques helpful:

1. Post charts in the classroom that students can use as guides. For example, you might create charts entitled "Techniques for a Good Book Club Discussion," "Literary Terms We Know and Use," and "Support for the Theme(s)." Allow students to contribute their ideas to these charts, particularly during community share discussions.

2. Review past lessons and present activities that reinforce what's already been learned. If you feel students are getting lazy in their book groups, you might revisit fishbowl.

3. Always address problems immediately.

4. To give students ownership, try to refer to their ideas (in their words) and use their work as examples.

5. Continue to model for students, using your work and their work.

6. Avoid burnout. Try to incorporate varying activities and response types on a weekly basis.

7. Whenever you can, empower your students with choice.

8. Move beyond typical school texts to include videos, songs, news articles, web sites, and magazines that relate to your unit.

 STUDENTS' CRITERIA

Students in one Book Club classroom generated the following criteria for a good book club discussion:

- Ask questions
- Voice own opinions
- Make comparisons
- Back up opinions with facts
- Good questions and responses
- Everyone talks
- Be polite
- Good book
- Speak clearly
- Some disagreement
- Don't jump around topics
- Make connections
- Good eye contact
- Good vocabulary
- Four or more people
- Don't overuse "like"
- Sit still

Using Inclusion Strategies

We are often asked if Book Club can meet the needs of all students—even those who traditionally need special support. In our experience, Book Club can work extremely well in heterogeneous classrooms that must meet the needs of diverse groups of learners. Below are some tips for helping special-needs students access literature written for their grade level.

- Developing an individualized plan that includes prereading strategies and guided reading can be key to helping a special-needs student succeed in a Book Club setting. If possible, collaborate with the special-education teacher to develop such a plan and to modify reading and writing activities for the student.

- Many students will benefit from activities and strategies that encourage them to preview their reading, connect new information to prior knowledge, visualize, ask questions, make predictions, identify and record main ideas, and review what they've read. Teaching strategies such as SQ3R, KWL, QAR, and reciprocal teaching are useful to all students and invaluable to struggling readers. (For more information on these strategies, see Chapter 3, pages 30–32.)

- Your unit plan for special-needs students should include providing plenty of background information, read-aloud sessions, and guided reading. Have adults, such as parents, special-education teachers, or tutors, preread selections with students so that they do not panic when they read on their own in class. In class, you can let them read as much as they can of the assignment, knowing they have already heard or read it once.

- Encourage partner reading. Special-needs students can follow along as stronger readers read aloud and serve as guides.

- Acquire, create, or have students create audiotapes of each chapter. Struggling readers can listen to and read along with the tapes.

- Allow time after class or at home for slower readers to catch up before discussing a section of text.

- If possible, conduct one-on-one discussions about the book. Review and summarize what students have already read and help them make predictions about upcoming chapters. If necessary, clue students in to major plot elements so that they will have context and additional background knowledge as they continue reading.

- By design, Book Club allows students to support each other in discussions and work together to find meaning in texts. Try to group stronger readers with students who need additional support. Stronger readers can model reading and discussion strategies. Also, special-needs students will gain confidence as they engage in real conversation and watch their peers regularly struggle to find meaning or express ideas. These students learn that reading and understanding literature is a process for everyone. Book Club also allows these learners to succeed by building on other strengths, such as verbal/speaking abilities.

Troubleshooting

As you incorporate Book Club in your classroom, you will inevitably encounter a few bumps in the road. Here are some tips for dealing with common problems.

Students Who Struggle with Sustained Silent Reading

We find that getting students to read silently for a period of time in class can sometimes be a challenge. Many of our students would love to have every novel read aloud to them! We know, however, that in order for them to succeed academically and develop into lifelong readers, they must learn to focus and build their sustained silent reading skills. To help students in this area, we sometimes cut back on the amount of time allocated to independent reading and then gradually increase this time over the course of the unit or school year. For example, at the start of a unit, we might read aloud part of a chapter and then have students read independently for five minutes. As students become better able to focus and absorb information on their own, we increase their independent reading time. Eventually, middle school students can be expected to read silently for 15 to 20 minutes.

Students Who Are Fast Readers

There may be students in your classroom who read much more quickly than others. Perhaps they read ahead and become "plot spoilers," or they finish their reading and writing assignments early and become disruptive. We require each student to obtain a related book from the classroom library and to read that book if he or she finishes the assigned reading and writing ahead of schedule. In addition to solving a classroom management problem, this gives students additional fodder for their logs and their discussions. You can even provide a list of generic questions that students can use to connect the main novel with their independent novel. For example, during a unit on *The Giver*, you might ask the following questions: How would the characters in your novel have reacted to the situation in *The Giver*? How are the settings of these two books alike or different? What job do you think your main character would be given in the society of *The Giver*, and why? How is the main character in your novel similar to or different from Jonas?

Disruptive Students

As you know, some students simply have more trouble working in a group than others. Nonetheless, we have found that all students can do well in Book

Club with appropriate guidance. Your role in organizing the discussion groups becomes extremely important when placing students who are either silent or disruptive. The following strategies have helped us deal with difficult students in our classrooms:

- **Give the student responsibility.** Provide clear directions and specific expectations for behavior, and define consequences. Ask the student on a daily basis if he or she can participate in the book club in an acceptable way. Observe the student closely in his or her book club. Have frequent conferences with the student to check on progress, gauge the student's attitude, and remind the student that he or she has choices.

- **Be prepared to remove the student from the group.** Prepare related alternative activities the student can do if he or she refuses to be a helpful member of the group and needs to be temporarily removed. You might have him or her write a character sketch, make a story map, or draw a favorite scene from the reading. The activity you assign in this situation should take about ten minutes to complete, and it should be related to the day's topic. The goal is to motivate and prepare the student to rejoin the group and act appropriately.

- **Allow the student to study how to participate in a positive way.** Give the student opportunities to observe other book clubs and take notes on what he or she sees. Then, in a conference with you, the student can share his or her observations. This process can often help students see ways in which they can successfully participate in book club discussions. Also, if the student has low self-esteem, he or she can observe that other students aren't perfect—that they, too, sometimes struggle to understand or find the right words.

Interrupting, Shouting, and Overlapping Speech

Of course, we hope for lively discussions and a classroom full of students who are eager to talk about books. However, students' enthusiasm may occasionally lead to discussion chaos—with interrupting, shouting, and overlapping conversations. You can try to correct such a situation by periodically reviewing the guidelines for good book club discussions that pertain to listening and responding. Give students the following guidelines:

- Always listen carefully to what group members say, and then respond. Sometimes it's helpful to wait a few seconds to think about what was said before responding.

- Overlapping speech is acceptable only if everyone in the group can still understand the whole conversation. It's not acceptable if nobody is listening to or understanding what others are saying.

DISCUSSION TIP

If students in a group continue to shout or talk over each other, you might consider choosing a student to serve as a "facilitator"—one whose job is to keep order during a discussion. Rotate the role so that each student in the group has a chance to oversee a discussion. Another option is to have students pass a "talking stick"—an item that signals whose turn it is to talk. Note that these strategies are last resorts and should be used only in a temporary way.

- Always keep voices at a reasonable level. Don't shout. Remember that you are supposed to be having a conversation that involves listening and responding, not a shouting match.

- Learn to "disagree agreeably," without getting angry. The point of book clubs is to share ideas openly, so don't take it personally if someone else disagrees with your ideas. Focus on ideas, not personalities.

Students Who Are Reluctant to Talk

Sometimes students participating in Book Club for the first time are hesitant to offer their opinions in a book discussion. They need to build confidence in themselves as readers and as people who can discuss books. To encourage students who are quiet and unsure of themselves, you might take some of the following steps:

- Review what makes a good conversation. Ask students to discuss conversations they've had with their friends and families. Encourage them to think about what makes a conversation interesting and enjoyable and to suggest various ways of participating in a conversation.

- Model talking with a group that includes either colleagues, former students, or current students who are comfortable in their book groups. See the discussion of "fishbowl" on pages 59–61.

- Using an overhead projector, present written transcripts of successful discussions. Highlight the words and phrases that people in the transcript use to talk about books. Also point out ways in which people interject their comments when they have something to say. Often, when students don't participate in discussions, it's because they can't find the right opportunity to jump in.

- Show a videotape of previous students in their book club groups.

- Enlist confident students to support more hesitant group members by directing questions to them and listening respectfully to their responses. Model how to bring someone into a conversation without making him or her feel embarrassed.

- Remind students that they can apply the ideas in books to their own lives and to movies and other books. If students feel they can connect to books on a more personal level, they may feel less intimidated.

Students Who Do Not Get Along

Even if you've taken great care to group your students as appropriately as possible, you'll still occasionally have to deal with disagreements and personality clashes. You can take the following steps to try to deal with these kinds of problems:

● **READING LOGS
IN DISCUSSIONS**

The ultimate goal of Book Club is to get students engaged in true conversations about books. Remind students that they should keep their logs handy during discussions so that they can refer to them periodically, but that they should not depend on them too heavily. If students continue to read directly from their logs and seem reluctant to converse, ask them to meet in their groups without their logs until they build their conversation skills.

- Act as a temporary facilitator to mediate a disagreement.

- Role play a book club discussion that includes a disagreement. Model for students how to give each other opportunities to express their ideas without interrupting or responding in anger. Teach students how to be mediators in their own discussions.

- Have students who haven't been getting along work on a short, specific project together—such as completing a share sheet or responding to a writing prompt. This will give the students practice working together toward a common goal and might help them discover areas of mutual interest.

- Remind students that their grade for the unit depends in part on the success of their book club discussions. Explain that learning to compromise, listen, and respect the opinions of others is an important component of Book Club. Developing these "people skills" will help them achieve success in the Book Club classroom and in life.

Students Who Have Gotten Off Task

A group of students having a discussion will inevitably lose focus every now and then. We've used a simple method for steering them back to task called "three leaps." If you notice that a group is off task, ask group members to explain in three leaps how they got from the book to their present topic. This usually works in getting students to refocus. If students are continually losing focus, you might be allowing discussions to continue for too long. One rule of thumb is that most students can carry on an effective discussion for roughly their age-equivalent in minutes. However, you may observe that some students can go longer, while others need to break sooner.

Final Thoughts

The key to success in Book Club is careful preparation, patience, and the ability to keep this most important goal in mind: building students' positive attitude toward reading. Putting the program into place for the first time involves a lot of decision making and an ability to manage complex issues. However, by dealing with these decisions and issues early, you can establish a successful Book Club program in your classroom. Book Club teachers have achieved success by staying focused on their own instincts and teaching styles, their students' needs and abilities, and their instructional goals.

Theme-Based Unit:
The Giver

Thematic Units for Beginning or Advanced Book Clubs

This chapter outlines a complete thematic unit contrasting conformity with individuality. At the center of the unit is Lois Lowry's Newbery Medal–winning novel *The Giver,* which students will read and discuss in book clubs. A variety of other texts and activities contribute to students' exploration of themes in the novel.

The Book Club lesson plans in this chapter are meant for a class using Book Club for the first time. The lessons teach and reinforce the skills that students need to participate successfully in literature discussions. If your class is already familiar with Book Club, we've provided an alternative set of lessons in Chapter 7. These lessons assume that students are comfortable with the format of Book Club and can focus more exclusively on aspects of the literature. Even if you plan to use the more advanced lesson plans in Chapter 7, read through page 81 of this chapter for information about the thematic unit as a whole.

Literacy Skill Instruction

Book Club allows you the flexibility to meet your own state, district, and/ or school curriculum standards. The mini-lessons you teach during opening community share can easily be adapted to your requirements as students work their way through the novel. For the purpose of our lesson plans, Book Club is divided into four curriculum areas: Language Conventions, Literary Aspects, Comprehension, and Composition (see Chapter 1, Achieving a Balanced Literacy Curriculum, page 5). The charts on pages 69 and 70 correlate these curriculum areas to individual Book Club lessons for *The Giver.*

Lessons are also correlated to language arts standards established by the National Council of Teachers of English and the International Reading Association. Numbers in parentheses refer to specific NCTE/IRA standards shown in the chart below.

NCTE/IRA Standards for the English Language Arts

1. Students read a wide range of print and nonprint texts to build an understanding of texts, of themselves, and of the cultures of the United States and the world; to acquire new information; to respond to the needs and demands of society and the workplace; and for personal fulfillment. Among these texts are fiction and nonfiction, classic and contemporary works.

2. Students read a wide range of literature from many periods in many genres to build an understanding of the many dimensions (e.g., philosophical, ethical, aesthetic) of human experience.

3. Students apply a wide range of strategies to comprehend, interpret, evaluate, and appreciate texts. They draw on their prior experience, their interactions with other readers and writers, their knowledge of word meaning and of other texts, their word identification strategies, and their understanding of textual features (e.g., sound-letter correspondence, sentence structure, context, graphics).

4. Students adjust their use of spoken, written, and visual language (e.g., conventions, style, and vocabulary) to communicate effectively with a variety of audiences and for different purposes.

5. Students employ a wide range of strategies as they write and use different writing process elements appropriately to communicate with different audiences for a variety of purposes.

6. Students apply knowledge of language structure, language conventions (e.g., spelling and punctuation), media techniques, figurative language, and genre to create, critique, and discuss print and nonprint texts.

7. Students conduct research on issues and interests by generating ideas and questions and by posing problems. They gather, evaluate, and synthesize data from a variety of sources (e.g., print and nonprint texts, artifacts, and people) to communicate their discoveries in ways that suit their purpose and audience.

8. Students use a variety of technological and information resources (e.g., libraries, databases, computer networks, video) to gather and synthesize information and to create and communicate knowledge.

9. Students develop an understanding of and respect for diversity in language use, patterns, and dialects across cultures, ethnic groups, geographic regions, and social roles.

10. Students whose first language is not English make use of their first language to develop competency in the English language arts and to develop understanding of content across the curriculum.

11. Students participate as knowledgeable, reflective, creative, and critical members of a variety of literacy communities.

12. Students use spoken, written, and visual language to accomplish their own purposes (e.g., for learning, enjoyment, persuasion, and the exchange of information).

Curriculum Correlation Chart

Curriculum Area	Lessons in Chapter 6

Language Conventions

Sound/Symbol
- Spell conventionally
- Read with fluency

Grammar
- Use appropriate language choices (verbs, syntax, punctuation) in oral reading, discussion, and writing

Interaction
- Work with peers to set goals
- Interact with peers in literacy contexts

Lessons 1–15: Book clubs (1, 3, 4, 11, 12)
Lesson 1: Introduction to Book Club (1, 3, 4, 11, 12)
Lesson 14: The Essay (5, 6)
Lesson 15: Collaborative Project (3, 5, 11)

Literary Aspects

Literary Elements

Theme
- Author's purposes
- Connections to life

Point of View
- Characters' POV
- Author's POV

Genre/Structures
- Story structure
- Expository structures
- Types of genres

Author's Craft
- Style
- Text features

Response to Literature

Personal
- Share experiences
- Share personal feelings
- Place self in situation
- Compare self to characters

Creative
- Ask "What if?" (change event in plot and explore impact)
- Dramatize events and characters' attitudes or actions
- Illustrate events and characters

Critical
- Explain changes in beliefs or feelings
- Use evidence from text to support ideas
- Critique texts using specific examples
- Discuss author's purposes
- Identify author's craft
- Use text as mirror of own life and as window into lives of others

Lesson 2: The Tripod Log Format (3, 4, 5, 6, 11)
Lesson 3: Extended Responses to Text (3, 4, 5, 6)
Lesson 5: Me and the Book (3, 4, 5)
Lesson 7: Author's Craft (3, 6)
Lesson 8: Dialogue (3, 5, 6)
Lesson 9: Favorite Story Part (3, 5, 6)
Lesson 10: Story Characters (3, 6)
Lesson 12: Author's Purpose and Genre (3, 4, 5, 6)
Lesson 13: Intertextual Connections—Theme (3, 4, 5, 6, 11)
Lesson 14: The Essay (5, 6)
Lesson 15: Collaborative Project (6, 12)

continued on next page

Curriculum Correlation Chart, continued

Curriculum Area	Lessons in Chapter 6
Comprehension	

Background Knowledge • Make predictions • Draw on prior knowledge • Build knowledge as needed • Use context clues • Make intertextual connections **Processing Text** • Summarize • Sequence • Build vocabulary • Organize and use knowledge of text structure • Analyze characters, setting, plot sequence **Monitoring Own Reading** • Ask questions • Clarify confusions	**Lesson 4:** Build Vocabulary (3, 9) **Lesson 6:** Compare and Contrast (3, 4, 6) **Lesson 11:** Sequence of Story Events (3, 5) **Lesson 13:** Intertextual Connections—Theme (3, 4, 5, 6, 11)

Curriculum Area	Lessons in Chapter 6
Composition	

Process • Plan • Draft • Revise **Writing as a Tool** **Writing from Sources** **On-Demand Writing**	**Lessons 1–12:** Log writing (4, 12) **Lesson 13:** Intertextual Connections—Theme (3, 4, 5, 6, 11) **Lesson 14:** The Essay (5, 6) **Lesson 15:** Collaborative Project (4, 5, 6, 11)

Integrating Instruction

Many language arts teachers are responsible for teaching skills in other curricular areas. If you're team teaching, for example, you may need to integrate science, math, or social studies content into your literature instruction. Teaching with *The Giver* provides many opportunities for cross-curricular connections, particularly with social studies. For your convenience, we've identified links with social studies content based on the ten thematic strands defined by the National Council for the Social Studies (NCSS). The chart on page 71 highlights the strands that relate most closely to *The Giver* and indicates which activities and lessons support each strand. You can use this chart as a starting point for correlating the unit to your own standards.

Correlation to Social Studies Standards

NCSS Thematic Strands

Lessons and Activities

1. **Culture**
   Social studies programs should include experiences that provide for the study of culture and cultural diversity.

   Chapter 6, Lessons 4, 5, 6, 14; Extended Unit, Weeks 1, 2

2. **Time, Continuity, and Change**
   Social studies programs should include experiences that provide for the study of the ways human beings view themselves in and over time.

   Chapter 6, Lessons 6, 8, 9, 14; Extended Unit, Weeks 1, 2, 7–8, 9–10

3. **People, Places, and Environments**
   Social studies programs should include experiences that provide for the study of people, places, and environments.

   Chapter 6, Lessons 1, 2, 6, 8, 15; Extended Unit, Weeks 1, 7–8

4. **Individual Development and Identity**
   Social studies programs should include experiences that provide for the study of individual development and identity.

   Chapter 6, Lessons 1, 4, 5, 8, 9, 10, 11, 13, 14; Extended Unit, Weeks 1, 2, 7–8, 11

5. **Individuals, Groups, and Institutions**
   Social studies programs should include experiences that provide for the study of interactions among individuals, groups, and institutions.

   Chapter 6, Lessons 1, 3, 4, 5, 8, 11, 13, 14; Extended Unit, Weeks 1, 2, 7–8, 9–10

6. **Power, Authority, and Governance**
   Social studies programs should include experiences that provide for the study of how people create and change structures of power, authority, and governance.

   Chapter 6, Lessons 4, 6, 8, 14; Extended Unit, Weeks 1, 2, 9–10

7. **Production, Distribution, and Consumption**
   Social studies programs should include experiences that provide for the study of how people organize for the production, distribution, and consumption of goods and services.

8. **Science, Technology, and Society**
   Social studies programs should include experiences that provide for the study of relationships among science, technology, and society.

   Chapter 6, Lessons 6, 8, 12; Extended Unit, Weeks 9–10

9. **Global Connections**
   Social studies programs should include experiences that provide for the study of global connections and interdependence.

10. **Civic Ideals and Practices**
    Social studies programs should include experiences that provide for the study of the ideals, principles, and practices of citizenship in a democratic republic.

    Chapter 6, Lesson 8; Extended Unit, Weeks 1, 2, 9–10

TEACHING TIP

If you plan to use Chapter 6 as the framework for your unit, you can use Chapter 7 as a source for additional instructional and writing options. This can be especially useful if you have a differentiated classroom, where some students may need less guidance with the components of the program and additional ways of examining the text.

Planning an Extended Theme-Based Unit

This chapter describes a theme-based unit with Book Club lessons focusing on *The Giver*. (See the Ten-Week Unit Overview on page 76.) While the Book Club lessons form an integral part of the unit as a whole, they can also stand alone if you choose not to teach the entire unit. In other words, you can use Lessons 1–15 to guide students' reading and discussion of *The Giver* without having completed the activities for Weeks 1–2 suggested in the overview. If you plan to teach the four-week Book Club segment only, you may skip to page 82 now. (Turn to page 103 if you wish to use the lesson plans for an experienced Book Club class.)

Unit Themes

For most young adolescents, the theme of individuality versus conformity is part of everyday life. Adolescents continually balance trying to establish their own identities with trying to "fit in." They crave structure and support, but they are often eager to test boundaries—especially those established by the adult world. In this unit, students will read *The Giver* in conjunction with other books, poems, and a film that examine issues surrounding individuality and conformity.

In *The Giver,* characters live in a protected world where individual choice has been eliminated and everything is done for the good of the community as a whole. As a result, theirs is a society that almost never experiences complications of any kind. There is no pain, hunger, or neediness. Everyone has a job and a family that has been carefully selected for him or her. Everyone is trained to behave according to strict codes and to use "precise" language. On the surface, this community makes perfect sense. But does it really? What is it missing? How perfect is a society that has no room for spontaneity, personal choices, or "messy" emotions like love? These are the questions that readers, along with the book's main character, will confront as the story unfolds. Help students identify these ideas in the book by integrating them into classroom discussions throughout the unit. You might display theme-related questions such as the following and use them to focus students' discussions.

When is it best to conform to the wishes or rules of others?

What problems are avoided when people conform?

What new problems does conformity create?

When is it important to act as an individual and stand up for one's own beliefs?

How important is it for people to have choices?

Read-Aloud Book List

When you read aloud, you create a common literary context for the whole class. The following books and poems focus on themes of individuality and conformity. As read-aloud materials, they are useful for building background knowledge, motivating students, and encouraging students to make intertextual connections. For source information on these materials, refer to the Bibliography (page 198).

Nonfiction
Looking Back: A Book of Memories by Lois Lowry
Newbery Medal Acceptance Speech (1994) by Lois Lowry

Novel
The Wave by Todd Strasser

Picture Books
The Big Orange Splot by Daniel Manus Pinkwater
Chester's Way by Kevin Henkes
Chrysanthemum by Kevin Henkes
Island of the Skog by Stephen Kellogg
The Sneetches by Dr. Seuss

Short Stories
"A Christmas Memory" by Truman Capote
"Dark They Were, and Golden-Eyed" by Ray Bradbury
"The Lottery" by Shirley Jackson

Poetry
"If I Were in Charge of the World" by Judith Viorst
"The Road Not Taken" by Robert Frost
"The Unknown Citizen" by W. H. Auden
"Warning" ("When I am an old woman, I shall wear purple . . .")
   by Jenny Joseph

Special Classroom Library

During a thematic unit, try to stock your classroom with a variety of theme-related literature. The following books dealing with conformity and individuality are appropriate for your classroom library during this unit.

1984 by George Orwell. This classic science-fiction tale describes a brutal totalitarian society in which Big Brother and the Thought Police monitor every person's thoughts and actions. The book's hero sees through the government's lies and methods of mind control that keep people in a state of unthinking conformity. He puts his life on the line to fight for truth and freedom.

The Chocolate War by Robert Cormier. Shy freshman Jerry Renault "disturbs the universe" at his prep school when he refuses to be bullied into selling chocolates for an annual fundraising drive. The novel examines mob cruelty and an unlikely hero's struggle to protect his personal freedom.

Fahrenheit 451 by Ray Bradbury. This classic science-fiction novel is about a totalitarian society in which books are systematically burned to prevent the free exchange of ideas. The book's hero is a book burner who discovers the tragedy of his work and of his society.

Freak the Mighty by Rodman Philbrick. In this story of friendship and nonconformity, two friends learn to value their differences and pool their individual strengths to conquer obstacles in their lives.

Gathering Blue by Lois Lowry. In this companion volume to *The Giver,* Lowry creates another mysterious world controlled by merciless, secretive authorities. Kira, the novel's hero, has an exciting but frightening opportunity to bring freedom and truth to her dark world.

The Last Safe Place on Earth by Richard Peck. Fifteen-year-old Todd Tobin learns the truth about his sheltered, picture-perfect suburban neighborhood, where hate groups and censors seek to eliminate anyone or anything that doesn't fit their views. This book explores the consequences of allowing hatred, censorship, and narrow-mindedness to go unchallenged.

A Place Called Ugly by Avi. Fourteen-year-old Owen Coughlin learns that developers plan to tear down his family's beloved summer cottage of ten years to make way for a resort. He decides to fight to protect the place that holds so many special memories.

A Wrinkle in Time by Madeleine L'Engle. A brother and sister travel through space and time to save their father from an evil force that threatens all that is good in the universe. After traveling to a world where a central brain controls everything, the children learn to face their imperfections and to value their unique traits.

Other Media

Connections can extend beyond written texts to include songs, movies, and personal experiences. We recommend the following film as an additional resource for this unit.

The Wave (VHS, 46 minutes). A history teacher wants to demonstrate for his students the atmosphere in 1930s Nazi Germany, so he devises an experiment. Acting as the leader of a movement called "The

Wave," he promotes totalitarian ideas about power, discipline, and superiority. His students are surprisingly willing to follow along, and the school becomes a frightening place where anyone who rejects the movement is punished. This television movie is based on real events in California in 1967. The Holocaust Resource Center and Archives at Queensborough Community College in Bayside, New York (718-225-1617) lends the film to teachers who send a written request on school letterhead. The video is also available for purchase from Social Studies School Service of Culver City, California (1-800-421-4246).

Weekly Activities

Students' reading and discussion of *The Giver* can take place in the context of a complete unit focusing on conformity and individuality. The chart on page 76 provides a brief overview of activities students may complete during an ten-week unit on this theme. They begin by conducting research, building background, and formulating their ideas about a "perfect world." Beginning in the third week, they read *The Giver* in their book clubs. After finishing the novel, they extend their study of unit themes, read other theme-related texts, revisit their ideas about a perfect world, write a poem, and hold a debate. Complete descriptions of weekly activities are provided below.

Week 1: Research/Introduction to Themes

- In a whole-class discussion, introduce the terms *individuality* and *conformity*. Ask students to name various ways people express their individuality. For example, students might talk about clothing, hairstyles, hobbies and activities, and political and social movements. Write their ideas on the chalkboard or on chart paper.

- Then invite students to discuss examples of conformity. Students might talk about dress codes, laws and rules, and activities and groups that promote conformity. Again, record students' ideas on the chalkboard or chart paper.

- Invite students to think about the pros and cons of conformity. When is it important or helpful to conform to certain rules and behaviors? When does conformity cause or add to other problems?

- Ask students what makes a person a "nonconformist." You might discuss synonyms such as *maverick, rebel, original, eccentric,* and *dissenter.* Then brainstorm a list of people—historical figures, entertainers, artists, political leaders, activists—who are known for "going against the grain" and being themselves without apology.

Ten-Week Unit Overview

This unit has been correlated with the NCTE/IRA Standards for the English Language Arts (see page 68). Numbers in parentheses refer to specific standards.

Week 1: Research/ Introduction to Themes

- Students research conformity versus individuality throughout history and across cultures. (1, 7, 8)

- Book groups focus on people who have stood up for beliefs, worked to change societal norms, or lived according to their own rules. (1, 7, 8)

- Students choose a book to read outside class that connects to the unit theme. (2)

Week 2: Background Building

- Teacher reads aloud theme-related writings, such as picture books, a poem, and a short story. Students discuss what the writings suggest about individuality, conformity, and choice. (2, 3, 9)

- Students give presentations to report the results of their research. (7)

- Students connect in-class and independent reading to overall conformity/individuality theme. (2)

- Teacher reads aloud "If I Were in Charge of the World" by Judith Viorst to start students thinking about what qualities their "perfect" world might have. (2, 3)

- Students list what they would do if they were in charge of the world. (4)

Weeks 3–6: Book Club

- Students form book clubs to read and discuss *The Giver.* (4, 11)

- Students keep reading logs as resources for group discussions. (3, 5, 12)

- Students analyze various literary elements and think about the author's style. (3, 6)

- Students create a variety of written responses and participate in a collaborative project. (4, 5, 6, 11)

- Students assess their own work and that of their peers. (6)

Weeks 7–8: Extension of Themes

- Students discuss the importance of memory, and teacher reads aloud Lois Lowry's memoirs. (2)

- Students organize, write, design, and present their own memoirs based on significant items that represent each year of their lives. (4, 5, 11)

Weeks 9–10: Completion of Theme Study

- Students continue to discuss the theme of individuality and conformity. (11)

- Students review and discuss the film or the book *The Wave.* (3)

- Students revise their "If I Were in Charge of the World" notes and write poems based on these notes. (4, 6)

- Students debate a theme-related topic. (4, 11)

- Divide students into their book club groups. Four or five students in each group is ideal. Tell students that you would like them to research individuality versus conformity through time and across cultures. Their research should focus on individuals who have fought for their beliefs, attempted to change the rules of society, or simply lived in a way that was considered strange or unique. Have each group concentrate on one person. If students need more direction, suggest that they look at writers and artists who were not part of mainstream life; religious communities; civil rights movements in various times and cultures; political, environmental, animal rights, and labor union movements; and even people in their own lives and communities.

- For their research, encourage students to use the library, the Internet, and interviews of people in the community. As they collect their information, they should think about why certain people have not fit into mainstream life, what specific conditions have prompted people to seek change or to rebel against mainstream society, and how people who are different have been received by society as a whole. They should also think about the personal qualities that nonconformists possess.

- In addition to their research, students may select a book related to the theme of nonconformity and individuality to read independently. Suggested titles are listed in the Special Classroom Library on page 73.

Week 2: Background Building

- Continue to build the theme by reading aloud from picture books, short stories, and poems that deal with conformity, individuality, and personal choices. Suggested titles include "The Lottery," *Chester's Way, The Sneetches,* and "The Road Not Taken." See the Read-Aloud Book List on page 73.

- As students continue their research, have them prepare to present their findings to the class. Each group should produce an opinion paper and a creative handout that introduces one individual to the class and explains why he or she is a nonconformist. They should also describe how the world was affected—for better or worse—by each individual. To give students ideas for designing a handout, you might pass out copies of Think Sheet 20, Presentation Handout.

- After students give their presentations, hold a class discussion about the following questions: What are the pros and cons of resisting an established norm? What does society gain and/or lose by allowing a variety of ideas and opinions?

- Encourage students to make connections between their group's research and their independent reading.

- Read aloud the poem "If I Were in Charge of the World" by Judith Viorst, which gives a young person's humorous perspective on how the world should be adjusted to fit his or her own tastes and needs.

- Ask each student to write a similar list of goals that he or she would work toward if given the chance to be in charge of the world. Tell students that they will revisit their lists after reading *The Giver* to see if their perspectives have changed at all.

Weeks 3–6: Book Club

See Book Club Lesson Plans, page 82 or page 106. Lessons beginning on page 82 are intended for students experiencing Book Club for the first time. The lessons suggest step-by-step methods for introducing reading log options, discussion techniques, and other components of the program to a class. Lessons in Chapter 7, starting on page 106, are intended for students who are already familiar with Book Club and can focus more exclusively on aspects of the novel.

Weeks 7–8: Extension of Themes

Memoir Project

- Remind students that in *The Giver,* Jonas comes to value his individuality when he receives memories. The memories teach him lessons, broaden his world, and bring him in touch with a whole range of emotions and experiences. They become part of who he is and leave him wanting more from life.

- Tell students that, in much the same way, our own memories form an essential part of our identities. They teach us lessons, tell us stories about the people and experiences we love, and remind us of who we are. Have each student freewrite for a moment about one personal memory that is particularly important to him or her. Invite students to share their memories and explain why they are so important.

- Tell students that a personal memoir is a record or account of the important moments in a person's life. A memoir usually includes stories, anecdotes, and photographs. As an example, read passages from Lois Lowry's memoir, *Looking Back.* Pass the book around the classroom and allow students to examine its organization and its collection of pictures. Ask students to think about what Lowry's memoir says about her life and her character.

- Tell students that they will be creating their own memoirs. Explain that you would like each student to bring in an artifact (picture, stuffed animal, postcard, souvenir, trophy, ticket stub, etc.) of significance for each year of his or her life. Tell students that they may photograph large objects that cannot easily be transported. Also, if students remember important items that they no longer have, they can draw pictures or write brief descriptions of them.

- Tell students to think of their items as keys to their most important memories. Explain that each student will write a detailed paragraph for each of his or her personal artifacts. (So, a student who is twelve years old will have twelve paragraphs in his or her memoir.) The paragraphs need not focus entirely on the items, but on what the items represent to each student. For example, a photograph might lead to a memory of a special person; a T-shirt might remind someone of a vacation; a toy might bring back a childhood memory.

- Explain that students may structure their paragraphs in various ways. They can create word pictures that are snapshots of important moments in time. They can incorporate dialogue to create brief scenes or conversations between people. They can begin a paragraph with an exciting lead and write it as a news story, or they can present a single important or difficult moment in slow motion—building suspense as they write. They can also shrink the events of a particularly important year into a paragraph. Every paragraph, however, should emphasize concrete details and the significance of a person, place, or thing in the student's life. For example, review some of the most important memories that The Giver passes on to Jonas in the novel. What kinds of details give these memories special meaning? Evaluation Sheet 5 can help you evaluate students' final products. Consider discussing this sheet with the class before students begin writing.

- You might want to share the excerpts from memoirs of other Book Club students shown on page 80.

- Tell students that they can design their memoirs—both the interior and the front and back covers—in any way they choose, using a variety of materials. If they have access to the technology, they may also choose to post their memoirs on a personal web site. (Be sure to review some rules of Internet safety first. For example, students should not publish their addresses, phone numbers, or last names or agree to meet people who contact them online.) Have students prepare to display their work for the class or for other students in the school.

- You might end the memoir project by having students write reflective essays explaining what they have learned from putting together a memoir and what others might learn by reading their personal memories. Students might also want to write about the people in Jonas's world and the restricted lives they lead. Does looking over their own rich collections of memories further emphasize what the people in Jonas's community are

TECHNOLOGY TIPS

- Some students may choose to present their final memoir projects electronically. They can create web pages or do a presentation using programs such as Hyperstudio, Corel Presentations, or Microsoft PowerPoint. Students who prefer to create a traditional book or album might consider using a drawing program or clipart to decorate their final products. They can develop special designs for their pages and for their front and back covers.

- Students may choose to use actual photographs in their memoirs, or they can scan images or use digital images if they have access to scanning and digital photography equipment.

▶ **Memoir Samples**

In this paragraph, the student focuses on a particularly significant and eventful period of her childhood. The events take place over a long period of time, but she is able to squeeze her most vivid memories into a paragraph in a way that shows their importance. The artifact for this paragraph was a photo of the student's six-year-old self with her mother.

6 Years Old—My Parent's Divorce

My parents got divorced when I was six years old. I'm not sure that I fully understood it at the time, but I remember them telling me. After that, my dad moved to an apartment. There was a swing on the porch and a bulletin board with lots of pushpins. It wasn't very big, so about a year and half later, he moved to another apartment. There was a big pool and there were several other kids that lived there. I soon made friends with most of them. There was an older girl from Romania, named Amy, a boy named Josh, who played hockey, little twin girls, and two sisters who were always fighting. After that, my dad got married to my step-mom, Hazel, who is a teacher. At my dad and Hazel's wedding, I wore shorts under my dress and did cartwheels down the aisle.

My Grandpa died at the age of 82. He had a heart attack which killed him instantly. Looking back, I wish I had talked to him more often. I always seemed to ignore him. I think his death has taught me to open up to my parents, because when they die, I want them to know how much I really love them. So, thanks Grandpa. Stay the same.

◀ This student focuses on a photograph of his grandfather and a friend. The photograph led him to reflect on what his grandfather meant to him and how memories of his grandfather continue to affect him.

missing? Give students time to share their memoirs with one another in class. You might ask them to read from their favorite pages. Then have students take their memoirs home to keep or to give as gifts.

Weeks 9–10: Completion of Theme Study

- Invite students to reflect on *The Giver* and on the other selections they've read during this unit. Ask them to think about why the theme of individuality versus conformity is addressed by so many writers in so many different ways. Discuss why this might be an important theme to examine throughout history and in today's world.

- Ask students if they believe their society could ever become like the society in *The Giver*. Then have the class view the movie *The Wave* or read aloud the novel that is based on the film. After watching the video or reading the novel, students may meet in their book clubs to discuss how the story relates to the theme of individuality versus conformity. What does the experiment say about the human inclination to follow the ideas of a group and a strong leader rather than follow one's own beliefs or sense of right and wrong? How might people balance conforming to the rules and customs of society with trying to remain freethinking individuals?

- Two possible ways to end the unit are described below.

Poetry

Have students review the lists they created in response to "If I Were in Charge of the World" by Judith Viorst. Ask them if they want to revise any of the ideas they had before the unit began. Then have each student transform his or her list into a poem about an ideal world. Have students read their poems aloud to the class. Discuss whether the poems seem to be influenced by everything the class has read during the unit.

Debate

ASSESSMENT OPTION

You might use a class debate as a basis for assessment. As students debate, evaluate how well they do the following: present ideas and support them with facts and reasons, use good listening and discussion skills, and draw from themes they've studied in the unit. A final debate can show how students' reading and discussion skills have progressed over the course of the unit.

Invite students to debate a theme-related topic. For example, introduce the arguments surrounding the pros and cons of dress codes in schools. Work with students to outline the most popular ideas on the topic. If possible, you and your students might want to try to locate newspaper editorials, magazine articles, or online information representing both sides of the school dress code debate. Divide the class into two groups: one arguing in favor of dress codes and one arguing against dress codes. Then have the groups debate this topic, either in a whole-class discussion or in smaller discussion groups. Encourage students to give concrete reasons and facts to support their opinions. Remind them that they can draw on personal experience, documented facts, and themes they've studied in this unit. To extend the assignment, have students choose other theme-related topics that they can research and debate.

Book Club Lesson Plans

If you plan to teach the full ten-week unit (see page 75), students should have completed activities for Weeks 1–2 before you begin teaching the lessons in this section. Page references throughout the lessons are from the Laurel-Leaf Newbery paperback edition of *The Giver*. A reminder: The lessons in this chapter are for students who are new to Book Club. Lesson plans for more experienced Book Club students are provided in Chapter 7.

Ten-Week Unit

> Throughout the lesson plans, you'll see features like this one designed for teachers who are following the complete ten-week unit. If you're using the Book Club lesson plans only, you may ignore these features.

The Giver: A Synopsis

Twelve-year-old Jonas will soon take part in his community's Ceremony of Twelve and receive his Assignment—the career he will have throughout his adult life. The community long ago eradicated poverty, fear, pain, and disorder of any kind. To maintain this "perfect" world, however, individual choice and freedom of expression are sacrificed. People are assigned careers by a Committee of Elders. Families are contrived units that operate under strict guidelines. Behavior and language are carefully monitored, and people deemed inferior or burdensome are "released" from the community, never to be seen again.

Jonas, like everyone else in the community, has never known any other life and is generally comfortable and content. At the Ceremony, however, Jonas's life changes more than he ever could have imagined. Instead of being assigned a typical job, such as Nurturer or Engineer, Jonas is singled out for the most honored job in the community: Receiver of Memory. He is to receive special training from a community Elder known only as The Giver. The Giver alone holds memories of another time—when lives were filled with pain and complications as well as colors, choices, and true pleasures. He must now pass these carefully guarded memories on to Jonas.

At first, Jonas is afraid to enter the strange world of memories. After several training sessions, however, he is thoroughly repulsed by his own world. He suddenly knows the abuses that occur in his controlled community and sees everything that he, his family, and his friends have been denied. One day Jonas, with the support of The Giver, boldly escapes the boundaries of his community in search of freedom and truth.

Language Conventions:
Introduction to Book Club

Objectives:
- Introduce students to the process and terms associated with Book Club.
- Acquaint students with the idea of responding to writing prompts and keeping a reading log.
- Model for students the features of a good book discussion using a picture book.

Assigned Reading:
The Big Orange Splot by Daniel Manus Pinkwater

Writing Prompts:
- Explain the effect Mr. Plumbean has on his neighbors and his street.
- Record some of the descriptive words and phrases the author uses to add humor to the story.
- Would you like to live on Mr. Plumbean's street? Why, or why not?

- To begin your first Book Club unit of the year, introduce students to the structure and special language of the program. As a general introduction, explain that they will be reading chapter books by various authors along with related stories, poems, and other readings. Each day they will read one or two chapters in class or as homework, or they will listen as you read aloud. Explain that they will be asked to respond to the reading by writing in their reading logs. Then they will meet in small groups called book clubs to discuss their ideas with other students.

- When introducing Book Club techniques to students for the first time, it's helpful to use a simple text that they can write about and discuss with confidence. Tell students that this first lesson will focus on the picture book *The Big Orange Splot,* which is related in theme to the novel they will be reading in their book clubs—*The Giver* by Lois Lowry.

- Before students hold their own book club discussions, you might gather a small group of adults to model discussion techniques in a fishbowl setting. For example, one Book Club teacher put together a discussion group that included a librarian, the principal, a reading specialist, and herself. (For more information on fishbowling, see page 59.) We've found that students benefit from observing experienced readers discussing books. If you are unable to gather such a group, you and a small group of your students can conduct the first fishbowl discussion. In this scenario, your role as a facilitator and guide is crucial.

- Read the picture book aloud, and then have students (and any adults participating in fishbowl) respond to the writing prompts. You might choose to discuss the prompts with the class before asking students to respond to them in their logs.

LOG RESPONSES

- **The writing prompts provided in this guide are suggestions for response for you to assign as you wish. Some students will be able to handle one per reading assignment; some might be able to respond thoughtfully to two or three. There will be times when you might want students to focus on writing an extended response to a single prompt.**

- **As students become more comfortable with the Book Club format, they will certainly have ideas and questions that go beyond the writing prompts given. Here and throughout all the lessons, you may want to consider giving students "free choice" as a log option. Think Sheet 1 gives students a variety of suggestions for response. Be sure that students are challenging themselves and continually thinking and responding in new ways. The tripod response format, outlined in Lesson 2, is one way of challenging students to approach their reading from more than one angle.**

- The fishbowl discussion should take place after everyone has had time to respond to the prompts. At that point, gather together your small group of adults or students. Generally, a group of four or five is best. Be sure to arrange the classroom so that all students can hear and see the discussion unfold. Group members should use their written responses as a starting point.

- Remember that the goal of fishbowl is to show students what a thoughtful conversation about text looks like. It's important for students to see how good readers use text, prior knowledge, and personal experience to make connections. It's also important for them to know that an effective book group has a conversational tone and an atmosphere that encourages a balanced exchange of ideas. Student observers with ideas might be invited to participate in the discussion by sitting in a "visitor chair" within the group.

- In closing community share, first invite students to share their responses to the book. Tie up any loose ends and ask students to give final thoughts about the book and their written responses. Second, ask the class to discuss what was accomplished in the fishbowl discussion. Encourage students to talk about what they like and what they believe might be challenging about participating in a book group.

Lesson 2

Response to Literature:
The Tripod Log Format

Objectives:
- Begin reading *The Giver*.
- Introduce tripod reading log page. (See Think Sheets 2 and 3.)

Vocabulary:
apprehensive
distracted
distraught

Assigned Reading:
Chapters 1–3
(pages 1–25)

Writing Prompts:
- Begin to list characters in the book. Write one line about each character.
- Identify places in the text where Lowry builds suspense or raises questions in your mind.

- To spark students' interest in *The Giver*, begin the day's lesson by asking students to respond briefly to this simple writing prompt: *Describe the perfect world*. Invite them to share their responses in a whole-class discussion. Responses to this prompt often describe a world without poverty, disease, war, pain, and unhappiness. You might ask students to think about how their perfect worlds could be achieved and write their ideas on the chalkboard or on chart paper. One Book Club teacher ends this discussion by passing out copies of *The Giver* and telling students, "Here it is: your perfect world."

- Your opening lesson might also include a discussion of vocabulary words (listed on the left) that will appear in the day's reading. Vocabulary words are selected because they are challenging and/or important to students' understanding of the novel. Students can also keep a running list of any words they find difficult, interesting, or funny as they read. Lesson 4 focuses more on vocabulary.

- At this point in your reading, does Jonas's community seem like a good place to live? Why?

NOTES:
- Reproducible Think Sheets and Evaluation Sheets, referred to throughout this unit, are provided in the back of the book after page 153. These sheets are used to focus and organize students' responses to their reading and to guide teacher assessment as well as students' assessment of their own work .
- All writing prompts in the lesson plans also appear on Think Sheet 4. Distribute copies of this sheet so that students can refer to it as they complete each reading assignment in *The Giver*.

- To introduce students to the book, consider reading the first chapter aloud. This sets a tone for the book and gives students a fluent voice as a model for their own reading. For Chapters 2 and 3, either continue reading aloud or ask students to read silently or with partners. Suggest that students keep track of their favorite and least favorite sections of the book as they read throughout the unit. They can write page numbers in their logs to help them find these sections later. (See Think Sheet 5.)

- Then pass out Think Sheets 2 and 3, which introduce students to the tripod format for responses. Explain that there are many ways to respond to a single piece of writing. The tripod encourages them to respond to one section of the book in three different ways. One part of the tripod focuses on text, or their understanding of the story; another on personal and creative response, or connecting the book to their lives; and another on critical response, or analyzing the text and the author's craft. Tell students that they can always refer to Think Sheets 1, 2, and 4 for ideas on how to respond in their logs.

- Have students respond to the three writing prompts using Think Sheet 3. Before they begin writing, you might discuss the prompts with the class. Explain how each prompt fits into the tripod format. If necessary, review the term *suspense,* helping students to define it as the feeling a reader has while wanting to find out what will happen next in a story. The feeling might be eagerness, anxiety, curiosity, or even dread, but it always keeps the reader turning pages.

 LOG RESPONSES

The tripod challenges students to respond to text in a variety of ways. It helps them strengthen their comprehension of the text, examine author's craft, and connect to the book on a personal level. When students are choosing writing prompts or exercising their "free choice" response option, encourage them to cover all three angles of response as often as possible. Especially in this first unit, it is worthwhile to remind students periodically of the tripod option.

- Then have a group of students hold a fishbowl discussion as the other students observe. Select students who did not participate in fishbowl in Lesson 1. Be ready to facilitate discussion and provide guidance if the conversation breaks down or loses focus. At this point and throughout the unit, observe students' use of their logs during book club discussions. They should not be so dependent on their logs that they always read from them rather than engaging in real discussion. If they are too dependent on their logs, have them leave them behind when they meet in their groups. One strategy is to have students review their logs before meeting with their groups and make notes and questions in the margins for quick reference during discussions. They can also use Think Sheet 7, Questions for My Book Club.

- In closing community share, invite other students to share their responses and comment on the chapters they read. Find out if students have any questions or concerns at this point in their reading. Then spend a moment discussing the success of the book discussion. What did the group members do well? What could they do better?

Lesson 3

Response to Literature:
Extended Responses to Text

Objectives:
- Encourage students to use their logs as thinking tools.
- Help students develop depth in their written responses.
- Have students construct extended responses and support their ideas with evidence from the text.
- Begin charting the features of a good book club discussion.

Vocabulary:
gravitating
primly
tabulated

Assigned Reading:
Chapters 4–5
(pages 26–39)

Writing Prompts:
- Would you want to be an elderly person in Jonas's community? Why?
- What reaction does Jonas get from his parents when he describes his dream? What do you suppose is the reason for this reaction?
- In Jonas's community, why do you think so much importance is placed on the sharing of feelings and dreams?

- In today's lesson, continue to focus on students' use of their reading logs. Beginning Book Club students often write quick responses and then put their pencils down. Tell students that they should use their logs as thinking tools. Whether they are responding to prompts in class or as homework, they should keep writing for at least 5–10 minutes. Tell them that they may be surprised by the ideas that surface when they keep their pencils moving for a set period of time. To encourage extended responses, you might require students to complete at least one page of writing per writing prompt.

- Another goal for students' reading logs is written responses that show evidence of "depth"—meaning that students include quotations, details, and specific examples to support their ideas. Explain to students that as they read, they should make note of interesting details, quotations, or scenes that seem important to the story. Doing this can help them formulate ideas and then write about what they read.

- Have students complete the day's reading either silently or in pairs. Then discuss the writing prompts. Each student should pick one prompt and then take several minutes to respond to it. Remind students to express their ideas in complete sentences and to support their responses with evidence from the text. To help students get started, suggest that they first write a brief statement in response to a prompt. Beneath each statement, they should list two or three supporting reasons, details, or quotations. Then they should create an extended response (at least a paragraph or two) from these notes. Being able to organize, support, and clearly articulate ideas will help students in their book discussions and in future writing assignments.

 TEACHING TIP

When Book Club is new to students, allocate shorter periods of time for each component. This will avoid frustrating students when they've run out of things to write or talk about. Expand the schedule as students become more comfortable with the program. Below is a sample schedule for a beginning Book Club class.

- **Opening Community Share: 5–10 minutes**
- **Reading: 15–20 minutes**
- **Writing: 5–7 minutes**
- **Book Clubs: 5–7 minutes**
- **Closing Community Share: 5–10 minutes**

- Organize another fishbowl discussion with a new group of students. Using their log responses as a starting point, students in the fishbowl can discuss Chapters 4 and 5 while the rest of the class observes. Continue to guide students, helping them keep their conversation focused and moving. The suggestions you offer at this point are tools students can carry with them when they begin meeting in their independent book clubs.

- In closing community share, begin creating a chart entitled "How to Have a Good Book Club Discussion" that you can hang in the classroom throughout the unit. Tell students that they will continue to add to this chart in subsequent discussions, as they have more book club experiences. Items on the chart might include the following.

  - Don't interrupt.

  - Back up opinions with facts.

  - Ask good questions.

  - Refer to your reading log—don't just read from it.

  - Build on each other's ideas.

  - Stay focused.

  - Make connections.

  - Be polite.

  - Speak clearly.

Lesson 4

Comprehension:
Build Vocabulary

Objectives:
- Help students notice and record interesting or confusing words as they read.
- Draw attention to the special language Lowry creates for Jonas's world.

Vocabulary:
interdependence
relinquish
reprieve

- Tell students that another way to respond to the book in their reading logs is to keep a list of words and phrases from their reading that they find interesting, fun, confusing, or unique.

- Explain to students that writing down interesting words can help them in a variety of ways. A particular word can remind a reader about an important event in a story or a feeling or idea that a character expressed. Writing down a difficult word can help a reader learn and remember the word's meaning. For everyone in a book club, thinking about language word-by-word is another way to understand the characters and story more fully.

Assigned Reading:
Chapters 6–7
(pages 40–58)

Writing Prompts:
- Find some interesting words in the chapters you've read so far.
- How would you describe the special language of Jonas's community, which includes words such as *Assignment* and *Stirrings?*
- In our own society, how do we use words to distance ourselves from things that are unpleasant or difficult to face (i.e., the phrase *passed away* for *died*)?

- Before students read, suggest ways for them to record words in their reading logs. Students can record words while reading or while looking back over the selection (after having read it once). You might want to model identifying some interesting words in today's assigned reading. For example, the word *Inadequate* (page 42) is interesting because Lowry capitalizes it—indicating that it is a label that carries a great deal of weight in the community. The word *chastisement* (page 53) is challenging and has an interesting collection of sounds.

- Point out to students that language and word choice play an important role in the world Lowry creates. The community continually stresses its own brand of "precise" language—a language that reveals a great deal about the community's values. For this reason, watching for interesting words and phrases is particularly useful in this unit.

- After students read and respond to the prompts, have them meet for the first time in their own book club groups. As students discuss the book and the words they've gathered from their reading, walk from group to group, helping students become familiar with the format. In the beginning, it is a good idea to visit each book group on a daily basis to guide students and facilitate discussion.

- In community share, have students discuss their final thoughts on the day's reading. If you plan to have a "word wall," begin building it using the words students recorded in their logs. You might want to leave students with these thoughts to ponder: What is the function of words and language in Jonas's world? Is their language actually precise, or does it simply cloud the truth in many cases?

TEACHING TIP

Throughout the unit, consider working with your students to create a "word wall"—a place for the class to record the definitions of interesting words and phrases that they encounter in their reading. It provides a public arena where students can explore and discuss the connections between words, their meanings, and their connotations. A word wall can take many forms, as long as it has an easy-to-use format and exists in a safe place where you can store information for the duration of the unit. For example, you may use a portion of a chalkboard, large pieces of chart paper attached to a wall, or a portable chart stand.

Lesson 5

Response to Literature:
Me and the Book

Objectives:
- Invite students to connect aspects of the book to their own lives.

- Remind students that books not only entertain us and introduce us to interesting new people, places, and ideas; they can also help us better understand ourselves. Ask students if any characters, events, or places in

- Have students craft personal responses that share experiences and personal feelings, place themselves in a situation, or compare themselves to characters.
- Encourage students to maintain in-depth discussions in their book clubs.

Vocabulary:
anxiety
benign
empowered
integrity

Assigned Reading:
Chapters 8–9
(pages 59–71)

Writing Prompts:
- If you could give Jonas one of your memories, what would it be and why?
- Put yourself in Jonas's place after he learns of his selection. How might you feel in this situation?
- "Now, for the first time in his twelve years of life, Jonas felt separate, different." Recall a time when you felt different and alone. In what ways was your experience similar to and different from Jonas's experience?
- Have you ever been given a responsibility that you felt you didn't deserve or worried you couldn't handle? Explain.
- In your opinion, what are the pros and cons of Jonas's world?

the book so far have reminded them of people, places, and events in their own lives. Tell the class that making personal connections with characters and situations in a book can deepen their understanding of both the book and themselves.

- Tell students that they can write in their logs about events or characters in the book that remind them of something in their own lives. Explain that writing about these characters and events can help them see connections between the book and their own experiences. Seeing these connections can make the book come alive and help readers enter the world the author creates. For example, one student might understand what it's like to feel different and therefore might be better able to express her feelings on the subject. Another student might remember a time when a major life experience caused him to feel frightened or uneasy. Still another student might have an interesting personal memory that could comfort Jonas as he transitions into his new Assignment.

- Explain to students that the best way to organize a personal response is to describe something in the book and then tell what it reminds them of in their own lives. (Think Sheet 6 can help them organize their ideas.) For this lesson, invite students to respond to three of the prompts or to think of their own personal connections.

- Tell students that they don't have to share in their book clubs specific experiences that make them feel uncomfortable. They can, however, share in a general way an insight they have reached or an idea they have formulated after writing a personal response.

- As you walk around the room and monitor students' book clubs, listen to find out if students are moving toward being able to sustain an in-depth conversation on a significant topic. The goal is to get students to focus on a meaningful topic and follow through with it before skipping to another topic. When book clubs are still new to students, they will need extra guidance in achieving this goal. Visit each group regularly to offer suggestions and to do some facilitating. You might use Evaluation Sheet 2 to jot down notes. You might also collect example comments from the book discussions that you can share with the class in closing community share.

- In closing community share, ask students how they feel about writing personal responses. Do they find it helps them understand and appreciate the book? Why, or why not? You might also invite volunteers to share their personal responses. End closing community share by checking in with students about their book club discussions. Ask them how they feel about their book clubs and share some of the observations you have made about their progress.

| Lesson | 6 | Comprehension: **Compare and Contrast** |

Objectives:
- Introduce the Venn diagram format for comparison and contrast.
- Remind students to continue using the tripod format for responses.
- Have students review all of their written responses and the chapters they've read and note specific topics or questions for book club discussions.

Vocabulary:
conspicuous
diminish
glee
obsolete
sensation

Assigned Reading:
Chapters 10–11
(pages 72–87)

Writing Prompts:
- In a Venn diagram, compare something from your life to something in Jonas's life. (Think about family, school, friends, etc.)
- Use the tripod format to respond to Jonas's first experience with The Giver. You might focus on the events of the meeting, words and phrases that give the meeting a feeling of mystery, and how you would feel if you were Jonas. Refer to Think Sheet 2 if necessary.
- Describe your first impression of The Giver. What details about this man and his function in the community stand out to you?

- In opening community share, discuss why it is helpful to compare and contrast two things. Ask students what they can learn by studying how two things are both alike and different. Encourage students to think about what sorts of details they could compare and contrast to understand a place or a situation better. For example, you might want to help students compare and contrast the education of children in *The Giver* with their own education. How do the educational methods used by people in *The Giver* meet the specific goals of that community?

- Discuss ways to record these kinds of comparisons. Draw a Venn diagram on the chalkboard and have students compare and contrast the education of children in our world with the education of children in Jonas's world. Then invite students to draw their own Venn diagrams in which they compare and contrast another aspect of life in *The Giver*, such as family life or community responsibility, with the same aspect of life in our world.

- Note that the Venn diagram is another writing option for students to keep in mind for their logs, and that it can be used whenever students want to record comparisons and contrasts they notice in a text. Students can continue to add to their Venn diagrams as they read further in the book and gather more details.

- At this time, you might also want to remind students of the tripod log option that they first used in Lesson 2. Encourage students to revisit this option periodically to practice using a variety of responses. To review what can be done in a tripod, have students refer to Think Sheet 2.

- Throughout this first Book Club unit, it's important to review book discussion techniques regularly. On this day, before students meet in their book clubs, have them review all of their written responses and the chapters they have read. They should note specific topics or questions for their book club discussions in the margins of their reading logs (or on Think Sheet 7) and plan to refer to their notes if there is a lull in the conversation. Tell them that they can use this strategy to manage the direction of their discussions and to make sure they don't forget to raise important issues from their reading.

- In closing community share, ask volunteers to share their Venn diagrams or their tripod responses. Talk about how these response options help them focus their thoughts on what they are reading.

You might want to point out that Venn diagrams can be used to make comparisons and contrasts across texts as well as within texts. If your students have read another book related to the theme of nonconformity and individuality in Week 1 of this unit, have them use what they learn in this lesson to compare and contrast the settings, characters, or events of the book to those of *The Giver.*

▶ Here is one student's Venn diagram; she compares and contrasts her family life with Jonas's.

| my family | The Giver family |

my family
two girls
parents are divorced
know my past
visit relatives
biological family
fight a lot
don't tell my mom everything
pick my name—my mom
marriage for love
know what is going on in the outside world
can't be released
have b-day party's after age 12

(both)
mom + dad
children
talk
eat together
have jobs
curfew
go to special occasions

The Giver family
no relatives
one girl + one boy
not biological mom or dad
your name is already picked
share everything at dream share
marriages are set up
always are nice to each other
have to take pills for stirrings
do whatever they are told
don't keep track of age

Lesson **7**

Literary Elements:
Author's Craft

Objectives:
- Help students understand techniques an author uses to create an interesting story, especially imagery, symbolism, and foreshadowing.
- Provide a scaffold for students' search for literary devices in the text.
- Have students write about a literary element they identify in the text.

Vocabulary:
admonition   vibrant
anguished   wryly
sparse

Assigned Reading:
Chapters 12–13
(pages 88–107)

Writing Prompts:
- Write about an image from Chapter 12 or 13 that you find particularly appealing or disturbing. What specific words and phrases bring this image alive for you?
- What sensory details (sight, sound, smell, touch, or taste) help you visualize Jonas's experiences on the sled?
- Draw a picture based on an image in *The Giver.*
- Jonas's fleeting glimpses of color begin to take on special meaning as he learns more about them. What does color come to symbolize?
- What do the bridge and the river symbolize for Jonas?
- The more Jonas learns, the more he begins to question. Find an example of foreshadowing in his conversations with The Giver.

- In this first Book Club unit, it's important to acquaint students with common literary devices that are part of an author's craft. Students can then look for literary techniques as they read, write about these techniques in their logs, and discuss them in their book clubs. In subsequent units, you might choose to focus an entire lesson on a single literary device. In this lesson, the goal is to introduce students to the author's use of imagery, symbolism, and foreshadowing. Each of these devices is prominent in *The Giver.*

- Explain to students that an author uses many literary techniques to draw readers into a story. Among other devices, a writer can use descriptive language to create images, or word pictures, that appeal to a reader's senses; describe something that symbolizes, or represents, an idea or feeling; and include details that foreshadow, or hint at, events to come.

- For example, review with students Chapter 11, pages 86–87. Read this section of the novel aloud, beginning with "Jonas obeyed cheerfully. . . ." Encourage students to think about imagery, symbolism, and foreshadowing as you read.

- When you have finished reading, ask students to note descriptive language that helps them to feel what Jonas is feeling. Students are likely to point out the mention of warmth, a stinging sensation, and a sharp pain in the crease of his arm. Then ask students to think about the old man's silent response to Jonas's statement "And now I understand better, what it meant, that there would be pain. . . ." What questions does the old man's silence raise in their minds? Students might say that his response hints at the pain that is in Jonas's future. Then encourage students to talk about what pain might represent in this situation. Guide students to understand that the pain represents Jonas's experience of being thrust into a world that is completely foreign and frightening to him.

- Tell students that as careful readers, they should start keeping their eyes open for authors' literary techniques. Explain that these techniques are part of what we call the author's craft. As students read, they can record these techniques in their logs and then explain why a particular technique helps them understand and enjoy a story. Think Sheets 8 and 16 can help students chart literary techniques as they read.

- The writing prompts for this lesson deal with literary devices in Chapters 12 and 13. You might want to spend time reviewing these prompts before students read. After students read the day's assignment, they should respond to two of these prompts. If they choose, they can also write about literary techniques that they spot on their own. In their book clubs, students can discuss the author's techniques in these chapters and in previous ones. Encourage students to explain how these techniques help their understanding of characters and situations in the story. Students can continue their discussion with the entire class during closing community share. Remind students to look for literary techniques as they continue reading.

Lesson 8

Responding to Literature:
Dialogue

Objectives:
- Encourage students to look for meaning in characters' dialogue and to respond in writing to this dialogue.
- Help students notice how characters reveal themselves through dialogue.
- Review criteria for good book clubs and add to the class list of criteria.
- Have students assess themselves and their book clubs based on class-established criteria for book club discussions.

Vocabulary:
assuage
excruciating
forsaken

Assigned Reading:
Chapters 14–15
(pages 108–120)

Writing Prompts:
- "If everything's the same, then there aren't any choices! I want to wake up in the morning and *decide* things!"
- "We really have to protect people from wrong choices."

- Explain to students that authors reveal information about characters, situations, and theme in a variety of ways. One of the most important ways is through dialogue. When characters speak to one another, they often reveal valuable information about their personalities, their feelings, and their views on the world around them.

- In opening community share, review the dialogue between The Giver and Jonas in Chapter 13, pages 97–99. Read their conversation aloud with a student (or choose two students to read aloud) with emotion and inflection. Then spend a few minutes talking about what readers learn from the conversation.

- Have students meet in pairs to read Chapters 14 and 15 aloud to each other. They should read the dialogue between The Giver and Jonas on pages 110–113 as a conversation.

- The quotations given as writing prompts come from the two conversations between Jonas and The Giver cited above. In their reading logs, students can respond to two of these or to any other quotations that caught their attention. Encourage students to explain the circumstances surrounding the dialogue and to tell what the words reveal about character or situation.

- Before students meet in their book clubs, take a moment to review the criteria for good book discussions that you began generating in Lesson 3. Add to the list if necessary; students might have new ideas based on their experiences in book clubs.

- Before closing community share, have students take a moment to evaluate themselves and their book clubs according to the class-established criteria

- "It gives us wisdom. Without wisdom I could not fulfill my function of advising the Committee of Elders when they call upon me."
- "But why can't *everyone* have the memories? I think it would seem a little easier if the memories were shared."
- "They selected me—and you—to lift that burden from themselves."
- "Back and back and back."

posted in the classroom. During closing community share, remind students to continue noticing dialogue in *The Giver* and to consider responding to quotations as an ongoing reading log option.

- This is a good time to have students complete formal self-assessments using Evaluation Sheet 9, Self-Assessment: Reading Log and Evaluation Sheet 10, Self-Assessment: Book Club. Explain to students that in the Book Club program, they are given opportunities to assess themselves. Self-assessment is a chance for them to think about the work they've done, take note of what has gone well, and decide what areas need extra work and improvement. Give students time to complete their forms thoughtfully and honestly and answer any questions they have about the forms.

- At this point in the unit, you might want to collect students' reading logs for evaluation. Write comments on the logs, telling students what they are doing well and what they need to improve. Explain to students that they will have a chance to revise their entries from the first half of the unit before your final evaluation.

Lesson 9

Response to Literature:
Favorite Story Part

Objectives:
- Encourage students to keep track of their favorite story parts in their reading logs.
- Help students identify why they like some parts of a story more than others.
- Review with students the importance of referring to the text in their discussion groups to clarify information and find supporting evidence.

Vocabulary:
perceive
vague
wisp

Assigned Reading:
Chapters 16–17
(pages 121–138)

- Remind students that readers bring a variety of experiences, attitudes, and opinions to their reading of a book. That is why two people can read the same book or the same chapter and have two totally different reactions to it. For example, a particular passage might have special meaning in the life of one reader. Another reader might be drawn to a particular character or style of writing. There might be places in a book that another reader simply feels are more interesting, powerful, or skillfully written than others. In Lesson 2, students learned the importance of keeping track of their favorite and least favorite story parts. Have students review any notes or page numbers they recorded in their reading logs or on Think Sheet 5. Remind students to continue to record the page numbers of story parts they especially like or dislike as they read.

 TEACHING TIP

You might choose to pair Truman Capote's "A Christmas Memory" with Chapters 16 and 17. Like the special memory that The Giver shares with Jonas, this story is rich with images of warmth, family rituals, and meaningful relationships. Students can compare and contrast this world with the world in which Jonas lives. You can also use this story to review imagery and symbolism. For example, guide students to think about the possible symbolism of the kites at the end of the story. (The kites symbolize the free spirits of Buddy and his cousin. Through the flying kites, the author implies that their friendship can rise above the obstacles that life presents.)

Writing Prompts:
- What have been your favorite and least favorite parts of the story so far? Explain your response.
- In The Giver's memory, Jonas sees candles and a fireplace. He recognizes that indoor fires are "risky" but at the same time enjoys their light and warmth. What might the fire symbolize for Jonas?
- "'There could be love,' Jonas whispered." Respond to this quotation.
- Explain why Jonas has such overwhelming feelings of loss and frustration when he sees his friends Fiona and Asher.

- While still in opening community share, invite students to mention some of their favorite and least favorite parts of the story so far. Brainstorming as a class will stimulate students' memories of earlier sections of the book.

- After students read the day's assignment, have them respond to the prompt asking for their favorite and least favorite part of the story. Students should also respond to the other prompts in the list or to a topic of their own choosing that relates to Chapters 16 and 17.

- Before students begin their book club discussions, take a moment to review the importance of supporting their ideas by referring to the text during discussion. This is especially helpful when they are trying to defend an opinion or remind other students of a specific section of the book. The text will help them clarify what they are saying and provide evidence to support their opinions.

- In closing community share, ask students what they achieved in their discussions. Did they talk about favorite and least favorite story parts? Did group members refer to the text to support their opinions or to clarify information? What other ideas came up during their discussions?

Lesson 10

Response to Literature: Story Characters

Objectives:
- Examine the importance of characters to a story.
- Focus on important and interesting details about the main characters in *The Giver*.
- Introduce creative formats for character descriptions.
- Revisit the tripod format and be sure students understand the various response types.

Vocabulary:
imploringly
luminous
ruefully
syringe

Assigned Reading:
Chapters 18–19
(pages 139–151)

- Explain to students that interesting characters are important to any story. Readers connect to a story through the words, actions, and thoughts of characters. A character might remind readers of people they've known, give valuable perspective on story events, or build suspense. Invite students to name the most interesting characters they've encountered in other stories. What makes these characters interesting? How did these characters help them connect to the story?

- Discuss details about major characters in *The Giver*. Tell students that they can learn about story characters in several ways. They can look for direct descriptions of characters' personalities, appearances, hobbies or jobs, homes, families, thoughts, and feelings. They can also pay attention to characters' words and actions and to how other characters react to them. Remind students that in *The Giver*, readers have direct access to Jonas's thoughts and feelings. They have to depend on other clues to understand most other characters.

Writing Prompts:

- Describe two characters from *The Giver* in creative ways (for example, a character profile or map, a personal ad, a job application, etc.).
- Discuss characters or events in Chapters 18–19 using the tripod format. For each section of the tripod, you may write about a topic of your own choosing or you may respond to these three topics.
  —Explain what happened to Rosemary and why.
  —How does Lowry show The Giver's feelings toward release?
  —Describe how you felt as you read about the release of the baby.

▶ This student chose to create a character profile of Jonas. Students could create this type of profile and continue to add to it as events in the novel unfold and they learn more about the character.

• Tell students that they can respond to characters in a variety of creative ways in their reading logs. For example, they can create a character map or profile, which is any kind of chart, list, or diagram in which students record interesting details about a particular character. Another option is a personal ad written from a character's point of view, in which the character highlights his or her strong points and interests. Still another option is creating a job application with information about a particular character. Invite students to suggest other creative ways of revealing information about characters. Explain that the purpose of these activities is to help students remember important details about characters as they read and to help them understand how an author creates characters.

• Have students complete the assigned reading and then respond to the writing prompts. Give them time to create their character descriptions and to respond to the chapters using the tripod format.

• After students meet in their book clubs, gather the class together to continue discussing characters or to address any questions about the reading or the tripod format. Remind students that they can revise or add to their character descriptions as the story progresses. You might want to use students' individual character descriptions to create a longer class character chart. Use the class chart to keep track of the novel's main characters as students read.

Chapter 8
Character Profile

Name: Jonas (#19)
Date of birth: date unknown
Assignment: Receiver of Memory
How he got this assignment:
  He was watched very closely. Everything that he did had to be done well. He was chosen by the committee.

How he feels about it?
  He is very proud because it is a very respectful assignment. He is a little sad because he will live alone. What does it mean? He will get special training from The Giver. He will learn about the outside world.

Ten-Week Unit

- Students who researched nonconformists at the beginning of the unit might want to review their work at this point. They can discuss what Jonas and The Giver have in common with the real-life characters they studied.

- Students can also consider whether any real events or situations experienced by their nonconformists resemble conditions in Jonas's community.

Lesson 11

Comprehension:
Sequence of Story Events

Objectives:
- Help students see that understanding the sequence of events in a story can help them better understand the story.
- Teach students to identify key story events and distinguish them from minor happenings.

Vocabulary:
chaos
efficient
emphatically
haphazard
stealthily

Assigned Reading:
Chapters 20–21
(pages 152–170)

Writing Prompts:
- Make a sequence chart of important events in the book so far.
- "She's very efficient at her work, your red-haired friend. Feelings are not part of the life she's learned." Explain what The Giver means in describing Fiona's attitude toward release, using your knowledge of Jonas's community.

- Understanding the sequence of events in a story is critical to story comprehension. Sequencing requires students to identify key story events and put these events in order—even if some are told out of order.

- Explain to students that it's important to understand and remember the order in which story events happen. Tell them that they can make a sequence chart, map, or list of these events in their reading logs. When they organize story events in their notes, they should focus on the most important events and leave out less important ones.

- If necessary, introduce the concept of sequencing using a picture book, another novel that students have read, a movie, or a poem. With students, generate a list of four or five key events. Help them understand the difference between a major event—one that truly moves the plot or series of events forward—and a small detail. Then have the class place the events in the order in which they happened. Explain that this is called a sequence of events. Mention that sequencing can help readers to understand a story and to retell or discuss the story later.

- Model various types of sequence charts using an overhead projector, a chalkboard, or chart paper. Tell students that a sequence chart can be anything that shows the order of events, including a storyboard or comic strip format, a flow chart with arrows, or a time line. Invite them to suggest their own formats for sequence charts.

- Another way to get students to focus on main ideas and the order of events in the novel is to have them name each of the novel's chapters. You might

- Do you understand Jonas's decision, or do you believe he is wrong? Explain your response.

have students complete this task individually, in groups, or as a class. Tell students that each chapter's title should reflect the main idea or a major event of the chapter. For a student sample of this activity, see page 117.

- When students are in their book clubs, observe their discussions of the sequence of events in *The Giver*. You can learn from these discussions how well they are reading and understanding the book. It's especially helpful to know which events they consider important and which they choose not to list. Address any problems and concerns in closing community share.

Lesson 12

Literary Elements:
Author's Purpose and Genre

Objectives:
- Analyze and discuss theme and author's purpose in relation to the book's ending.
- Encourage students to find their own interpretations of the book and its ending.
- Discuss the genre of science fiction and how *The Giver* fits into this genre.

Vocabulary:
landscape
tentatively
treacherously

Assigned Reading:
Chapters 22–23
(pages 171–180)

Writing Prompts:
- Describe images from Jonas's journey that help you understand his experience.
- What do you think happens to Jonas and Gabriel? What in the text makes you think this?
- Do you like the book's ending? If yes, explain why. If no, rewrite it.

- In opening community share, tell students that every author has a purpose for writing a novel. This purpose could include any and all of the following: to entertain, to teach, to express ideas or beliefs, to highlight problems in society.

- Encourage students to state what they believe is Lowry's purpose in *The Giver*. To help them focus, ask them to think about how she portrays aspects of Jonas's world—such as the language and behavior codes, Assignments, family, and release. Does she portray these things in a good light? Then ask them to think about feelings and ideas expressed by Jonas and The Giver on choices, pain, love, and personal freedom. Tell them that examining these details will lead them to the novel's important themes and to the author's purpose.

- Tell students that science fiction is a type of writing based on real or imaginary scientific developments and often set in imaginary, futuristic places. The purpose of science fiction writers is often to criticize, draw attention to, or raise concerns about aspects of technology or the modern world. Ask students to mention any science fiction stories they have heard, read, or seen in movies or on television. Talk about how these stories are similar to and different from *The Giver*. Invite students to think about which

TEACHING TIP

- At this point, you might want to read aloud Lois Lowry's 1994 Newbery Medal acceptance speech. Students can gain insight into the author's purpose by hearing what she has to say about her own writing. In the speech, Lowry directly addresses the ending of *The Giver*. She talks about what she hopes readers will take from the ending and describes the reactions of various readers.

- If you want to delve more deeply into a genre study, read aloud the short story "Dark They Were, and Golden-Eyed" by Ray Bradbury. Ask students to compare and contrast writing styles and themes in the short story and the novel.

- Describe what you think happens to Jonas's community after he leaves.
- What might the music that Jonas hears symbolize?
- Is *The Giver* a science fiction novel? Give details to support your opinion.

aspects of technology or the modern world are represented in the world Lowry creates.

- If possible, give students extra time to respond to the final chapter and discuss it in their book groups. As you walk around the room, observe how students' discussion skills have developed over the course of the unit. Listen to evaluate their understanding of the book's ending.

- Allow students to guide the course of discussion in closing community share. Often students want to debate what they believe happens in the final chapter. Encourage students to support their ideas about the novel's ending with solid reasons and details from the text. What do they believe happens to Jonas and Gabriel? What do they believe will happen to Jonas's community?

- Students interested in science fiction might want to discuss whether *The Giver* qualifies as science fiction. If they believe the novel is science fiction, encourage them to cite supporting details from the text. Examples include the mention of Climate Control on page 83 and the work of genetic scientists (page 95) to make everyone's hair and flesh the same tone. Ask them if the way memories work, including The Giver's method of transmitting them to Jonas, seems more like science fiction or fantasy. Also have them consider whether Lowry uses her story to comment on people's use of technology.

Lesson 13

Comprehension:
Intertextual Connections—Theme

Objectives:
- Read aloud two poems and connect their themes to *The Giver*.
- Discuss the three writers' different ways of dealing with the topic of individuality versus conformity.
- Encourage students to make intertextual connections in a group discussion and in writing.
- Have students write a poem on the subject of individuality versus conformity.

Assigned Reading:
None

- When students read various types of writing that deal with the same theme, they can approach the theme from several angles and develop a firmer and more complex understanding of it. Recognizing a theme from the main Book Club novel in other writings gives students confidence as readers.

- Tell students you are going to read aloud two poems that will remind them of *The Giver,* each in its own way. First read "Unknown Citizen" by W. H. Auden. If possible, make copies of the poem so students can follow along as you read. When you are finished, give students time to jot down their initial reactions to the poem.

- Ask students to explain how the Auden poem relates to an idea in *The Giver.* Which characters in the book are "unknown citizens"? What ideas

Writing Prompts:

- Write a poem like the one by Jenny Joseph. Your opening line should begin, "When I am an old woman, I shall" or "When I am an old man, I shall." Then insert details that reveal your individuality.
- Rewrite "Unknown Citizen," making the subject of the poem a nonconformist. Add interesting details to his life to distinguish him from other citizens.
- Write a letter from Jonas to any living "unknown citizen" whose life is like that of the person in Auden's poem. What advice might Jonas give this person?
- Compare statements in Jenny Joseph's poem with Jonas's statement "I want to wake up in the morning and *decide* things! A blue tunic, or a red one?"
- Imagine that the speaker in "Warning" is directing her words at a Committee of Elders from *The Giver*. Why would they consider her plans unacceptable and frightening?

are both Auden and Lowry trying to express about conformity and individuality? How does the Auden poem make you feel? Do characters in *The Giver* give you a similar feeling?

- Then read aloud "Warning" ("When I am an old woman, I shall wear purple . . .") by Jenny Joseph. Again, try to have copies available so students can follow along as you read. Ask students how this poem relates to the *The Giver*. What idea is the speaker trying to express? What do both she and Jonas understand about life?

- After the class discussion, give students time to respond to one or more of the writing prompts. Encourage them to try their hands at writing a poem as one response option. Suggest that they spend a few moments freewriting to gather ideas and details for their poems.

- After students have written their poems and responded to the other writing prompts, have volunteers read their poems and responses to the class. Ask students if it was helpful to connect themes in *The Giver* with themes in the two poems. Explain that making connections to other texts will be an important part of all Book Club units.

Ten-Week Unit

Students may want to revisit and discuss texts they read or heard at the beginning of the unit. These works might have more meaning to them now that they have read *The Giver*.

Lesson 14

**Composition:
The Essay**

Objectives:

- Teach students to organize their ideas about a topic in a multi-paragraph essay.
- Encourage students to support statements in their essays with solid reasoning and story text.
- Have students discuss and revise their writing in their book groups.

- Explain to students that writing an essay gives them a chance to explore a topic or theme in depth. Tell them that they will compose some kind of essay at the end of most Book Club units. In their essays, they might examine a character's development throughout the course of a novel, focus on one or more of an author's literary techniques, express an opinion about some aspect of a book, connect something in a book to their own lives, or compare and contrast a book with another text. Sometimes writing essays will be part of an essay test that will evaluate their understanding of a novel.

Assigned Reading:
None

Writing Prompts:
• Respond to one of the essay topics presented on Think Sheet 9. Support your ideas with evidence from *The Giver*.
• Respond to one of the quotations on Think Sheet 11. Explain what the quote means to you, tell whether you agree or disagree with the quote, and compare the quote to at least three other literary works.

• Think Sheet 9 offers eight essay topics directly related to *The Giver*. Think Sheet 11 asks students to respond to fresh text—two quotations that relate to the unit theme. Decide which type of essay you'd like your students to write. Then distribute and read aloud the relevant think sheet.

• Give students tips on organizing an essay. To begin, they should write a statement—called a thesis statement—that will be the focus of the essay. Then they can create an informal outline that lists the thesis statement followed by supporting ideas and details from the text. If necessary, demonstrate how to create such an outline based on a picture book or a poem that they've read. An example appears below.

> Thesis Statement: The Big Orange Splot expresses the view that people should follow their dreams.
>
> • After Mr. Plumbean changes his house, he enjoys it more. He loves to sit in the front yard and drink lemonade.
>
> • When his neighbors complain, Mr. Plumbean is not bothered. "My house . . . looks like all my dreams," he says.
>
> • Mr. Plumbean convinces his next-door neighbor to follow his own dream. The neighbor happily turns his house into a ship.
>
> • Mr. Plumbean convinces all of his neighbors to follow their dreams, and they proudly admit that their street is no longer "neat."

• Remind students that materials in their reading logs can help them focus on a topic and remember where to locate important parts of the novel. They should also review any notes they took during book discussions.

• After students have written their essays, have them work in their book clubs to begin the revision process. Think Sheet 10, Revision Checklist, can serve as a guide. You might use Evaluation Sheet 3 to assess students' final pieces.

Lesson 15

Responding to Literature:
Collaborative Project

Objectives:
- Have students collaborate to complete a project based on themes in the book.
- Encourage students to connect to themes in the novel and a picture book and then design a "dream house" sculpture based on these themes.
- Create a class community based on the idea of "Elsewhere" in *The Giver.*
- Have students write about the process of creating their final project.

Assigned Reading:
None

Writing Prompt:
Write about the process of creating your dream house and combining it with the work of other students. Describe the materials you chose and how you arranged them to express your individuality.

NOTES:
- At the end of the unit, students should conduct another formal self-assessment and set goals for future Book Club units. (See Evaluation Sheets 7–10.)
- If possible, meet with students individually to discuss their progress over the course of the unit and to give them their final grades. Share evaluation sheets or any other forms of assessment you used.

NOTE: This lesson will span several days as students create their dream houses and their class community and then write about the process.

- Remind students of the picture book they read at the beginning of the unit, *The Big Orange Splot.* Write the following quotation from the picture book on the board: "My house is me and I am it. My house is where I like to be and it looks like all my dreams." Tell students that they will be creating their own dream house sculptures using materials of their own choosing. Each student's house might show a personal hobby or interest, a personal belief, and/or favorite colors.

- Brainstorm ideas for dream houses. Give students time to think about what their houses could express to observers. Talk about materials that could convey their ideas. Then give students time to construct their sculptures. You might ask them to construct their houses as homework, but we've found that students benefit from impromptu discussions and critiques that arise during their process if they work on the project in class.

- When the houses are complete, ask students to arrange them to form a little community. Students can think of this community as "Elsewhere"— the place that Jonas dreams of finding beyond his community's boundaries. In a class discussion, discuss what the class's version of "Elsewhere" would be like. Write students' ideas about characteristics of the community on the chalkboard or chart paper throughout the discussion. Remind students to think of *The Giver* and what specific aspects of his community Jonas reacts against at the end of the novel. Encourage them to think about what he would like to see in "Elsewhere." Ask students if they think it was a good idea to focus on their individual houses first before thinking of them as part of a community. How does this idea relate to the novel and to the picture book?

- Then have each student write a few paragraphs explaining the process he or she followed in creating a dream house and the process the class went through in planning a community. What does his or her house represent? What does the community as a whole represent?

- If possible, display the houses and the process paragraphs in a more public area of the school. Or, have other classes visit your classroom to observe students' work. To use this project for assessment, see Evaluation Sheet 4.

Advanced Lesson Plans:
The Giver

A Unit for Experienced Book Club Students

The lesson plans in this chapter are geared toward students who have participated in Book Club before and are comfortable with the format of the program. If you plan to teach the extended theme-based unit described in Chapter 6 with an experienced class, these lessons are for you. As students become more comfortable with the basics of Book Club, your expectations for them will grow and change. Within the general framework of a Book Club unit, you have great flexibility in deciding which skills and activities will form the core of your curriculum. Our two sets of lesson plans for *The Giver* demonstrate how a unit can be adapted for use at any point during the school year, to meet the needs of a specific group of students.

The Curriculum Correlation Chart on page 104 shows how the lessons in Chapter 7 correlate to language arts standards established by the National Council of Teachers of English and the International Reading Association. Numbers in parentheses refer to specific NCTE/IRA standards; refer to page 68 for a complete list of the standards. For details about each curriculum area, refer to the chart in Chapter 1, page 6.

Ten-Week Unit

If you plan to teach the complete ten-week unit for *The Giver,* turn to page 75 of Chapter 6. There you will find prereading and postreading activities that you can use in combination with the four- week Book Club segment outlined in this chapter.

Curriculum Correlation Chart

Curriculum Area	Lessons in Chapter 7
Language Conventions	
	Lessons 1–15: Book clubs (1, 3, 4, 11, 12)
	Lesson 14: Incorporating Quotations (5, 6)
	Lesson 15: Dream House Project (3, 5, 11)
Literary Aspects	
	Lesson 1: Author's Craft—Word Choice (3, 11)
	Lesson 3: Setting (3, 11)
	Lesson 5: Imagery (3, 6)
	Lesson 6: Foreshadowing (3, 6, 11)
	Lesson 7: Static and Dynamic Characters (3, 5, 6)
	Lesson 9: Internal and External Conflict (3, 5, 6)
	Lesson 12: Genre Study—Fantasy and Science Fiction (3, 6)
	Lesson 13: Writing Poetry (3, 4, 5, 6, 11)
	Lesson 14: Incorporating Quotations (5, 6)
	Lesson 15: Dream House Project (3, 5, 11)
Comprehension	
	Lesson 1: Author's Craft—Word Choice (3, 9)
	Lesson 2: The Concept of Rituals (3, 5, 11)
	Lesson 4: Making Connections (3, 4, 11)
	Lesson 8: Loaded Statements and Symbolism (1, 3, 11)
	Lesson 10: Main Ideas and Sequencing (3, 5)
	Lesson 11: Answering the Big Theme Questions (3, 4, 5, 11)
Composition	
	Lessons 1–11: Log writing (4, 12)
	Lesson 13: Writing Poetry (3, 11)
	Lesson 14: Incorporating Quotations (3, 4, 11)
	Lesson 15: Dream House Project (3, 5, 11)

Integrating Instruction

This Book Club unit provides many opportunities for cross-curricular connections. If you're on a teaching team, you and your colleagues should plan how best to integrate your students' Book Club activities with other curricular areas. During the unit, encourage students to draw especially on their knowledge from social studies and civics classes to enrich their discussions. The chart on page 105 correlates Chapter 7 lesson plans and other activities in the *Giver* unit with ten social studies standards established by the National Council for the Social Studies (NCSS).

Correlation to Social Studies Standards

NCSS Thematic Strands

Lessons and Activities

1. **Culture**
   Social studies programs should include experiences that provide for the study of culture and cultural diversity.

   Chapter 7, Lessons 1, 2, 4; Extended Unit, Weeks 1, 2

2. **Time, Continuity, and Change**
   Social studies programs should include experiences that provide for the study of the ways human beings view themselves in and over time.

   Chapter 7, Lessons 7, 10, 11; Extended Unit, Weeks 1, 2, 7–8, 9–10

3. **People, Places, and Environments**
   Social studies programs should include experiences that provide for the study of people, places, and environments.

   Chapter 7, Lessons 1, 2, 3, 5, 8, 9, 10, 12, 14, 15; Extended Unit, Weeks 1, 2, 7–8

4. **Individual Development and Identity**
   Social studies programs should include experiences that provide for the study of individual development and identity.

   Chapter 7, Lessons 1, 2, 3, 4, 5, 8, 9, 12, 13, 14, 15; Extended Unit, Weeks 1, 2, 7–8, 9–10

5. **Individuals, Groups, and Institutions**
   Social studies programs should include experiences that provide for the study of interactions among individuals, groups, and institutions.

   Chapter 7, Lessons 1, 2, 4, 5, 12, 15; Extended Unit, Weeks 1, 2, 7–8, 9–10

6. **Power, Authority, and Governance**
   Social studies programs should include experiences that provide for the study of how people create and change structures of power, authority, and governance.

   Chapter 7, Lessons 1, 2, 3, 4, 5, 12, 15; Extended Unit, Weeks 1, 2, 9–10

7. **Production, Distribution, and Consumption**
   Social studies programs should include experiences that provide for the study of how people organize for the production, distribution, and consumption of goods and services.

8. **Science, Technology, and Society**
   Social studies programs should include experiences that provide for the study of relationships among science, technology, and society.

   Chapter 7, Lessons 3, 4, 12; Extended Unit, Weeks 9–10

9. **Global Connections**
   Social studies programs should include experiences that provide for the study of global connections and interdependence.

10. **Civic Ideals and Practices**
    Social studies programs should include experiences that provide for the study of the ideals, principles, and practices of citizenship in a democratic republic.

    Chapter 7, Lessons 3, 10, 15; Extended Unit, Weeks 1, 2, 9–10

Lesson **1**

Literary Elements:
Author's Craft—Word Choice

Objectives:
- Introduce students to the world of *The Giver.*
- Encourage students to consider word choice as part of the author's craft.
- Explore terms associated with word choice, such as *connotation, denotation,* and *euphemism.*

Vocabulary:
apprehensive
distracted
distraught

Assigned Reading:
Chapters 1–3
(pages 1–25)

Writing Prompts:
- Choose three or four words and phrases that you especially noticed in the first three chapters of *The Giver.* Explain why they stand out to you.
- As you enter the world of *The Giver,* what strikes you as interesting or strange?
- What possible conflicts do you see building in the story's plot?
- Identify places in the chapters where Lowry tries to build suspense or raise questions in your mind.

- Encouraging students to review previous units and learn from past mistakes and successes is an important part of Book Club. Begin the day's lesson by passing back students' reading logs and self-assessment sheets from the last Book Club unit. Have students evaluate their work and review the goals they set at the end of the unit for future reading logs and book club groups. Then ask them to plan for their logs and book discussions during this unit. Students can refer to Evaluation Sheets 7–10.

- To introduce *The Giver,* invite students to respond briefly to this simple writing prompt: *Describe the perfect world.* Invite them to share their responses in a whole-class discussion. Responses to this prompt often describe a world without poverty, disease, war, pain, and unhappiness. You might ask students to think about how their perfect worlds could be achieved and then write their ideas on chart paper or on the chalkboard. One Book Club teacher ends this discussion by passing out copies of *The Giver* and telling students, "Here it is: your perfect world."

- Continue the day's opening lesson by telling students that word choice is an important part of *The Giver.* Explain that word choice refers to a writer's process of carefully selecting words to create mood and meaning. Tell students that special language plays an important role in the world Lowry creates in *The Giver.* Then introduce students to the following terms:

  —**denotation:** the dictionary definition of a word

  —**connotation:** the ideas and feelings associated with a word

  —**euphemism:** a mild or pleasant expression that is used in place of one that is harsher or unpleasant

- To illustrate the meanings of *denotation/connotation,* write the words *frightened* and *apprehensive* on the chalkboard. Tell students that these two words appear in Chapter 1 of the novel. Explain that while their denotative meanings are similar, to many people their connotative meanings are quite different. Explore with students the denotative and connotative meanings of the words.

- To illustrate the meaning of *euphemism,* ask students to think about pleasant words and phrases in our own language that distance us from unpleasant things, such as *passed away* for *died.*

NOTES:
- Reproducible Think Sheets and Evaluation Sheets, referred to throughout this unit, are provided in the back of the book after page 153. These sheets are used to focus and organize students' responses to their reading and to guide teacher assessment as well as students' assessment of their own work.
- All writing prompts in the lesson plans also appear on Think Sheet 12. Distribute copies of this sheet so that students can refer to it as they complete each reading assignment in *The Giver*.

- To get students off to a strong start, read the first chapter of *The Giver* aloud. Encourage students to listen for interesting words and phrases. Have students read Chapters 2 and 3 independently and then respond to the writing prompts. Remind students to use all the writing time available. They can work through the list of prompts or select their own type of response.

- If necessary, before students meet in their book club groups, review the features of a good book discussion. (See Chapter 6, page 87.) As book club groups meet to discuss the opening chapters of the novel, walk through the classroom to monitor their discussion skills. If you find students are having trouble getting started, offer suggestions for discussion or reconvene the class for a more extensive review of book discussion strategies.

- In closing community share, begin to create two word charts that the class can complete over the course of the unit. One chart lists the denotations and connotations of interesting or meaningful words from the reading. The other keeps track of euphemisms students encounter as they read. For each euphemism, students should identify its special meaning in *The Giver* and its actual meaning. (See Think Sheets 13 and 14.) Remind students that the role of language is important in this novel. Looking closely at special words and phrases as they read will give them insight into the world Lowry creates.

LOG RESPONSES

- **The writing prompts provided in this guide are suggestions for response for you to assign as you wish. Some students will be able to handle one per reading assignment; some might be able to respond thoughtfully to two or three. There will be times when you might want students to focus on writing an extended response to a single prompt.**

- **As students become more comfortable with the Book Club format, they will certainly have ideas and questions that go beyond the writing prompts given. Here and throughout all the lessons, you may want to consider giving students "free choice" as a log option. Think Sheets 1 and 2 give students a variety of suggestions for response. Be sure that students are challenging themselves and continually thinking and responding in new ways. The tripod response format is one way of challenging students to approach their reading from more than one angle.**

Lesson 2

Comprehension:
The Concept of Rituals

Objectives:
- Help students define *rituals* and identify rituals in their own lives.
- Have students identify and explain rituals in *The Giver* and connect them to the rituals in their own lives.
- Encourage students to examine rituals in the novel to understand characters and ideas.

Vocabulary:
gravitating
primly
tabulated

Assigned Reading:
Chapters 4–5
(pages 26–39)

Writing Prompts:
- In a two-column chart, begin keeping track of rituals in Jonas's community and rituals in your own family, religion, or culture.
- Choose one ritual in your own life and explain its meaning and purpose.
- Naming is one example of a ritual. Why is naming so important to people? Why is naming particularly important in *The Giver*?
- In Jonas's community, why do you think so much importance is placed on the sharing of feelings and dreams?

- To begin the day's lesson, write the word *rituals* on the chalkboard. Explain to students that a ritual is a certain way of doing something that a person or group does the same way every time. Many cultural and religious customs are considered rituals. Explain that rituals can help bind together groups of people. To get students thinking about rituals, you might ask them to write briefly about a family or community ritual.

- Draw a two-column chart on the chalkboard or on a large sheet of paper. Invite the class to brainstorm a list of rituals from their own school, community, or religions. Ask them to discuss the meanings behind the rituals and to explain how the rituals help people to connect to one another. Record their ideas on one side of the chart.

- Before having students read the day's assignment, tell them that rituals play an important role in Jonas's community. Ask them to note these rituals as they read and to think about their meanings to Jonas's community. Tell students you would like them to create a two-column chart in their reading logs and use it to record rituals from both their own lives and the book.

- In closing community share, invite students to share the information from their charts. Record their ideas on the class chart. Below is a sample.

Rituals in Our World	Rituals in Jonas's Community
—Doing a group chant before the start of a baseball game	—The Ceremony of Twelve
—Making a wish and blowing out candles at a birthday party	—Sharing feelings at night
—Going to a parade on Memorial Day	—Celebrating "releases"
	—Telling about dreams

Ten-Week Unit

If you are teaching the complete unit (see the overview on page 76), you might refer back to this lesson in Weeks 7 and 8, when students begin their memoir projects. Recalling family, religious, and community rituals is one way to access important memories.

▶ This is one student's discussion of rituals in her own life.

Rituals

My family always goes to Christmas eve services at 11 pm. We also go to church every Sunday. I go to a conformation class every Wednesday. We always go to Christmas day and Easter services.

On birthdays we always go out to eat where ever the birthday person chooses. We always bake a cake and open presents at night. The birthday person also eats on a special plate.

We always go and see my grandma in the summer and thanksgiving or Christmas.

I always get 2 pairs of pants for Christmas and pick out a tree. I decorate the tree and our home. We put up lights and big candy canes around our house. We always sleep in + eat a big breakfast and then open presents.

Lesson 3

Literary Elements: Setting

Objectives:
- Understand the techniques authors use to develop setting.
- Examine the influence of setting on characters and events in a novel.

Vocabulary:
interdependence
relinquish
reprieve

Assigned Reading:
Chapters 6–7
(pages 40–58)

- Remind students that setting explains what's going on around the characters in a story. A story's setting can include details about historical period (past, present, or future); geographic location; time of year or day; weather conditions; or a set of beliefs, customs, and standards.

- Explain that an author can reveal a story's setting in a variety of ways. Sometimes a single, direct statement at the beginning of a story will establish time and place. Often, however, an author will pull readers into a fictional world more gradually, using descriptive language, concrete details, and the words and actions of characters to reveal the setting.

- To demonstrate an author's use of setting, review the first two pages of Chapter 1. On these pages, Jonas remembers the day a mysterious plane flew over his community. Ask students: From the details in this scene alone, what observations and judgments can be made about Jonas's community? Guide students to focus on what Jonas sees, hears, and wonders as the plane flies overhead, how Jonas and other community members

Writing Prompts:
- Describe the setting of *The Giver.* (Use Think Sheet 15.)
- How does setting affect characters and events in the novel?
- Explain the character of Asher. Why does he stand out in this community?
- Why might a community decide to choose jobs and families for its citizens? In your opinion, what are the pros and cons of such a system? Explain.
- Continue to chart interesting words, phrases, and euphemisms.

react to the plane, and the ultimate fate of the pilot. Ask students to describe the setting they imagine based on details and events from these two pages.

- Before students begin the day's reading assignment, point out that many settings are more than just a backdrop for the story events. A setting can be an important influence on characters and events. Tell students that they can analyze the importance of a story's setting by imagining what would happen if characters were moved to a different place and time. Would there still be a story? Ask students to pay close attention to details of setting in Chapters 6 and 7. How do these details add to what they have already learned in the first five chapters?

- You might distribute copies of Think Sheet 15 to encourage students to keep track of important details of setting as they read. When students meet in their book clubs, they can compare their notes and discuss the role of setting in *The Giver.*

 TEACHING TIP

To extend students' exploration of setting, you might ask them to create settings of their own based on real or imagined places. Encourage students to use descriptive language to pull readers into a time and place.

Lesson 4

Comprehension:
Making Connections

Objective:
- Encourage students to connect the novel to their own lives, to familiar books and movies, and to their prior knowledge.
- Introduce the elements of science fiction.

Vocabulary:
anxiety
benign
empowered
integrity

Assigned Reading:
Chapters 8–9
(pages 59–71)

- Remind students that good readers make connections as they read. For example, they connect characters and events to their own lives and to familiar books and movies. They also use their own knowledge and experience to figure things out and to make predictions about events to come. Tell students that making these kinds of connections as they read will help them understand, enjoy, and become more involved in their reading.

- Ask students what kinds of connections they have been making as they read. Do any of the characters remind them of people they know? Can they identify with any of Jonas's feelings? Do events in the novel remind them of other books they've read or movies they've seen? You might want to share with students any connections that you've made with the book so far.

- Tell students that you'd like them to focus on making connections to the text as they read the next two chapters. Think Sheet 6 can help them

Writing Prompts:

- If you could give Jonas one of your memories, what would it be and why?
- "Now, for the first time in his twelve years of life, Jonas felt separate, different." Recall a time when you felt different and alone. In what ways was your experience similar to and different from Jonas's experience?
- Does Jonas's situation or community remind you of any other books or movies? If so, explain the similarities.
- Predict the ways in which Jonas's new job might affect his relationships with his family and friends. Explain your response.
- Think about the instructions Jonas receives in his folder. What do they tell you about his future?
- Explain the mood, or atmosphere, at the ceremony when Jonas receives his Assignment.

make personal connections to the text. Encourage students to share their personal connections in their book clubs, but remind them that they need not share anything personal that causes them to feel uncomfortable.

- As students meet in their book clubs, walk through the classroom to make sure they are not relying too heavily on their reading logs. Their logs may be starting points for discussion, but students should be able to move away from their logs to have real conversations. Remind students that they can write questions and ideas in the margins of their logs for quick reference during discussion.

- In closing community share, continue to discuss students' connections to the text. You might also take time to add more words and phrases to the class word charts for denotation/connotation and euphemism.

- Because *The Giver* is sometimes considered a science fiction novel, this might be a good time to introduce briefly the elements of science fiction and write them on the chalkboard or chart paper. For example, you might write:

Science fiction is often

—set in imaginary, futuristic locations.

—based on real or imagined scientific discoveries or technological advances.

—critical of aspects of society.

—concerned about irresponsible uses of technology and science.

You might ask students to name science fiction books or movies with which they are familiar. Tell them that they should look for elements of science fiction in *The Giver* as they read, and that you will be returning to this topic later in the unit.

Ten-Week Unit

If you'd like to provide more opportunities for intertextual connections, refer back to the poems, picture books, and other works you read aloud at the beginning of the unit. Remind students to make connections to these pieces as they read.

Lesson 5

Literary Elements:
Imagery

Objectives:
- Be sure students can identify examples of imagery and explain the function of imagery.
- Alert students to the author's changing use of description in the novel.

Vocabulary:
conspicuous
diminish
glee
obsolete
sensation

Assigned Reading:
Chapters 10–11
(pages 72–87)

Writing Prompts:
- Choose a descriptive paragraph from one of Jonas's new memories and compare it to a descriptive paragraph from early in the book. What does the author do (and not do) to create certain images?
- Explain why, according to The Giver, snow and sunshine are not part of Jonas's world.
- What does The Giver mean when he tells Jonas that there is a difference between power and honor?
- Compare and contrast something from your life with something from Jonas's life.

- Remind students that a story's imagery is its collection of images, or word pictures. Images are words and phrases that describe things that can be seen, touched, tasted, heard, or smelled. Explain that imagery is a reader's window into the world created by an author.

- Read aloud the following passage from the first paragraph of *The Giver:*

    It was almost December, and Jonas was beginning to be frightened. No. Wrong word, Jonas thought. Frightened meant that deep, sickening feeling of something terrible about to happen. Frightened was the way he had felt a year ago when an unidentified aircraft had overflown the community twice. He had seen it both times. Squinting toward the sky, he had seen the sleek jet, almost a blur at its high speed, go past, and a second later heard the blast of sound that followed. Then one more time, a moment later, from the opposite direction, the same plane.

   Ask students to identify words and phrases that help them see and hear the plane and understand Jonas's feelings when the novel begins. Help students see how Lowry uses language to pull readers into Jonas's world.

- As students read the day's assignment, have them keep track of words and phrases that appeal to their senses and help them understand what Jonas experiences. Ask them to keep in mind the following questions: How is the world of memories different from the world in which Jonas lives? How does the author use language to draw attention to these differences? After students write in their reading logs, encourage them to explore answers to these questions in their book club groups.

- In closing community share, continue to discuss the author's use of imagery in Chapters 10 and 11. On the chalkboard, begin listing some of the most striking images that come from Jonas's experiences with The Giver. Continue listing sensory images as students read further in the book. Encourage students to think about what these images reveal about both worlds in which Jonas finds himself living.

Lesson 6

Literary Elements:
Foreshadowing

Objectives:
- Help students understand foreshadowing and suspense.
- Have students make predictions about the story based on the author's use of foreshadowing.

Vocabulary:
admonition
anguished
sparse
vibrant
wryly

Assigned Reading:
Chapters 12–13
(pages 88–107)

Writing Prompts:
- Find details in your reading that seem to foreshadow events to come. Explain your predictions, based on these hints.
- Explain Jonas's ability to "see-beyond."
- How does Jonas feel when he learns the truth about colors?
- "If everything's the same, then there aren't any choices!" Respond to this quotation. Do you believe choices are important?

- Remind students that foreshadowing is an author's way of hinting at events to come. An author might do this through dialogue between characters, through imagery, and through a character's thoughts and feelings.

- Explain that details of foreshadowing often create suspense—feelings of anticipation or expectation—in a reader. Invite students to discuss their experiences with foreshadowing and suspense in books they have read or movies they have seen. Then ask students when they experienced suspense in their reading of the novel so far. What specific moments or details created suspense, and why?

- As students read, they should think about details in the dialogue between Jonas and The Giver that create suspense and seem to hint at events to come. Think Sheet 16 can help students focus their reading.

- After students write in their logs, have them meet in their book clubs to discuss foreshadowing or any other issues that came up in their reading. Remind students that they can work in their book club groups to begin completing Think Sheet 16. They can return to this sheet throughout the novel, whenever they encounter examples of foreshadowing.

- In closing community share, continue the discussion of foreshadowing and suspense. Students might mention Jonas's growing anger and confusion as he learns more about the realities of his world. They might also mention The Giver's obvious frustration about how things are, the story of the failed Receiver, and Jonas's thoughts as he stands on the bridge and wonders about Elsewhere. Invite students to share their predictions based on foreshadowing in these chapters.

TEACHING OPTION

Your students may have read "The Road Not Taken" by Robert Frost at the beginning of the unit. Since this poem deals directly with the issue of making choices and dealing with the consequences of one's choices, you may want to revisit the poem. If students haven't yet read the poem, this is a good point at which to read it aloud. Ask students how Frost seems to feel about choices—both the difficulties and the rewards of making choices. Then ask how the idea expressed in this poem relates to Jonas's feelings as he learns about his lack of choices.

Lesson 7

Response to Literature:
Static and Dynamic Characters

Objectives:
- Help students distinguish between static and dynamic characters.
- Have students recognize and explain changes in the main character and the reasons behind these changes.

Vocabulary:
assuage
excruciating
forsaken

Assigned Reading:
Chapters 14–15
(pages 108–120)

Writing Prompts:
- What is Jonas's attitude toward his world at the beginning of the novel? How do his experiences with The Giver begin to change him?
- Why is The Giver forced to share pain with Jonas?
- In what ways is Jonas now different from the members of his family?
- What does Jonas do to soothe Gabriel? How does he feel about his action?
- Explain the memory Jonas is given in Chapter 15.

- Explain to students that one way to analyze a character is to look at how much that character seems to be affected by events in a story. A character who does not appear to change over the course of a story is known as a static character. A character who does change is called a dynamic character.

- Tell students that they can look for changes in characters by paying close attention to their responses to events in the novel. Careful readers examine characters' words, actions, and feelings as events in a story unfold.

- Encourage students to look for possible changes in Jonas as they read today's assignment. By Chapter 15, how is he different from the boy he was in Chapter 1? For contrast, ask them to think about how he is different from his family and friends at this point in the novel. Have they changed at all?

- Encourage students to explore these questions in their reading logs and in their book club groups. Students might also discuss how they believe Jonas will deal with the changes in his life and the new information he has.

- In closing community share, discuss the reasons why Jonas is a dynamic character. Encourage students to be aware of further changes in Jonas as the story continues.

- At this point in the unit, you might want to have students conduct a formal self-assessment. Distribute Evaluation Sheets 9 and 10 and ask students to complete the sheets honestly and thoughtfully. If necessary, review the importance of self-assessment and the purpose of the evaluation sheets.

- You might also collect students' reading logs for evaluation. Write comments on the logs, telling students what they are doing well and what they need to improve. Explain to students that they will have a chance to revise their entries from the first half of the unit before your final evaluation. Remember that you can use Evaluation Sheet 2, Book Club Observation Sheet, throughout the unit to evaluate students' progress in their book clubs.

Lesson 8

Comprehension:
Loaded Statements and Symbolism

Objectives:
- Encourage students to be aware of short statements and minor acts that are loaded with significant meaning.
- Help students recognize symbolism.
- Have students use loaded statements and symbolism to arrive at a deeper understanding of the text.

Vocabulary:
perceive
vague
wisp

Assigned Reading:
Chapters 16–17
(pages 121–138)

Writing Prompts:
- In The Giver's favorite memory, Jonas realizes that fire is both dangerous and wonderful. What might fire symbolize?
- At the end of Chapter 17, Jonas tells Gabriel, "There could be love." What does this statement reveal about Jonas and the new understanding he has about his life?
- Put yourself in Jonas's place. What would you do with your new knowledge of the world?
- Why are loving family relationships seen as dangerous in Jonas's world?

- Remind students that a symbol is a person, place, or thing that represents something beyond itself. For example, the heart is often used as a symbol for human emotions. A white dove carrying an olive branch is a symbol for peace. Tell students that writers use symbols in their writing to emphasize important ideas.

- Explain that writers also emphasize important ideas through loaded statements or actions. Explain that sometimes the shortest statements or most minor acts can be loaded with significant meaning.

- Read aloud the story "A Christmas Memory" by Truman Capote. This story relates to today's reading assignment in *The Giver*. It can also help you demonstrate the ways in which an author uses symbolism and loaded statements to emphasize ideas. For example, encourage students to look at the story's images of the fruitcakes and the kites. Students might say that the fruitcakes are symbolic of the characters' generous spirits, their enjoyment of life, and their common bond; the kites symbolize the free spirits of Buddy and his cousin. Through the flying kites, the author implies that the characters' friendship can rise above the obstacles that life presents. Loaded statements include "Buddy, the wind is blowing," "This is our last Christmas together," and "Oh my, it's fruitcake weather."

- To return students' focus to *The Giver*, ask students to consider what Jonas's glimpses of color might symbolize. How does his introduction to color relate to his growing awareness of the truth in other aspects of his life?

- As students read, they should be aware of symbolism and loaded statements and actions. They can jot down their ideas in their logs and then expand on these ideas using the writing prompts provided. In their book club groups, students can compare their notes on symbolism and help one another to explore symbols and loaded statements and actions in the novel.

- In closing community share, encourage students to make further intertextual connections between Chapters 16 and 17 of *The Giver* and "A Christmas Memory." Focus on big theme questions that relate to conformity, making choices, and occasionally rebelling against the norm. Guide students to look at Buddy's unusual friendship with his older cousin, the lack of choices he has in his own life, and Buddy and his friend's ability to have a genuine love of life and to find meaning in simple actions. Ask students to compare the Christmas memory in this story with the Christmas memory Jonas is given. Encourage students to look for more examples of symbolism and loaded statements and actions as the rest of the story unfolds.

Lesson 9

Literary Elements:
Internal and External Conflict

Objectives:
- Help students understand the two kinds of conflict in a story—internal and external.
- Encourage students to look at how conflict moves a story forward.

Vocabulary:
imploringly
luminous
ruefully
syringe

Assigned Reading:
Chapters 18–19
(pages 139–151)

Writing Prompts:
- In what ways does Jonas experience internal conflict once he has a bigger picture of the world in which he lives?
- With what internal conflict does The Giver struggle?
- What conflicts might Jonas face if he tries to act on some of his feelings?
- Explain what happened to Rosemary. Why does her experience put added pressure on Jonas and The Giver?
- What was your reaction to the release of the baby? Explain your response.

- Remind students that a conflict is any struggle between opposing forces. Tell students that conflict is what drives a story forward; if there were no conflict, there would be no story. In an external conflict, a character (or group) struggles against another character (or group) or against some outside force. An internal conflict takes place within a character's mind or soul.

- Ask students to think about conflicts in other books they have read and movies they have seen. Encourage students to identify both internal and external conflicts. Ask them: How does conflict work to drive the events of these stories forward?

- Then ask students to brainstorm a list of conflicts that move events in *The Giver* forward. What conflicts are faced by Jonas's community? Against whom or what does Jonas struggle, particularly after his training begins? You might create a graphic organizer on the chalkboard where you can record students' ideas. An example is shown below.

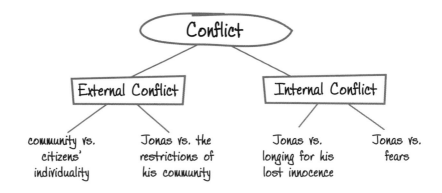

- Ask students to copy the class chart into their individual reading logs and to continue to add to the chart as they read. Explain that conflict plays an important role in Chapters 18 and 19.

- In closing community share, discuss how some of the conflicts in *The Giver* might be resolved. Record students' predictions and then revisit these predictions after they finish reading the book.

Lesson 10

Comprehension:
Main Ideas and Sequencing

Objectives:
- Encourage students to focus on major events of the story by creating sequence charts.
- Have students name important chapters in the novel by focusing on the main ideas and important events of each chapter.

Vocabulary:
chaos
efficient
emphatically
haphazard
stealthily

Assigned Reading:
Chapters 20–21
(pages 152–170)

Writing Prompts:
- Lowry chose not to use chapter titles in *The Giver*. Create titles for some of the most important chapters. Be sure each title reflects the chapter's main ideas or main events.
- Create a sequence chart that tells what has happened in the novel so far. Remember to concentrate on the most important events.
- Jonas does not want to believe that his good friend Fiona could ever be part of a person's release. The Giver responds by telling him, "Feelings are not part of the life she's learned." Explain what he means.
- Do you agree with Jonas's decision? Why?
- Explain how The Giver feels about Jonas's plan.

- At this point in the novel, it's helpful to look back on the important events that have taken place so far. A good way to do this is to have students create sequence charts that present in a visual way the most important events of the novel in the order in which they occur. Sequencing is an important skill because it asks students to distinguish major events and main ideas from minor ones. Tell students that after they read, they should create sequence charts. If necessary, review with students the different types of sequence charts. Basically, any graphic organizer that shows the order of events is helpful—examples include a comic strip or storyboard, a flow chart, and a numbered list of events.

- Another way to help students focus on main ideas is to ask them to create titles for the book's chapters. The titles should reflect main ideas and main events in each chapter. A student sample appears below.

> In *The Giver*, the chapters are not titled.
> Here is the list of titles that I would give them.
>
> Chapter 1: The Community
> Chapter 2: Family Talk
> Chapter 3: Babies
> Chapter 4: Home of the Old
> Chapter 5: "Stirrings"
> Chapter 6: Lilies Day
> Chapter 7: She Skipped Me
> Chapter 8: My Assignment

- In closing community share, have students share their sequence charts and their chapter titles. You might work from the students' individual charts to create a class sequence chart.

- You might also want to spend time discussing the events leading to the final chapters of the book. Do students agree with Jonas's decision to flee the community? Why does Jonas feel he can no longer stay? Spend time discussing the role of The Giver in Jonas's decision to leave. What is The Giver's attitude toward the community and the life he has lived? What clues indicate his attitude? End the discussion by asking students to predict what is going to happen to Jonas and how the novel might end.

Ten-Week Unit

In this chapter, Jonas makes a difficult and dangerous decision. Ask students who researched nonconformists at the beginning of the unit to revisit their research. Have them compare Jonas's situation and actions to the experiences of another nonconformist. What qualities and/or circumstances does Jonas have in common with some of the real-life nonconformists students studied?

Lesson **11**

Comprehension:
Answering the Big Theme Questions

Objectives:
- Encourage students to revisit the big theme questions for this unit.
- Invite students to analyze the book's ending.
- Have students revisit their predictions for the end of the novel.
- Read Lois Lowry's 1994 Newbery Medal acceptance speech, in which she comments on the book's ending.
- Have students write a critique of *The Giver*.

Vocabulary:
landscape
tentatively
treacherously

Assigned Reading:
Chapters 22–23
(pages 171–180)

- For this lesson, skip opening community share and have students begin reading Chapters 22 and 23 immediately. This will give students more time to respond to the prompts and you more time at the end of the lesson for wrap-up activities.

- If possible, give students extra time to respond to the reading prompts and to grapple with the book's ending in their book clubs. Encourage them to focus on their various interpretations of the final chapter and on whether or not the book provides its own answers to the unit's big theme questions.

- In closing community share, allow students to continue to share their responses to the writing prompts and to express their ideas on the book's ending. You might also discuss with students the predictions they made in Lesson 9 about how conflicts could be resolved. Ask students if they feel any conflicts were resolved in the final pages of the novel.

- Read aloud Lois Lowry's 1994 Newbery Medal acceptance speech, in which she discusses her own ideas about the book's ending. Invite students' comments on the speech. Ask them to explain whether or not Lowry's own insights help them appreciate the book's conclusion.

- As an additional writing assignment, you might have students write critiques of *The Giver*. Explain to students that good readers question what they read, evaluate a book's good points and weak points, and notice various author's crafts. Invite students to discuss famous critics in newspapers, in magazines, or on television and to discuss critiques they have read or heard. Ask them to identify the kinds of things critics like to examine or discuss, such as characters, story, language, and so on.

- Inform students that you would like them to write their own critiques of *The Giver*. Have the class discuss what they believe are the positive and negative aspects of the novel. You might have them refer to their notes about their favorite and least favorite story parts. Remind students that a good critic must always provide reasons for his or her opinions. Students can refer to their logs to remind themselves of various parts of the book.

- Give students a chance to read their reviews aloud, either to their book clubs or to the whole class. You might want to collect the completed reviews for assessment purposes.

Lesson 12

Literary Elements:
Genre Study—Fantasy and Science Fiction

- Return to the topic of science fiction, which was introduced in Lesson 4. Remind students that literature is often categorized by type, or genre. Suggest that *The Giver* is best characterized as a science fiction novel. Then review the characteristics of science fiction. Explain that science fiction is fiction based on real or imagined scientific discoveries or technological advances. Tell students that this type of fiction is often set in imaginary, futuristic locations.

- Remind students that many science fiction works criticize or condemn aspects of society. Science fiction writers are often concerned about irresponsible uses of technology and science that have negative effects on human beings.

- Invite students to talk about science fiction books or movies with which they are familiar. What do these science fiction works have in common? How do they differ?

- Discuss *The Giver* as a science fiction novel. You might write the following questions on the chalkboard or read them aloud: To what aspects of science and technology does *The Giver* draw attention? What might

Writing Prompts:
- What is your interpretation of the book's ending? Support your response with evidence from the text.
- Are you satisfied with the book's ending? If yes, explain why. If no, rewrite it.
- Describe what you think happens to Jonas's community after he leaves.
- What might the music that Jonas hears symbolize?
- How might Lois Lowry respond to the big theme questions for this unit? Support your response with evidence from the text.

Objectives:
- Build students' understanding of science fiction.
- Discuss why *The Giver* is considered a science fiction novel.

Assigned Reading:
None

Writing Prompts:
- To what aspects of science and technology does *The Giver* draw attention? What might Lowry be saying about these aspects of science and technology?
- What aspects of society might Lowry be critiquing in *The Giver*?

TEACHING TIP

You might want to read aloud "Dark They Were, and Golden-Eyed," a short story by Ray Bradbury. This piece illustrates what a typical science fiction story is like, and its theme of losing one's identity works well with *The Giver*.

Lowry be saying about these aspects of science and technology? What aspects of society might Lowry be critiquing in *The Giver*? Give students time to brainstorm ideas and then to respond to these questions in writing. Discuss their responses in community share.

Lesson 13

Response to Literature: Writing Poetry

Objectives:
- Connect the themes in two poems to themes in *The Giver.*
- Have students compose their own poems about conformity.

Assigned Reading:
None

Writing Prompts:
- Compare the statements in Jenny Joseph's poem with Jonas's statement "I want to wake up in the morning and *decide* things! A blue tunic, or a red one?"
- Explain how the theme of Auden's "Unknown Citizen" relates to themes in *The Giver.*
- Write an original poem about conformity or making choices.

- Begin the lesson by reading aloud the poems "Warning" ("When I am an old woman, I shall wear purple . . .") by Jenny Joseph and "Unknown Citizen" by W. H. Auden.

- Immediately after you read, give students time to respond to the first two writing prompts. This will give students practice in responding to fresh text, which they will be asked to do in the final lesson as part of assessment. After students respond, allow them to meet in their book clubs.

- In community share, discuss students' written responses and their ideas about the poems. Remind students that making intertextual connections can extend their understanding of important themes. Ask students how these poems help their understanding of *The Giver.*

- To reinforce the unit themes and to give students practice in creative responses, have students compose original poems on the themes of conformity versus nonconformity or having choices. Some students might choose to follow the style of other poems they have read; others might have their own ways of presenting their ideas. Remind students of the power of concrete details and vivid imagery.

Lesson 14

Language Conventions: Incorporating Quotations

Objectives:
- Have students organize their ideas about a topic in a multi-paragraph essay.
- Encourage students to incorporate quotations from the novel into their essays.

- Remind students that writing an essay gives them a chance to explore in a complete way a topic or theme in *The Giver.*

- Think Sheet 9 offers eight essay topics directly related to *The Giver.* Think Sheet 11 asks students to respond to fresh text—two quotations that relate to the unit theme. Decide which type of essay you'd like your students to write. Then distribute and read aloud the relevant think sheet.

- Review the proper ways to incorporate quotations.
- Have students discuss and revise their writing in their book groups.

Assigned Reading:
None

Writing Prompts:
- Respond to one of the essay topics presented on Think Sheet 9. Support your ideas with evidence from *The Giver.*
- Respond to one of the quotations on Think Sheet 11. Explain what the quote means to you, tell whether you agree or disagree with the quote, and compare the quote to at least three other literary works.

- Explain that one way to make an essay more effective is to support ideas with quotations from the text. Demonstrate for students how to use supporting quotations to strengthen the ideas of an essay. Write the following paragraph on the chalkboard:

> During training, Jonas often finds himself pulled in two different directions. One minute he is angry and desperate to make even the simplest decisions. He wants to change his drab world so badly he is ready to explode. The next minute, he turns back to the only life he has ever known. He tries to convince himself that his world is better because it is safe. He still can't help thinking about all that his friends and family are missing.

- Have students look through the text to find passages that would support the statements in this paragraph. Point out that they may choose lines of dialogue spoken by characters or statements made by the story's narrator. Here is one way to revise the sample paragraph:

> During training, Jonas often finds himself pulled in two different directions. One minute he is angry and desperate to make his own choices. He explodes to The Giver, "If everything's the same, then there aren't any choices! I want to wake up in the morning and *decide* things! A blue tunic, or a red one?" The next minute, he turns back to the only life he has ever known. He tries to convince himself that his world is better because it is safe. He still can't help thinking about all that his friends and family are missing. Lowry writes, "He found he was often angry, now . . . angry at his groupmates, that they were satisfied with their lives which had none of the vibrance that his was taking on."

- Invite students to discuss what the quotations add to the paragraph. If necessary, review proper punctuation of quotations and proper ways to introduce quotations in a paragraph. Use the sample paragraph as a model.

- After students have written their essays, have them work in their book clubs to begin revising their essays. Think Sheet 10 can help them in the revision process. Walk through the room, stopping to offer assistance and advice. Tell students that as editors for their classmates, they can look for places in each essay to add details, facts, or quotations to strengthen the writing. They should also think about whether each essay is well organized and focused on its topic. If possible, hold individual conferences with students over the course of a few days to discuss their essays and the essay-writing process. You might use Evaluation Sheet 3 to assess students' final pieces.

Lesson 15

Responding to Literature:
Dream House Project

NOTE: This lesson may span several days as students create their dream houses, build their class community, and then write about the process.

Objectives:
- Have students collaborate to complete a project based on themes in the book.
- Have students write about the process of creating their final project.

Assigned Reading:
None

Writing Prompt:
Write about the process of creating your dream house and combining it with the work of other students. Describe the materials you chose and how you arranged them to express your individuality.

NOTE:
- At the end of the unit, students should conduct another formal self-assessment and set goals for future Book Club units. (See Evaluation Sheets 7–10.)
- If possible, meet with students individually to discuss their progress over the course of the unit and to give them their final grades. Share evaluation sheets or any other forms of assessment you used.

- Read aloud the picture book *The Big Orange Splot* by Daniel M. Pinkwater. Talk about how this simple story relates to *The Giver.* Discuss why Mr. Plumbean creates a house that reflects his individuality and how he transforms his neighborhood.

- Write the following quotation from the picture book on the board: "My house is me and I am it. My house is where I like to be and it looks like all my dreams." Tell students that they will be creating their own dream house sculptures using materials of their own choosing. Explain that their dream houses will reflect each student's individuality, just as the houses in the picture book reflect the individuality of Mr. Plumbean and his neighbors. Each student's house might show a personal hobby or interest, a personal belief, and/or favorite colors.

- Talk about which materials could best convey students' ideas. Then give students time to construct their sculptures. You might ask students to construct their houses in class or as homework.

- When the houses are complete, tell students that you would like to arrange them in the classroom to form a community. Explain that they can think of this community as "Elsewhere"—the place beyond the boundaries of Jonas's community that he dreams of finding. In a class discussion, discuss what the class's version of "Elsewhere" would be like. Write students' ideas about the characteristics of this community on the chalkboard or on chart paper. Remind students to think of *The Giver* and what specifically Jonas reacts against in his own community at the end of the novel. Encourage them to think about what he would like to see in "Elsewhere." Ask students if they think it was a good idea to focus on their individual houses first before thinking about the houses as part of a community. How does this idea relate to the novel and to the picture book?

- Then have each student write a few paragraphs explaining the process he or she followed in creating a dream house and the process the class went through in planning a community. What does his or her house represent? What does the community as a whole represent?

- If possible, display the houses and the process paragraphs in a more public area of the school. Or, have other classes visit your classroom to observe students' work. To use this project for assessment, see Evaluation Sheet 4.

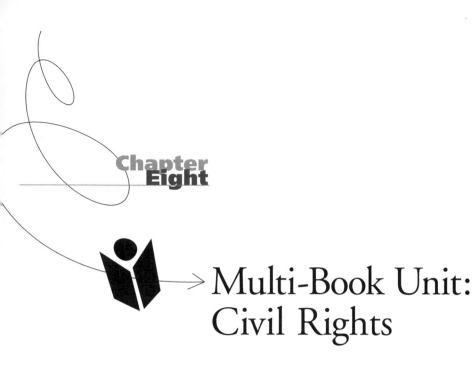

Chapter Eight

Multi-Book Unit: Civil Rights

Why Conduct a Multi-Book Unit?

The multi-book unit is a natural extension of Book Club. Instead of focusing on a single novel, the class focuses on several books linked by a theme or topic. These books are read simultaneously, with each book club reading a different title. Book clubs then come together to share their books and discuss relevant issues or themes with the whole class. In the unit outlined in this chapter, book clubs read four books related to the African American struggle for civil rights. Students gain valuable content knowledge, make intertextual connections daily, and deepen their understanding of literature—all while covering the curricular areas of language conventions, literary elements, response to literature, comprehension, and composition.

How Is a Multi-Book Unit Structured?

When you review the lesson plans in this chapter, you'll see that a multi-book unit functions in much the same way that a typical Book Club unit does. Most days begin with a lesson on a topic determined by your teaching objectives. Students then read their assigned books and write in their response logs. Book clubs maintain regular conversations, discussing their books and their written responses. Community share, however, functions to make links among the four books and build unit themes. The focus in closing community share shifts from comprehending a single title to developing a wider understanding of a theme or topic. In this unit, we use community share as a time for students to gain further content knowledge about events surrounding the civil rights movement, to model and make intertextual connections, and to explore various perspectives on the theme of civil rights.

Why Focus on Civil Rights?

America's civil rights movement, a controversial and relatively recent era in our nation's history, is rarely given in-depth treatment in our schools. Yet, the important lessons of these tumultuous times and the years leading up to them make the topic interesting and meaningful to today's adolescents. Many episodes in the African American struggle for civil rights are relevant to contemporary problems of racism, violence, and social change. Also, the compelling body of primary source materials, literature, and other resources from this period make it ideally suited for the classroom. Entertainer and civil-rights activist Harry Belafonte wrote about the world of civil rights and human rights: "In that world are many stories of loss, many stories of victory, and many stories that deal with the courage of those who stand up against injustice." A unit on civil rights will bring these kinds of stories to your classroom and provide students with much to contemplate and discuss.

How Are the Books Selected?

All four books chosen for this unit are relevant to the theme of civil rights in America. They present characters and situations to which students can relate. Because many classrooms have students at varied reading levels and maturity levels, we purposely selected books that accommodate a diverse classroom. *The Watsons Go to Birmingham—1963* and *Roll of Thunder, Hear My Cry*, both written specifically for young adult readers, are interesting yet accessible for students reading on or below grade level. Students assigned to read these books will find much to discuss and write about, yet they will not be overwhelmed by long reading assignments or difficult language.

To Kill a Mockingbird and *I Know Why the Caged Bird Sings* are for readers who can handle longer reading assignments, more challenging language, and more mature content. *I Know Why the Caged Bird Sings* is the coming-of-age story of a woman whose pivotal life experiences include being sexually assaulted as a young child. This title generally works well with a select group of mature girls. *To Kill a Mockingbird* paints a realistic picture of the culture of racism in a small, Depression-era Southern town. The main events of the novel surround the trial of a black man who is falsely accused of sexually assaulting a white woman. This book, too, is best reserved for students who can handle its language and content in a mature, thoughtful way. Depending on the community in which you teach, you might consider passing out permission slips for parents to sign before students begin reading either of these two books.

Synopses of all four books appear on pages 136–137. Although the books vary in reading level, they work well together in broadening students' understanding of the unit theme. The daily lesson plans beginning on page 138 will help you pace students' reading, facilitate whole-class discussions, and encourage students to make important intertextual connections.

● STUDENT CHOICE

A multi-book unit is a good opportunity to give students some choice about the books they will read and discuss. At the start of the unit, you might give a book talk, briefly describing to the class what each book is about. Then allow students to express their preferences, perhaps ranking their top three choices. Factor this information into your book assignments. Remember that students who read the same book will also be in the same book club, so you should also take into account any grouping concerns.

Literacy Skill Instruction

The chart below correlates Book Club curriculum areas to individual Book Club lessons in this civil rights unit. For details about each curriculum area, refer to the chart in Chapter 1, page 6. Lessons are also correlated to language arts standards established by the National Council of Teachers of English and the International Reading Association. Numbers in parentheses refer to specific NCTE/IRA standards (see page 68).

Curriculum Correlation Chart

Curriculum Area	Lessons in Chapter 8
Language Conventions	**Lessons 1–11:** Book clubs (1, 3, 4, 11, 12) **Lesson 13:** Round-Table Discussion of Big Theme Questions (1, 3, 4, 11, 12) **Lesson 14:** Review and Synthesis (3, 4, 5, 11)
Literary Aspects	**Lesson 1:** Setting (3, 4, 5, 6, 11) **Lesson 2:** Characterization (3, 7) **Lesson 3:** Point of View and Voice (3) **Lesson 4:** Plot and Sequencing (3, 9) **Lesson 5:** External and Internal Conflict (3, 11) **Lesson 6:** Symbolism (1, 3, 11) **Lesson 7:** Confronting Problems (3, 11) **Lesson 8:** Imagery (6) **Lesson 10:** Family Connections (3, 11) **Lesson 11:** Characters Coming of Age Through Experience (3,11) **Lesson 12:** Writing a Poem (3, 9, 11) **Lesson 13:** Round-Table Discussion of Big Theme Questions (1, 3, 4, 11, 12) **Lesson 14:** Review and Synthesis (3, 4, 5, 11)
Comprehension	**Lesson 4:** Plot and Sequencing (3, 9) **Lesson 14:** Review and Synthesis (3, 4, 5, 11)
Composition	**Lessons 1–11:** Log writing (4, 12) **Lesson 9:** Personal Letter (3, 4, 11) **Lesson 12:** Writing a Poem (3, 9, 11) **Lesson 14:** Review and Synthesis (3, 4, 5, 11)

Correlation to Social Studies Standards

NCSS Thematic Strands	Lessons and Activities
1. Culture Social studies programs should include experiences that provide for the study of culture and cultural diversity.	**Extended Unit, Weeks 1–4, 9**
2. Time, Continuity, and Change Social studies programs should include experiences that provide for the study of the ways human beings view themselves in and over time.	**Lessons 11, 14**
3. People, Places, and Environments Social studies programs should include experiences that provide for the study of people, places, and environments.	**Lesson 1; Extended Unit, Weeks 1–4, 9**
4. Individual Development and Identity Social studies programs should include experiences that provide for the study of individual development and identity.	**Lessons 2, 11, 14**
5. Individuals, Groups, and Institutions Social studies programs should include experiences that provide for the study of interactions among individuals, groups, and institutions.	**Lessons 5, 7; Extended Unit, Weeks 1–4**
6. Power, Authority, and Governance Social studies programs should include experiences that provide for the study of how people create and change structures of power, authority, and governance.	**Lesson 7; Extended Unit, Week 10**
7. Production, Distribution, and Consumption Social studies programs should include experiences that provide for the study of how people organize for the production, distribution, and consumption of goods and services.	
8. Science, Technology, and Society Social studies programs should include experiences that provide for the study of relationships among science, technology, and society.	
9. Global Connections Social studies programs should include experiences that provide for the study of global connections and interdependence.	
10. Civic Ideals and Practices Social studies programs should include experiences that provide for the study of the ideals, principles, and practices of citizenship in a democratic republic.	**Lesson 1; Extended Unit, Weeks 1–4, 10**

Integrating Instruction

This multi-book unit provides many opportunities for cross-curricular connections, particularly with social studies. For your convenience, we've identified links with social studies content based on the ten thematic strands defined by the National Council for the Social Studies (NCSS). The chart on page 126 highlights the strands that relate to the civil rights unit.

Unit Themes

Through this unit's readings, discussions, and research, students will become acquainted with the circumstances surrounding the civil rights movement in American history. Most importantly, they'll have opportunities to explore what it means to have civil rights, what it means to be denied such rights, and what is lost when a society doesn't value all of its citizens and treat them equitably. We suggest displaying the following theme-related questions to focus students' discussions throughout the unit.

What is the meaning of civil rights?

How and why do prejudices against groups of people develop?

In what ways are people affected by prejudice and racism?

How do people begin to overcome their prejudices?

What was the American civil rights movement? What were the goals and methods of people involved in the movement?

Read-Aloud Book List

Listed below are read-aloud books and poems that focus on the African American struggle for civil rights. The selections are useful for building background knowledge, motivating students, and encouraging students to make intertextual connections. For source information on these materials, refer to the Bibliography (page 198).

Nonfiction

The Eyes on the Prize Civil Rights Reader: Documents, Speeches, and Firsthand Accounts from the Black Freedom Struggle, 1954–1990, edited by Clayborne Carson, David J. Garrow, Gerald Gill, Vincent Harding, and Darlene Clark Hine

Freedom's Children: Young Civil Rights Activists Tell Their Own Stories, edited by Ellen Levine

Nationally televised speech by President John F. Kennedy, June 11, 1963 (see Think Sheet 17)

Rosa Parks: My Story by Rosa Parks with James Haskins

Through My Eyes by Ruby Bridges and Margo Lundell

Short Fiction

Song of the Trees by Mildred D. Taylor

Picture Books

I Have a Dream by Martin Luther King, Jr., and Coretta Scott King
White Socks Only by Evelyn Coleman
Richard Wright and the Library Card by William Miller

Poetry

"Caged Bird" by Maya Angelou
"A Black Man Talks of Reaping" by Arna Bontemps
"Dream Variations" and "I, Too, Sing America" by Langston Hughes

Song

"Lift Every Voice and Sing" by James Weldon Johnson (see Think
   Sheet 21)

Special Classroom Library

You might consider adding the following texts to your classroom library to assist students in their research, strengthen their understanding of the unit theme, and provide opportunities for intertextual connections with the books they're reading in their book clubs.

The Autobiography of Miss Jane Pittman by Ernest J. Gaines. This classic novel is presented as the tape-recorded memories of an African American woman who lived for 110 years. Her life spans many periods in American history, from slavery to the civil rights movement.

Civil Rights Act of 1964. The text of this landmark U.S. legislation is available online and at the Government Documents sections of many public libraries. Highly controversial when it was first proposed, the Civil Rights Act was created to end discrimination based on race, color, religion, or national origin.

Free at Last: A History of the Civil Rights Movement and Those Who Died in the Struggle by Sara Bullard. A clear and moving overview of the civil rights struggle in the United States. The book includes a short history of African Americans; examines the American civil rights struggle chronologically; profiles forty people, both black and white, who joined the movement; and features many archival photographs.

The Kid's Guide to Social Action: How to Solve the Social Problems You Choose—and Turn Creative Thinking into Positive Action by Barbara A. Lewis. A resource guide for young people who want to solve social problems at the community, state, or national level. The book includes sections on fundraising, picketing, lobbying, organizing petitions, and writing letters and speeches. It also includes a directory of relevant addresses and phone numbers.

Malcolm X: By Any Means Necessary by Walter Dean Myers. An introduction to the life of the controversial political and religious leader Malcolm X. It details his life and his work for civil rights and includes historical information about the times in which he lived.

Mississippi Bridge by Mildred D. Taylor. Set in Mississippi in the 1930s, this novel is told from the point of view of a ten-year-old white boy who is friendly with his African American neighbors. He recognizes the injustices his friends face on a daily basis, despite the fact that his own father is violently racist.

Now Is Your Time: The African-American Struggle for Freedom by Walter Dean Myers. A comprehensive look at African Americans' struggle for freedom and equality. Focusing on major events as well as the stories of important individuals, the book begins with the capture of Africans in 1619 and covers early America, slavery, the Civil War, the civil rights movement, and contemporary times.

Warriors Don't Cry: A Searing Memoir of the Battle to Integrate Little Rock's Central High by Melba Patillo Beals. A firsthand account of the integration of Central High School in Little Rock, Arkansas. Beals, along with eight classmates, faced violence and hostility when she began attending the all-white school in 1957.

Other Media

Literary connections can extend beyond written texts to include songs, movies, and personal experiences. We recommend the following films as additional resources for this thematic unit.

4 Little Girls, directed by Spike Lee. This 102-minute documentary tells, through interviews and personal testimonials, about the 1963 bombing of an African American church in Birmingham, Alabama, that killed four young girls attending Sunday school. The event alerted the nation to the problem of segregation and the intensity of racial hatred in the country.

A Time for Justice, directed by Charles Guggenheim. This 38-minute documentary about the civil rights movement was produced as part of Teaching Tolerance, a national education project dedicated to helping teachers foster equity and understanding in their classrooms.

GUEST SPEAKERS

Because the civil rights movement happened so recently, many of the people involved in it are alive today. Seek a person or persons from your community—perhaps relatives of your students—who would be willing to share their personal memories of the era with your class.

Weekly Activities

The chart on the next page outlines a complete ten-week unit focusing on civil rights. In Weeks 5–8 of this unit, students read and discuss four theme-related books with their book clubs. Detailed Book Club lesson plans begin on page 138. Activities to be completed in Weeks 1–4 and Weeks 8–10 are described below.

Week 1: Research/Building Background

- Tell students that in this Book Club unit, they will be focusing on four books that relate to the African American struggle for civil rights. Explain that three of the books are set in the South in the 1930s, and the other book is set in Michigan and Alabama in 1963.

- Ask students to share what they already know about the civil rights movement, recording their answers in a KWL chart. Then build students' knowledge of the social conditions in the United States that serve as the backdrop for the four books. Begin by explaining that although the Civil War (1861–1865) and the Reconstruction period that followed it (1865–1877) officially ended the system of slavery in the United States, African Americans were still not treated as equal citizens under the law. Discuss the terms *segregation* and *Jim Crow.* Explain that the practice of segregation kept black people and white people separate in all aspects of life. Jim Crow laws enforced racial segregation in the South from the years following Reconstruction through the 1950s. These laws dictated where African Americans could walk, shop, work, and go to school. In the Jim Crow south, African Americans were denied many of the basic rights and privileges that we all take for granted. Tensions built around this system of discrimination and oppression for many years, finally erupting into what we know as the American civil rights movement of the 1950s and 1960s.

- To illustrate these facts, share some stories of individuals and events of the period. Read aloud the book *Rosa Parks: My Story* and supplement it with related readings from *The Eyes on the Prize Civil Rights Reader,* including the interview with Rosa Parks (page 45) and the speech by Martin Luther King, Jr., at Hold Street Baptist Church (page 48), which he gave in response to this incident. Finally, read *Through My Eyes,* the story of six-year-old Ruby Bridges—the first black child to integrate an all-white school in New Orleans, Louisiana. Her story further illustrates the racial hatred that didn't spare even the youngest African American citizens.

- Distribute the 1963 speech by John F. Kennedy (Think Sheet 17). This speech is an excellent introduction to some of the issues that were being

Ten-Week Unit Overview

This unit has been correlated with the NCTE/IRA Standards for the English Language Arts (see page 68). Numbers in parentheses refer to specific standards.

Week 1: Research/Building Background

- Students learn about topics in African American history, particularly topics related to the struggle for civil rights. (1, 7, 8)

- Students read a variety of nonfiction texts and speeches that relate to the civil rights movement. (1, 2, 3, 12)

- Class discusses the origins of prejudice and racism and examines why people are denied civil rights. Students also discuss the courage required to fight such obstacles. (3, 12)

- Students consider possible topics for research. They begin to plan a research paper and presentation. (1, 2, 7, 8)

Weeks 2–3: Research Papers

- Students receive instruction in planning and writing a research paper. (4)

- Students produce a thesis statement, an outline, and a rough draft. During the revision process, students critique their own work, meet with their book clubs for peer support, and take part in teacher-student conferences. (3, 4, 5)

- Students begin planning their class presentations, in which they will present their papers and teach the class about their topics. (5, 11, 12)

- Students design handouts for their classmates to serve as quick-reference guides to their research topics. (11, 12)

Week 4: Oral Presentations

- Students continue the writing, revision, and planning process to complete their papers and presentations. (6, 11, 12)

- Students begin to give their presentations.

Weeks 5–8: Book Club

- Students meet in book clubs to read and discuss the four books. Each group reads a different book. (4, 11)

- Students keep reading logs as resources for group discussions. (3, 5, 12)

- Students analyze various literary elements and make intertextual connections. (3, 6)

- Students create a variety of written responses and examine the theme of civil rights through their reading and written responses. (3, 4, 5)

- Through a round-table discussion, students examine the varied points of view of characters in their books. (11, 12)

Week 9: Extending Themes

- Students continue to discuss the theme of civil rights, drawing from the books, speeches, and poems they've read throughout the unit. (2, 3)

- Teacher reads aloud *Song of the Trees*. Each student connects *Song of the Trees* to his or her book in a short essay. (2, 3)

- Students write creative pieces related to their books and the unit theme. (5, 12)

Week 10: Applying Themes

- Students listen to Martin Luther King's "I Have a Dream" speech and then discuss social change. (1, 2, 3)

- Students discuss ways in which people try to promote social change through words (protests, music, ads, editorials, etc.). Students are asked to give concrete examples. (1, 2, 6)

- Students apply their writing skills to solving a contemporary problem. (4, 6, 7, 8, 11, 12)

confronted by the federal government at that time. Tell students that President Kennedy gave this speech on national television after he was forced to send National Guard troops to the University of Alabama to ensure the peaceful admission of two African American students. Explain that although a federal court had ruled that the students must be admitted to the formerly all-white university, many people—including George Wallace, the governor of Alabama—tried to block their admittance.

- After each reading, give students time to jot down their thoughts and impressions. Ask students to compare these readings to what they already know about the struggle for civil rights in the United States. In class discussions, explore the causes of prejudice and racial tension. What does each reading tell them about the human capacity for both hatred and courage?

- Tell students that they will be exploring this topic further by writing research papers that they will present to the class. Explain that each student will research a person or event and then write a formal research paper. Each student will then teach the class about the topic by giving an oral presentation that includes visual aids and a handout of his or her own design. To get students thinking about possible topics, distribute copies of Think Sheet 18. This sheet will help them focus their thoughts and begin the research process.

● FILM CONNECTION

In addition to these background readings, you might have students view a film that illustrates people and events of the civil rights movement. Possible choices include *4 Little Girls* and *A Time for Justice* (see descriptions on page 129). Note that both of these films are quite intense, and you should preview them to make sure they're appropriate for your class.

Weeks 2–3: Research Papers

- As students focus on possible topics for their papers, spend time in class talking about what a research paper is and what you expect each student to accomplish. (Of course, expectations for this assignment will vary depending on your time limitations and the experience and ability levels of your students.) Tell them that the writer of a research paper gathers information about a specific topic from a variety of sources, not just from encyclopedias or a single book. While an encyclopedia article can provide a general introduction to a topic, students will gain deeper understanding of a topic and will find many more interesting facts and ideas by consulting a variety of sources. Remind students that they can use online resources, magazine

● INTERNET RESEARCH

You might want to review with students how to choose reliable sources. Point out that while the Internet seems to provide a wealth of information, researchers need to distinguish between truly informative sites and those that might contain misinformation or information that is one-sided or incomplete. You might list types of sites that are generally reliable, such as those run by the government, universities, museums, and reputable organizations. Also discuss types of sites that might not be reliable, such as personal home pages or sites run by organizations with particular agendas.

TEACHING OPTION

Review how to properly document sources and avoid plagiarism. Explain to students that plagiarism occurs when a writer either intentionally or unintentionally uses someone else's work as if it were his or her own. Tell students that carefully keeping track of their sources can prevent them from making this kind of mistake. Urge students to cite direct quotations as well as facts and ideas that are not common knowledge or that did not come from their own experiences or thought processes. For more information on documenting sources, refer students to the *MLA Handbook for Writers of Research Papers* or a similar resource.

and newspaper articles, interviews, and films in addition to books and historical texts. They can also conduct interviews with adults who experienced the civil rights movement firsthand.

- As they research, students should take notes on index cards or sheets of paper, carefully recording information about each source (author, person or organization sponsoring a web site, publication date, and page numbers from which information or quotations are taken). Explain that each student will need to include a bibliography and citations with his or her final paper.

- Have students prepare their research papers and presentations in stages—setting dates by which they will complete steps in their research and writing process. Students should turn in a thesis statement and rough outline, a rough draft, and then a final draft of the paper. If possible, meet with students individually after they begin their research to monitor their progress and offer suggestions. You can also have students meet in their book clubs for peer revision sessions. Think Sheet 19 features a revision checklist that should be helpful to both you and your students. Students can use it to check their own work, and you can use it to evaluate their work when it is complete.

- When students are close to completing their papers, they can begin thinking about how they will present their topics to the class. Tell students that they can use their choice of visual aids, such as maps, time lines, photographs, and art. They can also use audiovisual materials if they choose. One requirement of the presentation is a handout that gives information "at a glance" about each topic. Students will distribute these handouts to their classmates at the time of their presentations. See Think Sheet 20 for a guide to creating a presentation handout.

Week 4: Oral Presentations

What you do with this week will depend on your schedule and the progress of your students. Your students might need an additional week to complete their research, the writing of their papers, and the organizing of their presentations. If this is the case, you can hold presentations at various times during the Book Club portion of the unit. If students have completed their papers, you may use this week to hold presentations and to complete additional background reading.

Weeks 5–8: Book Club

See Book Club Lesson Plans, page 136.

Week 9: Extending Themes

- If you created a KWL chart at the beginning of the unit, return to it and fill in the third column. Have students list the most essential facts and ideas they've learned. Ask them to discuss whether their understanding of the term *civil rights* has changed as a result of the work they've done in this unit. If so, how?

- Read aloud the book *Song of the Trees* by Mildred D. Taylor. Students who read *Roll of Thunder, Hear My Cry* will recognize the characters as members of the Logan family. In this story, the Logans must stop a white businessman who tricks and intimidates Big Ma into selling the beautiful old trees on the family farm. The family must pull together and find the courage to protect their rights and their land.

ASSESSMENT OPTION

Use this week's writing assignments for assessment. Use Evaluation Sheet 3 to judge students' essays on themes in the book. Evaluate students' creative pieces based on care, thoughtfulness, and use of concrete details to express an idea.

- After the reading, ask students to write an essay comparing *Song of the Trees* to something they read in the unit or to an idea they discussed during the unit. Remind students to back up their ideas with quotations and details from the texts or from discussions.

- Then ask students to write a creative piece related to *Song of the Trees.* For example, a student might write a poem about a place that's important to his or her family, a descriptive piece about a particularly trying experience, or a character sketch of an unpleasant person he or she has encountered.

- Evaluate students' pieces and then invite them to share their work with the class. You might gather students' work to create a literary journal.

Week 10: Applying Themes

- In this unit, students learned about ways in which ordinary people fought injustice with words and actions. Point out that the written word is especially effective in moving people to find courage and work for change.

- Locate a recording of Martin Luther King, Jr.'s "I Have a Dream" speech and play it for the class. (If you don't have a recording, read the speech aloud.) With students, analyze why the speech is effective. Point out King's use of repetition, his inclusion of personal details, and his statements of hope for the future.

- Ask students to think about contemporary problems that attract attention and concern. Have them describe ways in which people address these problems (marches, editorials, music, advertisements, etc.). Invite students to give concrete examples.

- Ask students to bring in examples of the written word being used to solve contemporary problems. Spend time evaluating the items in class, discussing with students which are effective and which are not very effective.

- Have students work in pairs or small groups to create a project that addresses a contemporary problem. Students might select one or more of the following projects:

  —print ad campaigns

  —public service announcements

  —letters to government officials

  —letters to newspaper editors

  —special newspapers that address particular problems

  —protest poetry

  —petition drives

  —skits

  —children's books

  —persuasive essays

- Evaluate students on how they present their ideas and on how effective their projects are. Set aside a day when students can display their projects for the class and the rest of the school.

Book Club Lesson Plans

Detailed lesson plans—which include daily reading assignments, writing prompts, and closing community share discussion topics—begin on page 138. Note that students should complete the activities for Weeks 1–4 before you begin the Book Club lessons. These activities help students build background about civil rights and the American civil rights movement, which is essential to interpreting their Book Club readings in the context of the overall unit themes. Their discussions will be greatly enriched by the research and writing that they do in the early weeks of the unit.

Synopses of the Featured Books

I Know Why the Caged Bird Sings by Maya Angelou

Set in the 1930s and early 1940s, this first book in her series of autobiographies traces Maya Angelou's life from childhood to young adulthood. Until the age of eight, Angelou and her older brother Bailey live with their grandmother in the rural, segregated community of Stamps, Arkansas. When the children move to St. Louis to live with their mother, Angelou is sexually assaulted by her mother's boyfriend, Mr. Freeman. Mr. Freeman is murdered the day he is convicted of the crime, and young Angelou blames herself. She stops speaking to everyone but Bailey, and the children eventually return to Stamps to live with their grandmother. They remain in Stamps until Angelou is thirteen years old. As a teenager, Angelou moves to San Francisco to live with her mother, spends time with a group of homeless teenagers in a junkyard, fights against racist hiring policies in wartime San Francisco, succeeds in graduating from high school, and becomes a mother.

Roll of Thunder, Hear My Cry by Mildred D. Taylor

Ten-year-old Cassie Logan lives with her family on a farm in rural Mississippi in the early 1930s. The Logan family works hard to keep the precious piece of farmland they own—land that gives them a sense of security and independence in a segregated community filled with racial injustices. The Logans face trouble when they organize a boycott of a white family's store in response to a brutal attack on three local African American men. Cassie's mother loses her teaching job, her father's leg is broken during a violent attack, and the Logans are forced to pay back immediately a bank loan. Meanwhile, the children's thirteen-year-old friend T.J. gets into serious trouble when he begins hanging around two trouble-making white teenagers. Cassie learns yet another lesson about pride and personal strength when she watches her father risk his life and the family farm one night to protect the boy from a lynch mob.

To Kill a Mockingbird by Harper Lee

Jean Louise "Scout" Finch and her older brother Jem live with their widowed father Atticus, a respected lawyer, in rural Alabama during the Depression. For a time, the children's lives are filled with adventures surrounding their fascination with a spooky house on their street. Rumor has it that an Arthur "Boo" Radley has lived in the house for years without ever leaving. Life becomes much more complicated when Atticus makes the decision to defend Tom Robinson, an African American man accused of raping a white girl. The Finch family faces hostility from a community entrenched in the deep-seated racism of the times. Despite Atticus's evidence to the contrary, Tom is found guilty and dies trying to escape from prison. To punish Atticus for defending Tom, the father of Tom's accuser attacks Jem and Scout one night. The children are saved by none other than their secret friend—Boo Radley.

The Watsons Go to Birmingham—1963 by Christopher Paul Curtis

Ten-year-old Kenny Watson lives in Flint, Michigan, with his parents, older brother Byron, and little sister Joetta. Kenny is an excellent student who is often teased by other kids at school. Byron, on the other hand, is an "official juvenile delinquent" and a bully. Kenny's parents fear they are losing control of Byron and eventually decide to remove him from negative influences in Flint. The family travels to Birmingham, Alabama, where Byron will spend the summer with his strict grandmother. The trip introduces Kenny and Byron to Southern policies of racial segregation. It also changes the boys' relationship through two traumatic experiences. First, Byron saves Kenny from drowning in a whirlpool. Then, their younger sister is nearly killed in a racially motivated church bombing. Kenny is the most deeply affected, and it is Byron who helps Kenny confront his feelings when the family returns to Flint.

Lesson **1**

Literary Elements:
Setting

Objectives:
- Introduce students to the concept of a multi-book unit, to the unit theme, and to the four books that will be the focus of the unit.
- Review the literary term *setting* and encourage students to begin thinking about the setting of each book.
- Begin a community share chart that will help the whole class keep track of the four books.

Assigned Reading:
Caged Bird:
    Chapters 1–4
Roll of Thunder:
    Chapter 1
Mockingbird:
    Chapters 1–3
The Watsons:
    Chapters 1–2

Writing Prompts:
- What do you learn about setting (the time and place in which events occur) in this first reading assignment?
- Predict how the setting might relate to the theme of civil rights. (Think about how the lives of African Americans are portrayed.)

- As with any unit, begin by having students review past work and set goals for their reading logs and book clubs. However, let students know that this unit will be slightly different from the others in format. Instead of focusing on a single novel, the class will focus on four books connected by theme. Each book club will be in charge of reading one book. In closing community share, the class will come together to share ideas and to connect characters, events, and common themes in the four books.

- Give a brief introduction to each of the four books. Tell students that the books are tied together by the theme of civil rights—specifically the civil rights movement in American history. You might give your students a voice in selecting the books they will read—see the side note on page 124.

- Explain to students that *I Know Why the Caged Bird Sings; Roll of Thunder, Hear My Cry;* and *To Kill a Mockingbird* all take place in the 1930s, in a South entrenched in racial segregation and hostility toward African Americans. *The Watsons Go to Birmingham—1963* takes place at the height of the civil rights movement, when people were demanding that the racist policies of the first half of the twentieth century be overturned. You might distribute copies of Think Sheet 17, which features John F. Kennedy's 1963 speech promoting the Civil Rights Act. See the Read-Aloud Book List on pages 127–128 for other selections. Then ask students to discuss what *civil rights* means to them. Explain that the main goal of this unit is to build a stronger understanding of the concept of civil rights through the books that they will read and discuss.

- End opening community share with a discussion of the literary term *setting.* Explain that a book's setting is the time and place in which it occurs. Encourage students to look for details that illustrate time and place as they begin reading their books. Think Sheet 15 can help students organize their thoughts.

- Give students time to read their assignments and respond to the prompts. Before they meet in book clubs, remind them that each day they will share information about their books in closing community share. With their book clubs, they should sort out the most important information to share.

▼ LOG RESPONSES

In this lesson and throughout the unit, we provide a selection of general writing prompts that connect to all the books. These will help students make connections across texts. All prompts are reprinted on Think Sheet 22. Remind students that in addition to using these prompts, they can always write their own responses to their reading. You might have students review Think Sheets 1 and 2 to help them focus their responses.

- In closing community share, begin a chart in which students can record details of each book and compare and contrast their reading experiences. Students will update this chart as they read. Here is a sample format:

I Know Why the Caged Bird Sings
by Maya Angelou

- Setting:
- Characters:
- Point of View:
- Issues:

Roll of Thunder, Hear My Cry
by Mildred Taylor

- Setting:
- Characters:
- Point of View:
- Issues:

To Kill a Mockingbird
by Harper Lee

- Setting:
- Characters:
- Point of View:
- Issues:

The Watsons Go to Birmingham—1963
by Christopher Paul Curtis

- Setting:
- Characters:
- Point of View:
- Issues:

Lesson 2

Response to Literature:
Characterization

Objectives:
- Discuss authors' methods of characterization.
- Begin recording important details about major characters in the four books.
- Compare and contrast characters in the four books.

- Remind students that authors use a variety of techniques to reveal information about characters. These techniques include directly describing personality traits or physical characteristics, showing how a character behaves and interacts with others, using dialogue, revealing what a character thinks and feels, and showing how other characters react to the character.

- Tell students that connecting to characters is key to understanding events and issues in a story. Invite students to mention some of the characters they have encountered in their books so far and to explain their first impressions of the characters.

Assigned Reading:
Caged Bird:
    Chapters 5–6
Roll of Thunder:
    Chapter 2
Mockingbird:
    Chapters 4–5
The Watsons:
    Chapter 3

Writing Prompts:
- Describe an important character you've encountered in your reading so far. Explain how the author reveals this character's traits (provide details, sample dialogue, description, etc.).
- So far, which characters do you like, dislike, have trouble understanding, or relate to easily?
- How does setting seem to affect individual characters in the book?

- Ask students to pay special attention, as they read, to the details authors use to give information about characters. Encourage them to record these details in their reading logs. Remind them that having the details on hand will help them as they respond to the prompts and as they hold their book club discussions.

- In closing community share, have students share the information they gathered about characters. Record this information in the class chart. Discuss how the characters and situations in the four books are similar and different. Encourage students to make their own connections between books. If they need some guidance, ask them to think about the following:

—Scout's actions on her first day of school and the actions of Cassie and Little Man on their first day of school. What do these characters' actions reveal about them?

—Cassie's mother, Kenny's mother, and Marguerite's grandmother. How do they deal with their families and with others in the community, and what do their words and actions reveal?

—Sibling relationships: Kenny and Byron, Scout and Jem, Marguerite and Bailey, and Cassie and her brothers. What do these relationships say about the children and their lives?

—The relationships between African Americans and white people in all four books

LOG RESPONSES

Remind students that an ongoing log activity can be recording words from their reading that they find interesting, unusual, or challenging. You might create a "word wall" on which you record words from all four books. This activity is especially useful for students reading the more challenging titles, *I Know Why the Caged Bird Sings* and *To Kill a Mockingbird.*

Lesson 3

Literary Elements:
Point of View and Voice

Objectives:
- Discuss what the terms *point of view* and *voice* mean and examine these elements in the books.
- Analyze how a particular point of view affects the telling of a story.
- Continue to examine and get to know characters in the four books.

- Begin opening community share by explaining that point of view is the perspective from which a story is told. In a story told from the first-person point of view, the narrator refers to himself or herself as "I" and plays an active role in the story. A story told from the third-person point of view has a narrator who is outside the story's action and who refers to characters using such pronouns as *he, she,* and *they.*

- Explain that voice is an author or a character's special style or manner of speaking. Many factors affect voice. These factors include the author or

Assigned Reading:

Caged Bird:
Chapters 7–9
Roll of Thunder:
Chapter 3
Mockingbird:
Chapters 6–7
The Watsons:
Chapter 4

Writing Prompts:

- Describe the unique point of view and voice of the narrator in your book. Support your response with details, words, and phrases.
- In today's reading assignment, what struggle or problem does your narrator face? How does he or she react to the situation?
- How would the events in your reading be different if they were told from another character's point of view? Choose one other character and describe a scene in the book from this character's point of view.

character's age, life experiences, personal beliefs, surrounding influences, and level of education. Such factors also affect a story told from the first-person point of view, since the reader gains information about story events and characters through the subjective eyes of one character.

- Point out that each of the four books is told from the first-person point of view of a young person. *The Watsons Go to Birmingham—1963* and *Roll of Thunder, Hear My Cry* are narrated by children explaining events in their lives as these events unfold. *I Know Why the Caged Bird Sings* and *To Kill a Mockingbird* differ slightly in that they are told by adult narrators looking back on childhood experiences. Invite volunteers to read passages from their books that best illustrate the unique perspectives and voices of their narrators.

- Begin closing community share with a quotation from the character Atticus Finch in *To Kill a Mockingbird*. He says, "You never really understand a person until you consider things from his point of view—until you climb into his skin and walk around in it. . . ." Tell students that reading is another way of "climbing into another person's skin." Ask students to discuss the narrators in the four books and figure out what readers gain from each narrator's particular point of view. Ask students if they think a young narrator perceives and experiences events and situations differently than an older, more experienced narrator would. Invite students to share their log responses for the discussion. Add to the class chart during the discussion.

 TEACHING OPTION

To bring students back to the theme of civil rights, read aloud selections from *Freedom's Children: Young Civil Rights Activists Tell Their Own Stories* by Ellen Levine. Invite students to think about what is interesting and revealing about a young person's perspective on the issue of civil rights.

Lesson 4

Comprehension:
Plot and Sequencing

Objectives:

- Explore the plot structure of a novel.
- Begin sequence charts for each of the four books.
- Use knowledge of plot structure to predict future events in the books.

- Remind students that plot is the series of events related to a central conflict in a story. A plot revolves around the development and eventual resolution of a main conflict. Terms commonly used to describe the elements of plot include the following:

Exposition: The introduction to the story, when setting, characters, and the main conflict are introduced. The exposition sets the tone or mood of the story and provides necessary background information.

Writing Prompts:
- Describe an incident or event in your reading that has a strong effect on the narrator.
- What questions are raised in your mind by events in the book so far?
- What statements can you make about the world in which your narrator lives?

Rising Action: The problems and complications that occur as a result of the main conflict or conflicts. This is the part of the story that develops the conflict to a high point of intensity.

Climax: The highest point of interest or intensity in the plot. The climax is often a turning point in the story, when something happens to change the course of events dramatically.

Falling Action: Includes events following the climax. Tensions relax as the conflict begins to resolve.

Resolution: The point at which the central conflict is ended or resolved in some way.

Denouement: This part of the story, which follows the resolution, ties up loose ends and answers remaining questions for the reader.

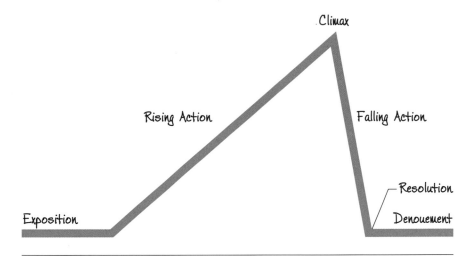

- Tell students that not all stories fit the plot diagram exactly. Because a novel is longer than a short story and often features numerous characters, its plot generally has more twists, turns, and conflicts. Usually, however, the reader can pinpoint one central conflict that drives the novel forward.

- Point out that *I Know Why the Caged Bird Sings* differs from the other three books in that it is nonfiction—a memoir rather than a novel. Because the author is describing events from her life, she does not have complete control over the plot structure of her book. Angelou demonstrates her skill as a writer by selecting events and scenes that create a coherent narrative with a plot structure similar to that of a novel.

- Have students copy the plot diagram in their logs and look for elements of plot as they read. Ask them to think about which events in each book fit the graph.

- In closing community share, create sequence charts for each of the four books. Guide students to focus on the most important and meaningful events of their books. Then discuss how these events fit into the plot diagrams they sketched in their logs.

- Have students predict what they think might happen later in their books. Suggest that they consider the events they've added to their plot diagrams and how those events might be building to a climax. Also have them think about the conflicts in their books and how these conflicts could be resolved.

Lesson 5

Literary Elements:
External and Internal Conflict

Objectives:
- Define *external conflict* and *internal conflict.*
- Help students identify the main conflicts in their books.
- Examine the roles of independence and self-respect in the lives of various characters.

Assigned Reading:
Caged Bird:
    Chapters 13–15
Roll of Thunder:
    Chapter 5
Mockingbird:
    Chapters 10–11
The Watsons:
    Chapter 7

Writing Prompts:
- Describe one external conflict and one internal conflict from your reading.
- What conflict seems to drive forward the events of your book?
- What do pride and self-respect mean to the characters in your book?
- Return to the theme of civil rights. What inequities do characters in your book live with on a daily basis?

- Introduce or review the terms *external conflict* and *internal conflict.* Tell students that an external conflict is a struggle that takes place between a character and some outside force, such as society, nature, or another character. An internal conflict takes place within a character. Explain that internal conflict can be caused by self-doubt, indecision, guilt, or frustration.

- Lead students to identify both types of conflict in their reading so far. Students might point out Marguerite's conflicting feelings toward Mr. Freeman and Kenny's conflicting feelings toward his friend Rufus as examples of internal conflict. Scout's struggle with her teacher and the battle between the Logan children and the bus full of white children are examples of external conflict.

- Help students see that many conflicts contribute to the rising action in their books. However, as they continue reading, they should be able to identify one conflict that is more important than all the others.

- In closing community share, introduce the topic of individual, family, and racial pride. Invite students to give examples of these kinds of pride in their books. In what ways do the circumstances that surround many of the characters increase or decrease feelings of independence and self-respect? Encourage readers from each book to comment.

- Relate your discussion of pride, independence, and self-respect to the theme of civil rights. Ask students to describe the effects that being denied civil rights might have on a person. When a society refuses to give one group of people the same rights that other groups enjoy, what happens to that group's sense of pride or self-respect? How does independence (political, social, economic) relate to civil rights?

Lesson 6

Literary Elements: Symbolism

Objectives:
- Define *symbolism* and discuss the role of symbolism in the books.
- Analyze the causes and effects of prejudice and racism.

Assigned Reading:
Caged Bird:
 Chapters 16–18
Roll of Thunder:
 Chapter 6
Mockingbird:
 Chapters 12–13
The Watsons:
 Chapter 8

Writing Prompts:
- Identify and write about an example of symbolism in your book.
- Write about the poem "A Black Man Talks of Reaping." Connect it to the unit theme or to a specific incident or event in your book.
- How do your characters describe prejudice? Collect quotations from your book.
- What is the most memorable or disturbing example of prejudice in your book so far?

- Explain to students that *symbolism* refers to an author's use of symbols—people, places, or things that represent or suggest something beyond themselves. Symbols often stand for ideas or feelings that cannot be seen. Invite students to discuss common symbols in our lives. Ask them to look for symbolism in their books as they read.

- Read aloud the poem "A Black Man Talks of Reaping" by Arna Bontemps. Explain that African Americans did much of the back-breaking labor that went into building the economy of the United States in its early years. As students know from their reading and from their study of the civil rights struggle, African Americans did not reap any rewards for their work. Talk about the symbolism of the land and of the "bitter fruit" that the speaker is forced to consume. Ask students to think about this poem as they continue reading their books.

- In closing community share, explore some of the causes and effects of prejudice. Read aloud or have a student read aloud the passage from *Roll of Thunder, Hear My Cry* in which Cassie's mother explains Mr. Simms's hatred for African Americans (pages 127–129: "White is something just like black is something. . . . For him to believe that he is better than we are makes him think that he's important, simply because he's white"). Do students agree with Mrs. Logan's assessment of one man's prejudice? Invite students to share ideas from their own reading or from their own experiences. If your students have gathered quotations about prejudice, you might write these on a class chart. You might also invite students to read their written responses to the Bontemps poem.

Ten-Week Unit

Students might refer to their research from Weeks 1–4 and to handouts by classmates to gain insight into the poem and events in the books.

Lesson 7

Response to Literature:
Confronting Problems

Objectives:
- Have students identify problems characters face and analyze how the characters handle these problems.
- Discuss important events that unfold in each book and continue adding to plot diagrams and sequence charts.
- Have each student compare and contrast a character's handling of a problem to his or her own handling of a problem.

Assigned Reading:
Caged Bird:
   Chapters 19–21
Roll of Thunder:
   Chapter 7
Mockingbird:
   Chapters 14–16
The Watsons:
   Chapter 9

Writing Prompt:
- Characters in your book face a variety of problems and struggle to find solutions. Create a problem/solution chart in which you can keep track of the ways in which different characters respond to problems in their lives.
- Continue charting important events in the plot of your book.
- Write about a time when you were forced to confront a problem or a difficult situation. Compare and contrast your response to the problem with the way a character in your book responds to a problem.

- In opening community share, discuss the importance of facing problems head-on and trying to solve them. Ask students why some people choose to ignore things that are wrong or problematic while others struggle to confront problems. Invite them to discuss incidents in their own lives. Have they ever tried to run from a problem rather than facing it? Why did they respond in this way? Have they ever felt satisfaction after trying to fix a problem, even if it seemed impossible to overcome?

- Remind students that the characters in their books face a variety of struggles—both large and small—on a regular basis. Guide students to give examples from their reading. For example, students might recall how the Logans in *Roll of Thunder, Hear My Cry* react to the worn textbooks given to African American students. They could avoid criticism by simply accepting the books—but then how would they feel about themselves? In *To Kill a Mockingbird,* Atticus decides to defend Tom Robinson despite the fact that his decision is unpopular in the community. He decides that "before I can live with other folks I've got to live with myself." In *I Know Why the Caged Bird Sings,* Marguerite's grandmother deals with the young people who come to harass and embarrass her by standing tall. Kenny's mother in *The Watsons Go to Birmingham—1963* decides that it's important to help Kenny save his friendship with Rufus.

- Distribute Think Sheet 23, a problem/solution chart that students can use to track events throughout their reading. Tell students that they will be asked to share their charts in community share discussions.

- Tell students that, as they read, they should think about how characters confront problems. They should analyze the reasons behind the characters' actions and decide whether or not they respect these actions.

- In closing community share, have students share their charts and their responses to the writing prompts. Encourage students to make connections across texts as the class examines characters in all four books.

Ten-Week Unit

Have students recall their research at the beginning of the unit and discuss ways in which people confronted real problems and issues in the struggle for civil rights. Have them compare and contrast historical people and events with characters and situations in their books.

Lesson 8

Literary Elements:
Imagery

Objectives:
- Teach or review the meaning of the literary term *imagery*.
- Encourage students to explore the uses of imagery in the four books.
- Have students discuss the imagery in a poem and song lyrics that connect to the unit theme.

Assigned Reading:
Caged Bird:
  Chapters 22–24
Roll of Thunder:
  Chapter 8
Mockingbird:
  Chapters 17–19
The Watsons:
  Chapter 10

Writing Prompts:
- What images does the author use to help readers experience a scene in the book? Note specific words and phrases that stand out to you.
- Explain any evidence of racism or racial tension in today's reading assignment.
- Connect the poem "Dream Variations" to a theme or idea in your book or to something discussed in class.

MUSIC CONNECTION

If possible, let students hear "Lift Every Voice and Sing" performed as a song. Students familiar with it might sing the song as a group. Or, you could play a recorded version.

- Explain to students that *imagery* refers to descriptive words and phrases that appeal to a reader's senses. A story's imagery is made up of images, or single described objects, that can be experienced with one or more of the senses. An image might help readers experience a mountain in the distance, a person sitting in a particular place, a loud noise, or the smell of something cooking. Invite students to give examples of images that appeal to each sense—sight, hearing, touch, taste, and smell.

- Help students understand that writers depend on imagery to draw readers into a particular scene or moment. In literature, imagery works together with dialogue and descriptions of action to create a complete picture of a scene. Explain that some literary genres, such as poetry and song lyrics, rely more heavily on imagery than other genres.

- Read aloud the poem "Dream Variations" by Langston Hughes. As you read, have students close their eyes and take in the image Hughes describes. Ask students what they see, feel, and hear in the poem. Guide students to think about the sensation of flinging one's arms wide or the feeling of the warm sun or a cool evening. Have them imagine the sight and sound of a man dancing and then sitting beneath a tree at nightfall.

- Discuss the theme of the poem. Guide students to understand the speaker's wish for freedom and a sense of belonging. Tell students that you would like them to think about this theme as they read their books. Also encourage students to look for examples of imagery in the day's reading assignment. Students should think about how the authors' images bring them closer to scenes and events in their books.

- In closing community share, invite students to share some of the most striking examples of imagery that they discovered in their reading. You might create four class webs on the chalkboard that capture imagery from the four books. Invite students to make connections between the Hughes poem and their books.

- Distribute Think Sheet 21, which features James Weldon Johnson's song "Lift Every Voice and Sing." Students reading *I Know Why the Caged Bird Sings* will recognize it from their reading as the song Marguerite hears at her school graduation. The song, which has become known as the Black National Anthem, fills Marguerite with a sense of wonder. Have students read the poem carefully and underline images that appeal to the senses and that give the song meaning. Discuss these images as a class.

Ten-Week Unit

Students completing the final project in Week 10 might want to revisit this poem and compare it to Martin Luther King, Jr.'s "I Have a Dream" speech. Both pieces are strong examples of how the written word can be used to inspire hope and promote change.

Lesson 9

Composition: Personal Letter

Objectives:
- Encourage students to focus on characters whom they admire and want to support, or on characters whose ideas they wish to change.
- Have students write detailed personal letters addressed to their chosen characters.
- Update class charts and revisit the big theme questions.

Assigned Reading:
Caged Bird:
  Chapters 25–29
Roll of Thunder:
  Chapter 9
Mockingbird:
  Chapters 20–23
The Watsons:
  Chapters 11–12

Writing Prompts:
- Focus on your favorite or least favorite character. Write a letter to this person, explaining why you admire or disagree with him or her. Use concrete details from the text to support your ideas, and give the character advice if appropriate.
- Review the predictions you made earlier. Have you been surprised by anything? Explain. Then make more predictions for the end of your book.

- Explain to students that characters sometimes inspire strong feelings in readers. When this happens, it means that an author has done his or her job in creating characters that are interesting and real to readers. Invite students to discuss some of their favorite and least favorite characters. Encourage them to recall concrete details and examples that illustrate what each character is like.

- Have students reflect back on the ideas they had about characters in Lesson 2. Have their feelings and ideas about these people changed and/or grown? In students' opinions, what have been some pivotal or defining moments for these characters?

- Explain that, after the day's reading, each student will compose a letter to his or her favorite or least favorite character. Tell students that each letter should express exactly why a character has behaved either admirably or badly. Students should support their opinions with concrete details from the texts and from their own experiences. Students should also explain how a character's words and actions have affected situations and other characters, for better or worse. They may give the character helpful advice, if appropriate. Remind students that they can discuss and revise their letters in their book clubs.

- In closing community share, ask for volunteers to share their letters with the class. Discuss the views students hold about what makes a person admirable and worthy of respect, and what makes a person worthy of disdain or criticism.

- Before ending the whole-class discussion, take time to review the class charts and add any new information. You might also revisit the big theme questions (page 127) to see if students have any new insights about them.

Lesson 10

Response to Literature:
Family Connections

Objectives:
- Analyze the importance of family ties in the four books.
- Have students discuss how difficult circumstances can drive families apart and bring families closer together.
- Encourage students to make connections to their own lives.

Assigned Reading:
Caged Bird:
    Chapters 30–32
Roll of Thunder:
    Chapter 10
Mockingbird:
    Chapters 24–27
The Watsons:
    Chapters 13–14

Writing Prompts:
- Describe the importance of family in your book. How are the characters' experiences in their families both challenging and rewarding?
- How do events in your book bring family members closer together? How do these events strain relationships between family members?
- Compare and contrast a relationship you have with someone in your family to a relationship between characters in the book.

- Begin the lesson by suggesting that family relationships are an important part of each of the four books. Encourage students to respond to this statement, drawing upon concrete examples from the books. You might guide students to think about Kenny's complicated relationship with his brother in *The Watsons Go to Birmingham—1963,* Marguerite's strong feelings toward her grandmother and her brother in *I Know Why the Caged Bird Sings,* the relationship between Scout and Jem in *To Kill a Mockingbird,* or the bond between members of the Logan family in *Roll of Thunder, Hear My Cry.*

- Encourage students to analyze how individual characters are affected by their relationships with family members. What do characters learn from people in their families? In what ways do family members give one another strength? In what ways do family members drain one another? Are there any characters in the books who fail or who seem lost because they don't have strong family ties? Ask students if they believe the difficult circumstances in all four books make the families stronger. If yes, why?

- As students begin today's reading, encourage them to keep these questions in mind. You might also ask them to think about the family relationships in their own lives and how they compare with those in the books.

- In closing community share, invite students to discuss their written responses, revisit the questions concerning family above, and review the events that unfolded in their reading assignments. Encourage them to compare and contrast the experiences of characters in the four books. You might also ask them to evaluate each author's success in creating believable families. Do the relationships and interactions between family members in each book ring true when compared with students' own experiences?

Response to Literature:
Characters Coming of Age Through Experience

Objectives:
- Read aloud two picture books about enlightening, coming-of-age experiences in the lives of young characters.
- Explore how characters grow and change throughout the course of each book.
- Complete the books and discuss how the unit theme ties the four books together.
- Complete the class charts.

Assigned Reading:
Caged Bird:
  Chapters 33–36
Roll of Thunder:
  Chapters 11–12
Mockingbird:
  Chapters 28–31
The Watsons:
  Chapter 15, Epilogue

Writing Prompts:
- Discuss the experiences of characters in the picture books. Compare and contrast their experiences to those of a character in your book.
- Choose one character and explain how he or she has been affected and/or changed by events in your book.
- What have you learned from events in your book?
- Review the predictions you made for the final chapters of the book. Were you surprised by anything? Explain.

- Read aloud, or invite students to read aloud, the picture books *White Socks Only* by Evelyn Coleman and *Richard Wright and the Library Card* by William Miller. In *White Socks Only,* a sheltered young girl confronts the realities of racism for the first time and is forever changed. *Richard Wright and the Library Card* shows how gaining access to a local library, with the help of a white friend, gave the life of young Richard Wright new meaning.

- Tell students that many books in literature explore a young character's "coming of age." Explain that this term refers to a character's experience of moving toward a clearer, more mature outlook on life. A character's coming of age is usually prodded along by a series of difficult learning experiences. To begin conversation on this topic, discuss the coming-of-age experiences of the characters in the picture books. Then prompt students to examine the main characters in their books. Ask them to think about how the characters' lives and outlooks are changed by their experiences. What do the characters learn about themselves? What do they learn about people, society, and human nature? Encourage students to think about these questions as they finish their books and discuss the final chapters in their book clubs.

- In closing community share, read the passage on pages 199–200 of *The Watsons Go to Birmingham—1963:* "'Why would they do that, Byron?' . . . 'I don't know, Kenny. Momma and Dad say they can't help themselves, they did it because they're sick, but I don't know. I ain't never heard of no sickness that makes you kill little girls just because you don't want them in your school. I don't think they're sick at all, I think they just let hate eat them up and turn them into monsters.'" Have students who are reading *The Watsons* explain the events surrounding this conversation between Kenny and Byron. Explain that this conversation represents a pivotal, coming-of-age moment for Kenny. He learns about the realities of racism and the effects of hate on seemingly ordinary people.

- Have students examine important moments for characters in the other books, inviting them to refer to their written responses and to any other thoughts that occur to them. In *To Kill a Mockingbird,* Scout's coming-of-age moment includes finally meeting Boo Radley and learning that most people are nice "when you finally see them." Guide students to think about how racism, fear, and hate prevent people from truly "seeing" others in this book and in the other books. In *Roll of Thunder, Hear My Cry,*

Cassie is affected by her father's decision to sacrifice his own safety and some of the family's land in order to save a young boy's life. She learns from her family that preserving self-respect and doing the right thing is sometimes more important than taking an easy and safe route. In *I Know Why the Caged Bird Sings,* the main character learns that it's up to her and her alone to determine the course of her life and to succeed. She doesn't let a series of hardships dampen her spirit or her will to survive.

- Guide students to see how the books connect to one another and to the unit theme of civil rights. Tie up loose ends and give students a chance to voice questions and concerns about their books and the unit theme. Take some time to put the finishing touches on the class charts and to review students' plot diagrams.

Lesson 12 — Response to Literature:
Writing a Poem

NOTE: The next three lessons might take longer than other lessons to complete. You'll probably need to allow extra days for students to complete their projects and assessment activities.

Objectives:
- Read aloud two poems that connect thematically to the unit.
- Have students work on original poems inspired by their reading or by their discussions of the unit theme.
- Have students work in their book clubs to discuss and revise their poems.
- Hold a class poetry reading in which students discuss their work.

Assigned Reading:
None

Writing Prompt:
Write an original poem in any style you choose. Focus on a detail or idea in your book or on the larger theme of civil rights.

- Read aloud the following statement from page 184 of *I Know Why the Caged Bird Sings:* "We survive in exact relationship to the dedication of our poets (include preachers, musicians, and blues singers)." Explain that Angelou is talking about the power of the written word and the ways in which it can comfort, enlighten, and inspire change. Tell students that the struggle for civil rights in the United States inspired many poets and writers to capture with words their personal experiences and the experiences of all African Americans.

- Read aloud the poems "Caged Bird" by Maya Angelou and "I, Too, Sing America" by Langston Hughes. Guide students to understand that Angelou's poem captures both her personal journey toward finding her voice again and the journey of all African Americans toward freedom and recognition. Point out that the Hughes poem focuses on a simple idea—the idea of being sent out of sight to eat in the kitchen—to explore the African American experience of being excluded by white America.

- Tell students that you would like them to compose poems of their own, based on ideas they've developed throughout the unit. Remind them that poetry can focus on a small detail or image—such as the image of a caged bird or the image of eating in the kitchen, to express a larger idea.

- Give students time to brainstorm ideas for their poems. Encourage them to flip through their books, look back over their written responses, and review their notes from discussions.

- Allow students to meet in their book clubs to read aloud the first drafts of their poems and get feedback from their peers.

- When the poems are completed, hold a class poetry reading in which all students can read and discuss their poems. Compare and contrast the different ways in which students express themselves and the different details and ideas on which students chose to focus. Also discuss how the poems connect to the theme of civil rights, and how each poet's work has been informed and influenced by the literature read in this unit.

Lesson 13

Response to Literature:
Round-Table Discussion of Big Theme Questions

Objectives:
- Have students take on the roles of characters in their books to discuss big theme questions.
- Encourage students to explore how characters in the book would respond to the theme questions.

Assigned Reading:
None

Writing Prompt:
None

- Tell students that you would like to revisit the big theme questions in an interesting way. Explain that each student will assume the role of a character from one of the four books and attempt to answer the questions from that character's perspective.

- If you have a large class, you might split it into two or three groups so that each student has a chance to participate in discussion. To assign roles, you can have students draw names out of a hat. Try to limit roles to major characters so that students have enough information on which to base their performances.

- After students are assigned characters, give them time to review their characters' beliefs, personal experiences, and manners of speaking. Allow them to make notes to which they can refer during discussions. Students' notes should include personal anecdotes that will support their responses to the questions.

- As students hold their discussions, walk through the room and make notes of your own. Assess how well students understand their characters and the questions.

- When the discussions are over, hold a debriefing session. Ask students what they enjoyed or found challenging about this method of exploring characters and themes.

Lesson 14

Assessment:
Review and Synthesis

Objectives:
- Discuss students' work during the multi-book unit on civil rights.
- Synthesize important ideas in the books and in the unit as a whole.
- Assess students' understanding through a writing activity.

Assigned Reading:
None

Writing Prompt:
None

- Give students time to complete the self-assessment questions on Evaluation Sheets 9 and 10. Encourage them to respond to the questions as honestly and thoroughly as possible.

- If possible, meet with students individually to discuss their performance during the unit. Use Evaluation Sheets 1 and 2 to guide your discussions. Review the self-assessment sheets that students completed and work with them to set goals for the next unit. Ask students what they learned from the civil rights unit and what they might do differently in the future.

- To evaluate students' abilities to connect ideas within a text, to interpret and analyze information, and to understand class discussions, ask them to respond to one of the following writing prompts:

  —What is the main conflict of the book? In what way is this conflict resolved, and how does it relate to the theme of civil rights?

  —How is the setting of the book important to the events and the overall theme of the book?

  —Select one character from the book and analyze the author's use of characterization to develop him or her. In what way is this character changed by his or her experiences?

  —This book has received awards, has been given excellent reviews, and has become very popular with readers. What about this book makes it outstanding and meaningful to so many people?

  —Books often have many smaller conflicts, or stories within stories. Give some examples of this from the book.

  —What did this book teach you about the effects of racism and prejudice on individuals and on society?

  —Compare and contrast the four books featured in this unit. Draw from your own reading as well as class discussions.

Ten-Week Unit

The activities in Weeks 9 and 10 offer opportunities for students to synthesize what they've learned throughout the unit and further explore unit themes. See pages 134–135 for details.

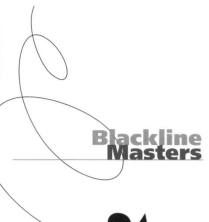

Think Sheets

The think sheets in this section are blackline masters that you can copy for your class. A few of the sheets are specific to the units outlined in Chapters 6–8, but most of them can be used with any Book Club unit.

What Can I Do in My Reading Log?

Picture
Every time I read, I get a picture in my head about the story. I can draw the picture in my log and write a sentence or two under my picture telling what it is and why I drew it.

Feelings
Sometimes a book makes me feel a certain way. I can write about that feeling and why the book makes me feel that way. I can also discuss how characters in the book feel.

Intertextuality
Sometimes what I read makes me think about another work—a book I've read or a movie I've seen. I can tell what other work this story makes me think of and why it makes me think of it.

Me & the Book
Sometimes what I read makes me think about my own life. I can write about an event or a character in a book that reminds me of my life. I need to tell what is in the book and what it reminds me of in my life.

Title Explanation
Whenever I look at a new book or chapter title, I try to predict what the book or chapter will be about. After I read the book or chapter, I usually have a different idea of why the author used those titles. I can write about the titles—what I think they mean before reading, and what they actually mean after reading. Some authors do not name their chapters. I can make up my own chapter titles and explain them.

Special Story Part
When I find a part in the book that I really like, I can write the page number in my log so I can remember where to find it. I can write a few sentences about why I think it is so special.

Interpretation
When I read, I think about what the author is saying to me, what he or she hopes that I'll take away from the story. I can write down my interpretation in my reading log and share what I'm thinking with the rest of the group. I need to listen to others' interpretations to see if they have similar, the same, or different ideas.

Critique
Sometimes when I'm reading, I think to myself, "This is really great!" Other times I think, "If I were the author, I would do this differently." I can write about things the author did well and things he/she could do better.

Tripod Response Options

► Here are some ideas for what you can write in your log. If your class develops new response types, add them to the chart.

Text

- Describe the plot line.

- Describe literary elements and devices that I notice in the text.

- Define new or interesting vocabulary words from the text.

- Explain how this text fits into a particular genre, such as historical fiction, nonfiction, realistic fiction, fantasy, or science fiction.

- Poems and Picture Books: Describe how the layout of the text contributes to the meaning.

- Make intertextual links—connections to other plots, characters, and themes.

Critical Response

- Critique the author's choice of certain words.

- Discuss the structure and/or style that the author uses.

- Critique the author's use of literary devices.

- Discuss the author's purposes for writing the text.

Personal and Creative Response

- Explain how the story, the character(s), or the theme(s) relate to my own life.

- Describe something that this story reminds me of.

- Express my opinion of the story, the character(s), or the theme(s).

- Respond to what I read with creative pieces—letters to the characters, poetry, brochures, etc.

Tripod Reading Log Page

Responding to *The Giver*

Big Theme Questions

- When is it best to conform to the wishes or rules of others?

- What problems are avoided when people conform?

- What new problems does conformity create?

- When is it important to act as an individual and stand up for one's own beliefs?

- How important is it for people to have choices?

Readings   Reading Log/Discussion Ideas

▶ **Chapters 1–3**

- Begin to list characters in the book. Write one line about each character.
- Identify places in the text where Lowry builds suspense or raises questions in your mind.
- At this point in your reading, does Jonas's community seem like a good place to live? Why?

▶ **Chapters 4–5**

- Would you want to be an elderly person in Jonas's community? Why?
- What reaction does Jonas get from his parents when he describes his dream? What do you suppose is the reason for this reaction?
- In Jonas's community, why do you think so much importance is placed on the sharing of feelings and dreams?

▶ **Chapters 6–7**

- Find some interesting words in the chapters you've read so far.
- How would you describe the special language of Jonas's community, which includes words such as *Assignment* and *Stirrings*?
- In our own society, how do we use words to distance ourselves from things that are unpleasant or difficult to face (i.e., the phrase *passed away* for *died*)?

This think sheet corresponds to Chapter 6 in teacher's guide.

Think Sheet 4

Responding to *The Giver*

Reading Log/Discussion Ideas

▶ **Chapters 8–9**

- If you could give Jonas one of your memories, what would it be and why?

- Put yourself in Jonas's place after he learns of his selection. How might you feel in this situation?

- "Now, for the first time in his twelve years of life, Jonas felt separate, different." Recall a time when you felt different and alone. In what ways was your experience similar to and different from Jonas's experience?

- Have you ever been given a responsibility that you felt you didn't deserve or worried you couldn't handle? Explain.

- In your opinion, what are the pros and cons of Jonas's world?

▶ **Chapters 10–11**

- In a Venn diagram, compare something from your life to something in Jonas's life. (Think about family, school, friends, etc.)

- Use the tripod format to respond to Jonas's first experience with The Giver. You might focus on the events of the meeting, words and phrases that give the meeting a feeling of mystery, and how you would feel if you were Jonas. Refer to Think Sheet 2 if necessary.

- Describe your first impression of The Giver. What details about this man and his function in the community stand out to you?

▶ **Chapters 12–13**

- Describe an image from Chapter 12 or 13 that you find particularly appealing or disturbing. What specific words and phrases bring this image alive for you?

- What sensory details (sight, sound, smell, touch, or taste) help you visualize Jonas's experiences on the sled?

- Draw a picture based on an image in *The Giver*.

- Jonas's fleeting glimpses of color begin to take on special meaning as he learns more about them. What does color come to symbolize?

- What do the bridge and the river symbolize for Jonas?

- The more Jonas learns, the more he begins to question. Find an example of foreshadowing in his conversations with The Giver.

Readings

Reading Log/Discussion Ideas

▲ Chapters 14–15

Respond to the following quotations.

- "If everything's the same, then there aren't any choices! I want to wake up in the morning and *decide* things!"
- "We really have to protect people from wrong choices."
- "It gives us wisdom. Without wisdom I could not fulfill my function of advising the Committee of Elders when they call upon me."
- "But why can't *everyone* have the memories? I think it would seem a little easier if the memories were shared."
- "They selected me—and you—to lift that burden from themselves."
- "Back and back and back."

▲ Chapters 16–17

- What have been your favorite and least favorite parts of the story so far? Explain your response.
- In The Giver's memory, Jonas sees candles and a fireplace. He recognizes that indoor fires are "risky" but at the same time enjoys their light and warmth. What might the fire symbolize for Jonas?
- "'There could be love,' Jonas whispered." Respond to this quotation.
- Explain why Jonas has such overwhelming feelings of loss and frustration when he sees his friends Fiona and Asher.

▲ Chapters 18–19

- Describe two characters from *The Giver* in creative ways (for example, a character profile or map, a personal ad, a job application, etc.).
- Discuss characters or events in Chapters 18–19 using the tripod format. For each section of the tripod, you may write about a topic of your own choosing or you may respond to these three topics.
  —Explain what happened to Rosemary and why.
  —How does Lowry show The Giver's feelings toward release?
  —Describe how you felt as you read about the release of the baby.

Responding to The Giver

Readings Reading Log/Discussion Ideas

▶ **Chapters 20–21**

- Make a sequence chart of important events in the book so far.
- "She's very efficient at her work, your red-haired friend. Feelings are not part of the life she's learned." Explain what The Giver means in describing Fiona's attitude toward release, using your knowledge of Jonas's community.
- Do you understand Jonas's decision, or do you believe he is wrong? Explain your response.

▶ **Chapters 22–23**

- Describe images from Jonas's journey that help you understand his experience.
- What do you think happens to Jonas and Gabriel? What in the text makes you think this?
- Do you like the book's ending? If yes, explain why. If no, rewrite it.
- Describe what you think happens to Jonas's community after he leaves.
- What might the music that Jonas hears symbolize?
- Is The Giver a science fiction novel? Give details to support your opinion.

Think Sheet 5

Special Book Part

When you come across a part of the book that you really like or that raises questions in your mind, write the page number(s) in your log to help you find it again later. Also write a few sentences or details about why you think that part is special, unusual, troubling, etc.

Page	Why I Want to Remember This Part

Me and the Book

Sometimes characters or events in a book remind you of things in your own life. Connecting to the book in a personal way increases your understanding and enjoyment of it. In your reading log, describe the part in the book and tell what it reminds you of in your life.

THE BOOK When I Read This:		MY LIFE I Was Reminded of This:
	⟺	
	⟺	
	⟺	
	⟺	

Questions for My Book Club

As you read, you might find things in the story that you wonder about or want to discuss. When this happens, write down questions to ask people in your group. They might be able to help you to understand something or think about it in a new way. Then record some of the responses you get from your group.

Question	Responses

Think Sheet 8

Charting Imagery and Symbolism

Imagery	Symbolism

The Giver
Essay Topics

▶ Choose one of the topics below and write an essay on it. Use the text of *The Giver,* your reading log, class discussions, and notes from your book club discussions as resources for detailed paragraphs.

- Explain both the benefits and the disadvantages of "sameness" in Jonas's community. Do you believe that giving up personal choices and individuality is worthwhile?

- Over the course of the novel, Jonas goes through a transformation. His beliefs and understanding of the world change significantly from the beginning to the end of the story. Explain how and why he changes.

- At one point in his training, Jonas observes that allowing people to have feelings such as love can be a dangerous way to live. What does he mean? Describe the relationships Jonas has with his family and his best friends and then the relationship he builds with The Giver. Which of these relationships would be considered dangerous by the community's standards? Why?

- What is the definition and the purpose of family in Jonas's community? In what ways do families in the novel differ from families in your world?

- Explain the idea of "release" in Jonas's community. Who gets released and why? In what ways does this practice reflect the community's attitude toward people?

- Discuss symbolism in *The Giver.* Think about the meanings behind colors, music, the river and bridge at the edge of the community, and the role of memory.

- Compare and contrast some of the images from Jonas's new memories with the images of his actual community. Why do community leaders want to protect the community from these memories—both the good ones and the bad ones?

- Compare and contrast Jonas with one of the nonconformists you researched and wrote about before the unit began.

© 2001 Small Planet Communications

Revision Checklist

Essay Topic: _____

Does the writer state the topic clearly? _____

Does the writer support ideas and opinions with facts from the text? _____

Where is supporting information needed? _____

_____

_____

_____

Is the piece written in paragraphs? _____

Does each paragraph present a new idea? Explain. _____

_____

_____

_____

Would I like to know more about anything? Is anything left out? Explain. ____

_____

_____

_____

Does the writer capitalize the first word of every sentence? _____

Does the writer use complete sentences and punctuate every sentence? _____

What is your general impression of the essay? _____

_____

_____

_____

The Giver

Book Club Essay

"You must try to forget all you have learned. You must begin to dream. From this time on you must shut your ears to the roaring of the voices."

—Sherwood Anderson, "Hands"

"To be nobody but yourself in a world which is doing its best, night and day, to make you everybody else— means to fight the hardest battle which any human being can fight: and never stop fighting."

—e. e. cummings

► To be part of something larger is believed by some to be a human need. Yet, to conform can squash individuality. Choose one of the quotes above. Write a composition that:

- explains what the quote means to you—i.e., describe its meaning in your own words (possibly providing your own examples) and tell whether you agree or disagree with the quote.

- compares the quote to at least three other literary works we studied this term.

► Show evidence of brainstorming, outlining, or some other form of prewriting.

Responding to *The Giver*

Big Theme Questions

- When is it best to conform to the wishes or rules of others?

- What problems are avoided when people conform?

- What new problems does conformity create?

- When is it important to act as an individual and stand up for one's own beliefs?

- How important is it for people to have choices?

Readings   Reading Log/Discussion Ideas

▶ Chapters 1–3

- Choose three or four words and phrases that you especially noticed in the first three chapters of *The Giver*. Explain why they stand out to you.

- As you enter the world of *The Giver*, what strikes you as interesting or strange?

- What possible conflicts do you see building in the story's plot?

- Identify places in the chapters where Lowry tries to build suspense or raise questions in your mind.

▶ Chapters 4–5

- In a two-column chart, begin keeping track of rituals in Jonas's community and rituals in your own family, religion, or culture.

- Choose one ritual in your own life and explain its meaning and purpose.

- Naming is one example of a ritual. Why is naming so important to people? Why is naming particularly important in *The Giver*?

- In Jonas's community, why do you think so much importance is placed on the sharing of feelings and dreams?

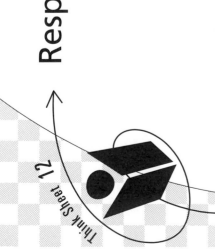

Reading Log/Discussion Ideas

▶ Chapters 6–7

- Describe the setting of *The Giver*. (Use Think Sheet 15.)
- How does setting affect characters and events in the novel?
- Explain the character of Asher. Why does he stand out in this community?
- Why might a community decide to choose jobs and families for its citizens? In your opinion, what are the pros and cons of such a system? Explain.
- Continue to chart interesting words, phrases, and euphemisms.

▶ Chapters 8–9

- If you could give Jonas one of your memories, what would it be and why?
- "Now, for the first time in his twelve years of life, Jonas felt separate, different." Recall a time when you felt different and alone. In what ways was your experience similar to and different from Jonas's experience?
- Does Jonas's situation or community remind you of any other books or movies? If so, explain the similarities.
- Predict the ways in which Jonas's new job might affect his relationships with his family and friends. Explain your response.
- Think about the instructions Jonas receives in his folder. What do they tell you about his future?
- Explain the mood, or atmosphere, at the ceremony when Jonas receives his Assignment.

▶ Chapters 10–11

- Choose a descriptive paragraph from one of Jonas's new memories and compare it to a descriptive paragraph from early in the book. What does the author do (and not do) to create certain images?
- Explain why, according to The Giver, snow and sunshine are not part of Jonas's world.
- What does The Giver mean when he tells Jonas that there is a difference between power and honor?
- Compare and contrast something from your life with something from Jonas's life.

Responding to *The Giver*

Reading Log/Discussion Ideas

▶ **Chapters 12–13**

- Find details in your reading that seem to foreshadow events to come. Explain your predictions, based on these hints.
- Explain Jonas's ability to "see-beyond."
- How does Jonas feel when he learns the truth about colors?
- "If everything's the same, then there aren't any choices!" Respond to this quotation. Do you believe choices are important?

▶ **Chapters 14–15**

- What is Jonas's attitude toward his world at the beginning of the novel? How do his experiences with The Giver begin to change him?
- Why is The Giver forced to share pain with Jonas?
- In what ways is Jonas now different from the members of his family?
- What does Jonas do to soothe Gabriel? How does he feel about his action?
- Explain the memory Jonas is given in Chapter 15.

▶ **Chapters 16–17**

- In The Giver's favorite memory, Jonas realizes that fire is both dangerous and wonderful. What might fire symbolize?
- At the end of Chapter 17, Jonas tells Gabriel, "There could be love." What does this statement reveal about Jonas and the new understanding he has about his life?
- Put yourself in Jonas's place. What would you do with your new knowledge of the world?
- Why are loving family relationships seen as dangerous in Jonas's world?

▶ **Chapters 18–19**

- In what ways does Jonas experience internal conflict once he has a bigger picture of the world in which he lives?
- With what internal conflict does The Giver struggle?
- What conflicts might Jonas face if he tries to act on some of his feelings?
- Explain what happened to Rosemary. Why does her experience put added pressure on Jonas and The Giver?
- What was your reaction to the release of the baby? Explain your response.

Reading Log/Discussion Ideas

▶ Chapters 20–21

- Lowry chose not to use chapter titles in *The Giver*. Create titles for some of the most important chapters. Be sure each title reflects the chapter's main ideas or main events.

- Create a sequence chart that tells what has happened in the novel so far. Remember to concentrate on the most important events.

- Jonas does not want to believe that his good friend Fiona could ever be part of a person's release. The Giver responds by telling him, "Feelings are not part of the life she's learned." Explain what he means.

- Do you agree with Jonas's decision? Why?

- Explain how The Giver feels about Jonas's plan.

▶ Chapters 22–23

- What is your interpretation of the book's ending? Support your response with evidence from the text.

- Are you satisfied with the book's ending? If yes, explain why. If no, rewrite it.

- Describe what you think happens to Jonas's community after he leaves.

- What might the music that Jonas hears symbolize?

- How might Lois Lowry respond to the big theme questions for this unit? Support your response with evidence from the text.

Denotation/Connotation

▶ As you read, keep track of the denotations (dictionary meanings) and connotations (ideas and feelings associated with a word) of interesting words.

Word	Denotation	Connotation

Euphemism

► A euphemism is a mild or pleasant expression that is used in place of another—especially one that is harsh or unpleasant. When you encounter a euphemism, think about what it means in the story and how you might rephrase it to make it more precise and to the point.

Euphemism:

What I Would Say:

Euphemism:

What I Would Say:

Euphemism:

What I Would Say:

Euphemism:

What I Would Say:

Euphemism:

What I Would Say:

Name: _____   Date: _____

Analyzing Setting

► Keep track of important details about setting as you read. When you have gathered plenty of details, write a description of the story's setting. You might have to update your description as you continue reading.

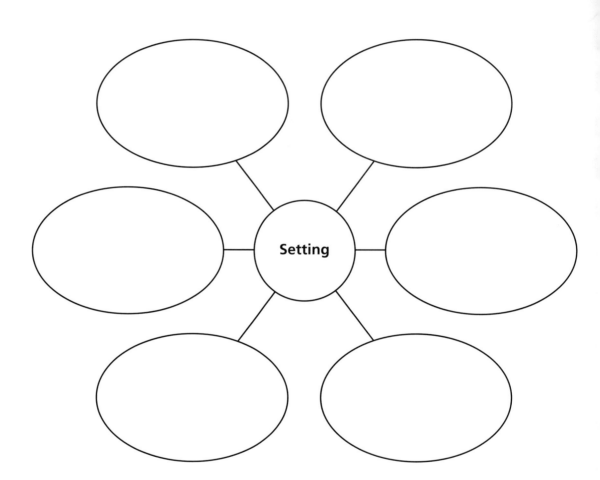

Setting

Description of setting based on details:

....

....

....

....

Foreshadowing

► Sometimes authors give clues about events that will happen later in the story. This is called foreshadowing. Record words and actions that seem to foreshadow future events. Make predictions based on that information and then, later, go back and check your predictions.

Page	Foreshadowing Clues	Prediction

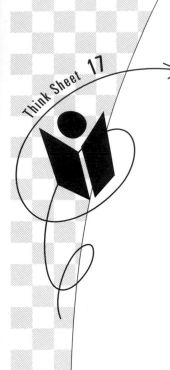

Nationally Televised Speech by President John F. Kennedy

June 11, 1963

This nation was founded by men of many nations and backgrounds. It was founded on the principle that all men are created equal; and that the rights of every man are diminished when the rights of one man are threatened.

It ought to be possible, therefore, for American students of any color to attend any public institution they select without having to be backed up by troops. It ought to be possible for American consumers of any color to receive equal service in places of public accommodation, such as hotels and restaurants, and theaters and retail stores, without being forced to resort to demonstrations in the street.

And it ought to be possible for American citizens of any color to register and to vote in a free election without interference or fear of reprisal.

It ought to be possible, in short, for every American to enjoy the privileges of being American without regard to his race or his color.

This is not a sectional issue. Difficulties over segregation and discrimination exist in every city, in every state of the Union, producing in many cities a rising tide of discontent that threatens the public safety.

Nor is this a partisan issue. In a time of domestic crisis, men of goodwill and generosity should be able to unite regardless of party or politics.

This is not even a legal or legislative issue alone. It is better to settle these matters in the courts than on the streets, and new laws are needed at every level. But law alone cannot make men see right.

We are confronted primarily with a moral issue. It is as old as the Scriptures and is as clear as the American Constitution. The heart of the question is whether all Americans are to be afforded equal rights and equal opportunities; whether we are going to treat our fellow Americans as we want to be treated.

If an American, because his skin is dark, cannot eat lunch in a restaurant open to the public; if he cannot send his children to the best public schools available; if he cannot vote for the public officials who represent him; if, in short, he cannot enjoy the full and free life which all of us want, then who among us would be content to have the color of his skin changed and stand in his place?

Who among us would then be content with the counsels of patience and delay? One hundred years of delay have passed since President Lincoln freed the slaves, yet their heirs, their grandsons, are not fully free. They are not yet freed from the bonds of injustice; they are not yet freed from social and economic oppression.

Nationally Televised Speech by President John F. Kennedy
continued

And this nation, for all its hopes and all its boasts, will not be fully free until all its citizens are free.

Now the time has come for this nation to fulfill its promise. The events in Birmingham and elsewhere have so increased the cries for equality that no city or state or legislative body can prudently choose to ignore them.

The fires of frustration and discord are burning in every city, North and South. Where legal remedies are not at hand, redress is sought in the streets in demonstrations, parades and protests, which create tensions and threaten violence—and threaten lives.

We face, therefore, a moral crisis as a country and a people. It cannot be met by repressive police action. It cannot be left to increased demonstrations in the streets. It cannot be quieted by token moves or talk. It is time to act in the Congress, in your state and local legislative body, and, above all, in all of our daily lives.

I am, therefore, asking the Congress to enact legislation giving all Americans the right to be served in facilities which are open to the public— hotels, restaurants and theaters, retail stores and similar establishments. This seems to me to be an elementary right.

I'm also asking Congress to authorize the Federal Government to partici- pate more fully in lawsuits designed to end segregation in public education. We have succeeded in persuading many districts to desegregate voluntarily. Dozens have admitted Negroes without violence.

Other features will also be requested, including greater protection for the right to vote.

But legislation, I repeat, cannot solve this problem alone. It must be solved in the homes of every American in every community across our country.

In this respect, I want to pay tribute to those citizens, North and South, who've been working in their communities to make life better for all.

They are acting not out of a sense of legal duty but out of a sense of human decency. Like our soldiers and sailors in all parts of the world, they are meeting freedom's challenge on the firing line, and I salute them for their honor—their courage.

(Source: *The Eyes on the Prize Civil Rights Reader.* New York: Viking Penguin, 1991.)

Civil Rights Unit

Planning Guide for Research Paper

► Listed below are some topics related to the civil rights movement. Write a research paper on one of these topics or one of your own choosing. Use the questions that follow the list to focus your topic.

Medgar Evers

Maya Angelou

Freedom Riders

Addie Mae Collins, Denise McNair, Carole Robertson, and Cynthia Wesley

Detroit and Newark Riots

Black Panthers

Desegregation

Montgomery Bus Boycott

Emmett Till

Martin Luther King, Jr.

Brown v. Board of Education

Malcolm X

Jesse Jackson

Bayard Rustin

Bloody Sunday/Selma

Civil Rights Act

Protests, Sit-ins, Marches

White Supremacist Groups

Segregation and Jim Crow Laws

Mohandas K. Gandhi

Langston Hughes

NAACP

Civil War

The Great Depression and African Americans

54th Massachusetts Regiment

Harlem Renaissance

Sixteenth Avenue Baptist Church

Thurgood Marshall

Central High School in Little Rock, Arkansas

Governor George Wallace

Name: _____ Date: _____

Civil Rights Unit
Planning Guide for Research Paper
continued

What do you already know about your topic?

_____

_____

_____

Where will you go to begin your search?

_____

_____

_____

As you begin your research, fill in these basic facts about your topic.

Who? _____

What? _____

When? _____

Where? _____

Why? _____

How? _____

Notes on source materials:

_____

_____

_____

_____

Revision Checklist for Research Paper

Content and Organization

_____ Paper supports or proves the thesis statement.

_____ Paper has a clear introduction, body, and conclusion.

_____ Ideas fit together logically.

_____ Introduction captures the reader's attention.

_____ Introduction introduces the thesis statement or main idea of the paper.

_____ Body of the paper presents evidence from a variety of reliable sources.

_____ All ideas and opinions are supported with evidence from the research.

_____ No unnecessary or unimportant pieces of information are included.

_____ Conclusion restates the thesis or main idea of the paper.

_____ Conclusion summarizes the main points of the paper.

Grammar, Usage, and Mechanics

_____ Wordiness has been eliminated.

_____ Sentence variety is achieved.

_____ Run-on sentences and sentence fragments have been eliminated.

_____ There are no slang expressions or first-person pronouns such as *I* or *me*.

_____ All sentences begin with a capital letter and end with a proper punctuation mark.

Documentation

_____ Every summary, paraphrase, or quotation is credited with a source.

_____ A complete bibliography appears in the correct format.

Think Sheet 20

Presentation Handout

▶ Here's a template for a handout to support an oral presentation. You can design your handout in any way you'd like, but try to include each of the elements on this sheet.

Title or Topic ....

← 1900   1950   2000   2050 →

Time line of significant events

Make your handout as interesting, appealing, and informative as possible. Cover all your information in a way that looks good and makes the reader want to read it. This handout might also be an overhead. For parts of the overhead that you want to be readable, use 18-pt. or larger fonts.

WHITES ONLY

COLORED

Include graphics with captions.

Important Fact File

• Bulleted list

• Most important facts about your topic

• 5 *W*s and 1 *H*

You might include a paragraph that tells about your topic.

Famous or Powerful Quotations

"Most of my life has been spent working in the world of civil rights and human rights. In that world are many stories of loss, many stories of victory, and many stories that deal with the courage of those who stand up against injustice."

—Harry Belafonte in foreword to Through My Eyes by Ruby Bridges

For More Information

1. List sources where you found your information.

2. Include books, web sites, etc.

3. Use standard bibliography format.

"Lift Every Voice and Sing"

by James Weldon Johnson

Lift every voice and sing
Till earth and heaven ring,
Ring with the harmonies of Liberty;
Let our rejoicing rise
High as the listening skies,
Let it resound loud as the rolling sea.
Sing a song full of the faith that the dark past has taught us,
Sing a song full of the hope that the present has brought us.
Facing the rising sun of our new day begun,
Let us march on till victory is won.

Stony the road we trod,
Bitter the chastening rod,
Felt in the days when hope unborn had died;
Yet with a steady beat,
Have not our weary feet
Come to the place for which our fathers sighed?
We have come over a way that with tears has been watered,
We have come, treading our path through the blood of the slaughtered,
Out from the gloomy past,
Till now we stand at last
Where the white gleam of our bright star is cast.

God of our weary years,
God of our silent tears,
Thou who hast brought us thus far on the way;
Thou who hast by Thy might
Led us into the light,
Keep us forever in the path, we pray.
Lest our feet stray from the places, our God, where we met Thee,
Lest, our hearts drunk with the wine of the world, we forget Thee;
Shadowed beneath Thy hand,
May we forever stand.
True to our God,
True to our native land.

Responding to the Readings

Big Theme Questions

- What is the meaning of civil rights?
- How and why do prejudices against groups of people develop?
- In what ways are people affected by prejudice and racism?
- How do people begin to overcome their prejudices?
- What was the American civil rights movement? What were the goals and methods of people involved in the movement?

Readings Reading Log/Discussion Ideas

▶ Lesson 1

- What do you learn about setting (the time and place in which events occur) in this first reading assignment?
- Predict how the setting might relate to the theme of civil rights. (Think about how the lives of African Americans are portrayed.)

▶ Lesson 2

- Describe an important character you've encountered in your reading so far. Explain how the author reveals this character's traits (provide details, sample dialogue, description, etc.).
- So far, which characters do you like, dislike, have trouble understanding, or relate to easily?
- How does setting seem to affect individual characters in the book?

▶ Lesson 3

- Describe the unique point of view and voice of the narrator in your book. Support your response with details, words, and phrases.
- In today's reading assignment, what struggle or problem does your narrator face? How does he or she react to the situation?
- How would the events in your reading be different if they were told from another character's point of view? Choose one other character and describe a scene in the book from this character's point of view.

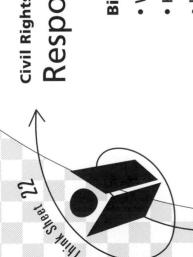

Responding to the Readings

Reading Log/Discussion Ideas

Readings

▲ Lesson 4

- Describe an incident or event in your reading that has a strong effect on the narrator.
- What questions are raised in your mind by events in the book so far?
- What statements can you make about the world in which your narrator lives?

▲ Lesson 5

- Describe one external conflict and one internal conflict from your reading.
- What conflict seems to drive forward the events of your book?
- What do pride and self-respect mean to the characters in your book?
- Return to the theme of civil rights. What inequities do characters in your book live with on a daily basis?

▲ Lesson 6

- Identify and write about an example of symbolism in your book.
- Write about the poem "A Black Man Talks of Reaping." Connect it to the unit theme or to a specific incident or event in your book.
- How do your characters describe prejudice? Collect quotations from your book.
- What is the most memorable or disturbing example of prejudice in your book so far?

▲ Lesson 7

- Characters in your book face a variety of problems and struggle to find solutions. Create a problem/solution chart in which you can keep track of the ways in which different characters respond to problems in their lives.
- Continue charting important events in the plot of your book.
- Write about a time when you were forced to confront a problem or a difficult situation. Compare and contrast your response to the problem with the way a character in your book responds to a problem.

▲ Lesson 8

- What images does the author use to help readers experience a scene in the book? Note specific words and phrases that stand out to you.
- Explain any evidence of racism or racial tension in today's reading assignment.
- Connect the poem "Dream Variations" to a theme or idea in your book or to something discussed in class.

Readings

Reading Log/Discussion Ideas

▶ Lesson 9

- Focus on your favorite or least favorite character. Write a letter to this person, explaining why you admire or disagree with him or her. Use concrete details from the text to support your ideas, and give the character advice if appropriate.
- Review the predictions you made earlier. Have you been surprised by anything? Explain. Then make more predictions for the end of your book.

▶ Lesson 10

- Describe the importance of family in your book. How are the characters' experiences in their families both challenging and rewarding?
- How do events in your book bring family members closer together? How do these events strain relationships between family members?
- Compare and contrast a relationship you have with someone in your family to a relationship between characters in the book.

▶ Lesson 11

- Discuss the experiences of characters in the picture books. Compare and contrast their experiences to those of a character in your book.
- Choose one character and explain how he or she has been affected and/or changed by events in your book.
- What have you learned from events in your book?
- Review the predictions you made for the final chapters of the book. Were you surprised by anything? Explain.

Name: _____   Date: _____

Problem/Solution Chart

Character	Problem	Steps Taken to Deal with the Problem

Blackline Masters

Evaluation Sheets

The evaluation sheets in this section provide assessment tools for both you and your students. Some sheets give you a framework for observing and assessing your students' work. Others guide students to set learning goals for their participation in Book Club and then to self-assess their progress. For more on assessment in the Book Club program, see Chapter 4.

Reading Log Evaluation

NOTE: This form assumes that the teacher has written comments on students' log entries for the first half of the novel and that students have had the chance to revise those entries to earn extra points.

- - - - - - ✂ -

Reading Log Evaluation

Student: _____ Date: _____

_____ Entries reflect a variety of response types. (10)

_____ Entries are well focused and coherent. (20)

_____ Entries focus on major themes, issues, questions, or characters. (20)

_____ Entries for the first half of the book are very strong or have been improved based on teacher feedback. (20)

_____ Entries for the last half of the book include details from text, notes, and/or discussions. (30)

_____ Total (100)

- - - - - - ✂ -

Reading Log Evaluation

Student: _____ Date: _____

_____ Entries reflect a variety of response types. (10)

_____ Entries are well focused and coherent. (20)

_____ Entries focus on major themes, issues, questions, or characters. (20)

_____ Entries for the first half of the book are very strong or have been improved based on teacher feedback. (20)

_____ Entries for the last half of the book include details from text, notes, and/or discussions. (30)

_____ Total (100)

Book Club Observation Sheet

Student's Name	Shares Log	Shares Ideas	Listens & Responds	Questions	Off-Task Behaviors

Each ✔ means the student exhibited this behavior.

Overall rating (Mark next to name.)

✳ exceptional
✚ good/okay
— not good
○ not participating at all

Off-Task Behaviors Key

1. writing in log
2. playing with pencil or other object
3. digging in desk
4. talking with someone else in group, not about Book Club topic
5. getting out of group to wander

Comments:

_____

_____

_____

_____

Essay Evaluation

Essay Evaluation

Student: _____   Date: _____

_____ Does the writer grab the reader's attention? (5)

_____ Does the writer clearly state his or her opinion on the issue? (5)

_____ Does the writer correctly use paragraphs? (5)

_____ Are there enough supporting details? (5)

_____ Is the writer's reasoning sound? (5)

_____ Does the writer use proper punctuation and capitalization? (5)

_____ Does the writer use correct sentences? (5)

_____ Does the writer use a variety of sentence structures? (5)

_____ Total (40)

✂ -

Essay Evaluation

Student: _____   Date: _____

_____ Does the writer grab the reader's attention? (5)

_____ Does the writer clearly state his or her opinion on the issue? (5)

_____ Does the writer correctly use paragraphs? (5)

_____ Are there enough supporting details? (5)

_____ Is the writer's reasoning sound? (5)

_____ Does the writer use proper punctuation and capitalization? (5)

_____ Does the writer use correct sentences? (5)

_____ Does the writer use a variety of sentence structures? (5)

_____ Total (40)

The Giver

Dream House Evaluation

Student: .... Date: ....

Quality

.... How well does the dream house express a particular idea, belief, or personality? (10)

.... How well does the student describe his or her process? (10)

Creativity/Design

.... Does the dream house have visual appeal? (5)

.... Is it constructed in a way that shows thought and care? (5)

Responsibility

.... Did the student meet the deadline? (5)

.... Did he or she participate effectively in the group component of the project? (5)

Comments:

....

....

....

....

....

Total points (40): ....

The Giver

Memoir Evaluation

Student: .... Date: ....

.... **Presentation** (neatness, effort, originality, decor) (20)

Comments: ....

....

....

.... **Mechanics** (correct sentences, sentence variety, punctuation, capitalization) (20)

Comments: ....

....

....

.... **Content** (artifacts and writing) (10)

.... years of artifacts and paragraphs

.... **Quality of Writing** (50) (Tell which year is the best example of each technique.)

.... strong opening sentence

.... use of concrete details

.... word picture of an object or scene

.... dialogue

.... scene in slow motion (suspense)

.... skillful summary of a year's worth of events

.... character description

Total points (100): ....

Language Skills Checklist

Reading Strategies	1	2	3	4
Predicting				
Sequencing				
Organizing				
Representation				
Identifying key ideas				
Revising				
Drawing conclusions				

Comprehension	1	2	3	4
Recognizes story themes				
Recognizes purpose				
Synthesizes information across texts				

Expressive Abilities: Oral	1	2	3	4
Evaluates text using specific ideas				
Expresses ideas clearly				

Expressive Abilities: Written	1	2	3	4
Evaluates text using specific ideas				
Expresses ideas clearly				

Comments: First Grading Period

Comments: Second Grading Period

Comments: Third Grading Period

Comments: Fourth Grading Period

Key: **+** Excellent ✔ Satisfactory **−** Needs Improvement

Setting Goals for My Reading Log

▶ Look through the reading log entries you created during your last Book Club unit. Pick out one of the best entries. What do you like about it? Describe why you think the entry is good.

_____

_____

_____

▶ Now pick a log entry that you think is not so good. What don't you like about it? How could it be improved?

_____

_____

_____

▶ Set some goals for yourself as you create your log for the next unit. (Complete at least three of the following sentences.)

To remember the events that happen in the story, I will _____

To help me understand characters in the book, I will _____

To make connections between ideas, I will _____

To learn and remember interesting new words, I will _____

To help me understand things about the book that seem confusing, I will _____

To connect the book to my own life, I will _____

To use my log to prepare for book club discussions, I will _____

Setting Goals for My Book Club

► Set some goals for yourself as you meet with your book club during this unit.

To get a conversation going, I will _____
_____
_____

To show respect for others in my group, I will _____
_____
_____

To encourage everyone to join the discussion, I will _____
_____
_____

To avoid problems I've noticed in groups before, I will _____
_____
_____

List any other goals that you have for your book club discussions during this unit.
_____
_____
_____
_____

Now that you've set some goals, it's your responsibility to meet them. As the unit goes on, return to this page to review your goals and assess how well you are achieving them.

Self-Assessment: Reading Log

▶ Use this page to critique your work in your reading log.

This critique refers to my log entries for Chapter(s) _____

▶ Answer "yes" or "no" to the following questions. Support all "yes" answers with concrete evidence from your entries. Use highlighters to identify the evidence directly in your log.

1. Do I use examples? (yellow) _____
   _____

2. Do I quote from or paraphrase the story? (orange) _____
   _____

3. Do I state my ideas clearly with strong organization? (green) _____
   _____

4. Do I use a variety of response types? Do I focus on major themes, issues, questions, or characters? (List at least three different response types in your log.)

   _____

   _____

   _____

   _____

   _____

Give yourself a grade for this portion of your log: _____

Summarize why that is a fair grade: _____

   _____

   _____

   _____

Self-Assessment: Book Club

► Answer the questions below and provide evidence for any "yes" answers. (I need proof, so be specific.) Then turn in one group self-assessment sheet for the group with signatures from everyone.

1. Do we go beyond the words in our journals?

....

....

2. Do we respond to what others are saying?

....

....

3. Do we use the book and quote sections when we debate?

....

....

4. Is everyone prepared and willing to participate?

....

....

5. Do we use polite discussion manners?

....

....

► On a separate sheet of paper, have everyone in your group give himself or herself a personal grade and assign a group grade for book club progress. Each person should back up the two grades with a sentence or two of reasoning.

Bibliography

Student Literature—Books

Angelou, Maya. *I Know Why the Caged Bird Sings.* New York: Bantam Books, 1993.

Avi. *A Place Called Ugly.* New York: William Morrow & Company, 1995.

Beals, Melba Patillo. *Warriors Don't Cry: A Searing Memoir of the Battle to Integrate Little Rock's Central High.* New York: Pocket Books, 1995.

Bradbury, Ray. *Fahrenheit 451.* New York: Ballantine Books, 1995.

Bridges, Ruby, and Margo Lundell. *Through My Eyes.* New York: Scholastic, 1999.

Bullard, Sara. *Free at Last: A History of the Civil Rights Movement and Those Who Died in the Struggle.* New York: Oxford University Press, 1993.

Carson, Clayborne, David J. Garrow, Gerald Gill, Vincent Harding, and Darlene Clark Hine, eds. *The Eyes on the Prize Civil Rights Reader: Documents, Speeches, and Firsthand Accounts from the Black Freedom Struggle, 1954–1990.* New York: Viking Penguin, 1991.

Coleman, Evelyn. *White Socks Only.* Morton Grove, IL: Albert Whitman & Company, 1996.

Cormier, Robert. *The Chocolate War.* New York: Bantam Doubleday Dell, 1986.

Curtis, Christopher Paul. *The Watsons Go to Birmingham—1963.* New York: Bantam Doubleday Dell, 1995.

Gaines, Ernest J. *The Autobiography of Miss Jane Pittman.* New York: Bantam Books, 1972.

Gibaldi, Joseph. *MLA Handbook for Writers of Research Papers,* 5th ed. New York: Modern Language Association of America, 1999.

Henkes, Kevin. *Chester's Way.* New York: Mulberry Books, 1997.

Henkes, Kevin. *Chrysanthemum.* New York: Mulberry Books, 1996.

Kellogg, Stephen. *Island of the Skog.* New York: Dial Books for Young Readers, 1993.

King, Jr., Martin Luther, and Coretta Scott King. *I Have a Dream.* New York: Scholastic Trade, 1997.

L'Engle, Madeleine. *A Wrinkle in Time.* New York: Yearling Books, 1973.

Lee, Harper. *To Kill a Mockingbird.* New York: Warner Books, 1988.

Levine, Ellen, ed. *Freedom's Children: Young Civil Rights Activists Tell Their Own Stories.* New York: Puffin Books, 2000.

Lewis, Barbara A. *The Kid's Guide to Social Action: How to Solve the Social Problems You Choose—and Turn Creative Thinking into Positive Action.* Minneapolis: Free Spirit Publishing, 1998.

Lowry, Lois. *Gathering Blue.* Boston: Houghton Mifflin, 2000.

———. *Looking Back: A Book of Memories.* Boston: Houghton Mifflin, 1998.

Miller, William. *Richard Wright and the Library Card.* New York: Lee and Low Books, 1997.

Myers, Walter Dean. *Malcolm X: By Any Means Necessary.* New York: Scholastic Paperbacks, 1994.

———. *Now Is Your Time: The African-American Struggle for Freedom.* New York: HarperCollins, 1991.

Orwell, George. *1984.* New York: Signet Classics, 1990.

Parks, Rosa, with James Haskins. *Rosa Parks: My Story.* New York: Penguin Putnam Books for Young Readers, 1999.

Peck, Richard. *The Last Safe Place on Earth.* New York: Bantam Doubleday Dell, 1996.

Philbrick, Rodman. *Freak the Mighty.* New York: Scholastic, 1995.

Pinkwater, Daniel M. *The Big Orange Splot.* New York: Scholastic, 1997.

Seuss, Dr. *The Sneetches.* New York: Random House, 1988.

Strasser, Todd. *The Wave.* New York: Laurel-Leaf, 1981.

Taylor, Mildred D. *Mississippi Bridge.* New York: Penguin Putnam, 2000.

———. *Roll of Thunder, Hear My Cry.* New York: Puffin Books, 1997.

———. *Song of the Trees.* New York: Laurel-Leaf, 1996.

Student Literature—Short Works

Angelou, Maya. "Caged Bird." In *Shaker, Why Don't You Sing?* New York: Random House, 1983.

Auden, W. H. "The Unknown Citizen." In *Collected Poems,* edited by Edward Mendelson. New York: Vintage Books, 1991.

Bontemps, Arna. "A Black Man Talks of Reaping." In *American Negro Poetry,* edited by Arna Bontemps. New York: Hill and Wang, 1963.

Bradbury, Ray. "Dark They Were, and Golden-Eyed." In *The Stories of Ray Bradbury.* New York: Alfred A. Knopf, 1980.

Capote, Truman. "A Christmas Memory." In *Breakfast at Tiffany's.* New York: Vintage Books, 1993.

Frost, Robert. "The Road Not Taken." In *The Poetry of Robert Frost: The Collected Poems, Complete and Unabridged.* New York: Henry Holt, 1979.

Hughes, Langston. "Dream Variations" and "I, Too, Sing America." In *The Collected Poems of Langston Hughes.* New York: Alfred A. Knopf, 1994.

Jackson, Shirley. "The Lottery." In *The Lottery and Other Stories.* New York: Modern Library, 2000.

Joseph, Jenny. "Warning." In *When I Am an Old Woman I Shall Wear Purple,* edited by Sandra Haldeman Martz. Watsonville, CA: Papier-Mache Press, 1991.

Lowry, Lois. "Newbery Medal Acceptance." *The Horn Book Magazine* 70, no. 4 (July–August 1994).

Viorst, Judith. "If I Were in Charge of the World." In *If I Were in Charge of the World and Other Worries.* New York: Atheneum Books for Young Readers, 1981.

Media Resources

4 Little Girls. Directed by Spike Lee. 102 minutes. 40 Acres & A Mule Filmworks, 1997. Videocassette.

A Time for Justice. Produced and directed by Charles Guggenheim. 38 minutes. Guggenheim Productions, 1994. Videocassette.

The Wave. Directed by Alexander Grasshoff. 46 minutes. Embassy Films, 1981. Videocassette.

Teacher Resources—Books

Atwell, Nancie. *In the Middle: Writing, Reading, and Learning with Adolescents.* Portsmouth, NH: Heinemann, 1987.

Davidson, Judith, and David Koppenhaver. *Adolescent Literacy: What Works and Why.* Garland Reference Library of Social Science, vol. 828. New York: Garland Publishing, 1993.

Erikson, Erik H. *Childhood and Society.* New York: W. W. Norton & Company, 1950.

Goodlad, John I. *A Place Called School: Promise for the Future.* New York: McGraw-Hill, 1984.

Harris, Theodore L., and Richard E. Hodges, eds. *The Literacy Dictionary: The Vocabulary of Reading and Writing.* Newark, DE: International Reading Association, 1995.

Harvey, Stephanie, and Anne Goudvis. *Strategies That Work: Teaching Comprehension to Enhance Understanding.* Yourk, MN: Stenhouse Publishers, 2000.

Jackson, Anthony W., and Gayle A. Davis. *Turning Points 2000: Educating Adolescents in the 21st Century.* New York: Teachers College Press, 2000.

Keene, Ellin Oliver, and Susan Zimmermann. *Mosaic of Thought: Teaching Comprehension in a Reader's Workshop.* Portsmouth, NH: Heinemann, 1997.

Knowles, Trudy, and Dave F. Brown. *What Every Middle School Teacher Should Know.* Portsmouth, NH: Heinemann, 2000.

Lipsitz, Joan. *Successful Schools for Young Adolescents.* New Brunswick, NJ: Transaction Books, 1984.

McMahon, Susan I., and Taffy E. Raphael, with Virginia L. Goatley and Laura S. Pardo. *The Book Club Connection: Literacy Learning and Classroom Talk.* New York: Teachers College Press, 1997.

National Middle School Association. *This We Believe: Developmentally Responsive Middle Level Schools.* Columbus, OH: National Middle School Association, 1995.

Turck, Mary. *The Civil Rights Movement for Kids: A History with 21 Activities.* Chicago: Chicago Review Press, 2000.

Teacher Resources—Articles and Chapters

Alvermann, Donna E. "Peer-Led Discussions: Whose Interests Are Served?" *Journal of Adolescent & Adult Literacy* 39, no. 4 (1995): 282–289.

Alvermann, D. E., J. P. Young, D. Weaver, K. A. Hinchman, D. W. Moore, S. F. Phelps, E. C. Thrash, and P. Zalewski. "Middle and High School Students' Perceptions of How They Experience Text-Based Discussions: A Multicase Study." *Reading Research Quarterly* 31, no. 3 (1996): 244–267.

Anderson, Richard C., Paul T. Wilson, and Linda G. Fielding. "Growth in Reading and How Children Spend Their Time Outside of School." *Reading Research Quarterly* 23, no. 3 (1988): 285–303.

Armbruster, Bonnie B., and Thomas H. Anderson. "Does Text Structure/Summarization Instruction Facilitate Learning from Expository Text?" *Reading Research Quarterly* 21, no. 3 (1987): 337–346.

Book Club *Plus* Network, The. "What Counts as Teacher Research?: An Essay." *Language Arts* 77, no. 1 (1999): 48–52.

Colvin, Carolyn, and Linda Kramer Schlosser. "Developing Academic Confidence to Build Literacy: What Teachers Can Do." *Journal of Adolescent and Adult Literacy* 41, no. 4 (1997/1998): 272–281.

Flood, James, and Diane Lapp. "Reading Comprehension Instructions for At-Risk Students: Research Practices That Can Make a Difference." In *Struggling Adolescent Readers: A Collection of Teaching Strategies,* edited by David W. Moore, Donna E. Alvermann, and Kathleen A. Hinchman. Newark, DE: International Reading Association, 2000.

Florio-Ruane, Susan, and Taffy E. Raphael. "Reading Lives: Creating and Sustaining Learning About Culture and Literacy Education in Teacher Study Groups." In *Talking Shop: Authentic Conversation and Teacher Learning,* edited by Christopher M. Clark. New York: Teachers College Press, 2001.

Kintsch, Walter, and Teun A. Van Dijk. "Toward a Model of Text Comprehension and Production." *Psychological Review* 85 (1978): 363–394.

Langer, Judith. "Examining Background Knowledge and Text Comprehension." *Reading Research Quarterly* 19 (1984): 468–481.

Ogle, Donna. "K-W-L: A Teaching Model That Develops Active Reading of Expository Text." *The Reading Teacher* 39 (1986): 564–570.

Palinscar, Annemarie Sullivan. "Reciprocal Teaching of Comprehension Fostering and Comprehension Monitoring Activities." *Cognition and Instructions* 2 (1984): 117–175.

Palinscar, Annemarie Sullivan, and Ann Brown. "Reciprocal Teaching Activities to Promote Reading with Your Mind." In *Reading, Thinking, and Concept Development: Strategies for the Classroom,* edited by Theodore L. Harris and Eric J. Cooper. New York: College Entrance Examination Board, 1985.

Pearson, P. David, and Taffy E. Raphael. "Toward a More Complex View of Balance in the Literacy Curriculum." In *Literacy Instruction for the New Millennium,* edited by W. Dorsey Hammond and Taffy E. Raphael. Ann Arbor, MI: Center for the Improvement of Early Reading Achievement & Michigan Reading Association, 2000.

Pearson, P. David, and Laura Roehler. "Developing Expertise in Reading Comprehension." In *What Research Has to Say About Reading Instruction,* edited by S. Jay Samuels and Alan E. Farstrup. Newark, DE: International Reading Association, 1992.

Raphael, Taffy E. "Balancing Literature and Instruction: Lessons from the Book Club Project." In *Reading for Meaning: Fostering Comprehension in the Middle Grades,* edited by Barbara Taylor, Michael F. Graves, and Paul van den Broek. New York: Teachers College Press, 1999.

———. "Book Club Workshop: Learning About Language and Literacy Through Culture." In *The Literacy Educators' Handbook,* edited by Joyce Many. Mahwah, NJ: Lawrence Erlbaum Associates, 2001.

———. "Question-Answering Strategies for Children." *The Reading Teacher* 36, no. 2 (1982): 186–190.

———. "Teaching Question-Answer Relationships, Revisited." *The Reading Teacher* 39, no. 6 (1986): 516–522.

Raphael, Taffy E., Karen Damphousse, Kathy Highfield, and Susan Florio-Ruane. "Understanding Culture in Our Lives and Work: Teachers' Literature Study in the Book Club Program." In *Literacy in the New Age of Pluralism and Multiculturalism.* Vol. 9 of *Advances in Reading/Language Research,* edited by Patricia R. Schmidt and Peter B. Mosenthal. Greenwich, CT: JAI Press (in press).

Raphael, Taffy E., Susan Florio-Ruane, and MariAnne George. "Book Club *Plus*: A Conceptual Framework to Organize Literacy Instruction." *Language Arts* (in press).

Raphael, Taffy E., Susan Florio-Ruane, Marcella Kehus, MariAnne George, Nina Hasty, and Kathy Highfield. "Thinking for Ourselves: Literacy Learning in a Diverse Teacher Inquiry Network." *The Reading Teacher* 54, no. 6 (2001): 596–607.

Raphael, Taffy E., James R. Gavelek, and Virginia Daniels. "Developing Students' Talk About Text: An Initial Analysis in a Fifth-Grade Classroom." *National Reading Conference Yearbook* 47 (1998): 116–128.

Index

Printed in Canada